CHRISTIANITY AND THE PROBLEM OF HISTORY

Christianity

AND THE PROBLEM
OF HISTORY

By ROGER LINCOLN SHINN

CHARLES SCRIBNER'S SONS

New York 1953

901
Sh6c

31515
June '54

PRINTED IN THE UNITED STATES OF AMERICA

To
KATHARINE
and to
CAROL *and* MARY BETH
who gave up all too much husbandly and fatherly attention
while this book was being written

PREFACE

PART of history is personal history. And part of my own personal history has been almost two decades of puzzling about the wider problems of history.

That puzzling is far from over. But parts of it can be mentioned in the past tense. There was youthful hopefulness, combined with lurking doubts as to whether hopefulness—my own or that of the authoritative voices of the times—was justified. There was the intoxicating effect of Spengler, who seemed sometimes so uncannily right, sometimes so perversely wrong. There were other ideas, but there was not—as in most of the Christian church there was not—much awareness of the rich tradition of biblical and Christian thought on this particular subject.

Then came the discovery of St. Augustine and some aspects of the Bible that were new to me. With them came the months leading up to World War II. Exciting and troubling events smashed some dreams, knocked down barriers to some strains of wisdom from the past. For more than four years I stopped studying the problems of history and became a minor actor in one of history's more spectacular dramas. In those years I read scarcely a book and harbored few scholarly thoughts. But I returned from the battlefields of Europe with some Christian conceptions about history burned far more deeply into me than ever before.

Some years of studying and teaching both Christian and non-Christian philosophies followed. Practical and intellectual problems moved about in conscious and subconscious thought. It was becoming clear to everyone that history had not shoved disaster and confusion into the past. Any account of history had to allow for their continuing presence and future possibility. But, despite the shouting despair of some, it seemed clear also that history was not *solely* disaster and confusion.

So out of these mixed activities and thoughts developed this book with its attempt to find guidance in Christianity for dealing with "the problem of history."

Christian tradition offers its wealth of materials for a study like this. I have had no ambition to trace the history of doctrines, but have taken from the past whatever offered help in meeting the problem. Similarly I have examined present-day writings of some of the world's most penetrating religious thinkers. I have not aimed to summarize their beliefs and certainly have not tried to develop a rival interpretation. But I have frequently investigated their ideas, sought to relate them to the central stream of Christian thought, looked for their likenesses and their challenges to the prevailing themes of secularism. I hope a reader may find here, not something strikingly new, but some help to understanding and appropriating past and present Christian thought about history.

My debt is obvious to a host of thinkers throughout the ages. Thinking only of those who have given me personal help and counsel on this specific manuscript, I should mention a few who have been teachers, senior colleagues, and friends: John C. Bennett and Richard Kroner of Union Theological Seminary, and Herbert W. Schneider and Horace Friess of Columbia University. Above all I should thank Reinhold Niebuhr, who, while working on his own superbly stimulating *Faith and History*, shared his thoughts with me in many a friendly conversation. Needless to say, this diverse group does not join in endorsing all that I have written.

If I were to be completely honest in thanking those men of our time who have stirred me to think about history, I suppose I should have to record a debt of sorts to such protagonists of history as Hitler and Stalin, who have forced me to face problems that I would gladly have avoided. But I am willing enough to let that debt go unpaid.

ROGER L. SHINN

ACKNOWLEDGMENTS

A number of scattered sentences and paragraphs of this book have previously appeared, in a different context, in my essay, "Religious Faith and the Task of the Historian," in *Liberal Learning and Religion*, a symposium edited by Amos N. Wilder. I am grateful to Harper and Brothers for permission to use them here. An occasional sentence is also used in "The Christian Gospel and History," in the symposium, *Christian Faith and Social Action*, edited by John A. Hutchison. Scribners have graciously allowed their repetition.

My thanks also go to the several publishers who have permitted quotation from their publications at many places in this volume. These citations are footnoted where they appear.

* * *

A Note on Abbreviations

A number of abbreviations of titles of books are used in the footnotes to Chapters III and VIII. These may be identified in the appropriate chapter references of the *Guide to Literature* at the end of the volume.

TABLE OF CONTENTS

CHRISTIANITY AND THE PROBLEM OF HISTORY

Introduction

CHAPTER I

THE PROBLEM

IT MAY be, as Hegel said in his *Philosophy of History*, that the one thing history teaches is that "peoples and governments never have learned anything from history." A more encouraging, though still portentous view, is expressed in the saying that those who do not study history are doomed to repeat it. Whichever judgment comes closer to truth, men do often ponder over their history, worry about it, and try to puzzle out its direction and meaning.

Our modern era, sensitive and self-conscious, has turned its interests upon itself in an unprecedented way. Through the studies of Sigmund Freud and his followers man has penetrated far into the inner workings of his own mind and personality. Similarly man has tried to probe the inner working of his social life and history, as is evident in the wide response to works like those of Spengler and Toynbee.

Neither of these interests is entirely new. In Socrates' "Know thyself," and the Psalmist's "What is man that Thou art mindful of him?," the ancients raised the question of man's nature. And the reader of modern psychology may find many an illuminating insight in the Platonic or biblical writings. Similarly the inquirer into the meaning and workings of history may find paths marked out by the seers of Apollo and the prophets of Israel's God. But modern thought is unique in combining with intense personal and historical self-concern a mastery of techniques for determining what goes on within the human being and within history.

The fact of this modern interest is itself part of the evidence in the problem. Only an age that is unsure of its grip, shaken by catastrophes and puzzled by the direction its history is taking, could produce the writings of our time. In periods when old assurances are vanishing, men have frequently taken concern for their destiny—sometimes for the destiny of all history.

I. THE PROBLEM OF UNDERSTANDING HISTORY: EVIDENCE AND INTERPRETATION

The baffling problem of our own age in its attempt to understand its history has been stated by Winston Churchill in his address at the Mid-Century Convocation of the Massachusetts Institute of Technology:

... we entered this terrible Twentieth Century with confidence. We thought that with improving transportation nations would get to know each other better. We believed that as they got to know each other better they would like each other more and that national rivalries would fade in a growing international consciousness.

We took it almost for granted that science would confer continual boons and blessings upon us. ... In the name of ordered but unceasing progress, we saluted the Age of Democracy expressing itself ever more widely through parliaments freely and fairly elected on a broad, or universal franchise. ... The whole prospect and outlook of mankind grew immeasurably larger, and the multiplication of ideas also proceeded at an incredible rate.

But there was another side to the picture, as Churchill points out:

This vast expansion was unhappily not accompanied by any noticeable advance in the stature of man, either in his mental faculties, or his moral character. His brain got no better, but it buzzed the more. ... While he nursed the illusion of growing mastery and exulted in his new trappings, he became the sport and presently the victim of tides and currents, of whirlpools and tornadoes amid which he was far more helpless than he had been for a long time.

Here in the focus of the twentieth century is the problem of history which has bewildered so many generations of mankind. Henry Adams had stated it some years before: "One sought only a spool on which to wind the thread of history without breaking it." But what spool can bring any order into so knotted and many-stranded a thread? What logic can find coherence in the tangled, dimly known past? And who can penetrate the unknown and unknowable future? Who a century, a generation, or even a month ago foresaw what happens today? Frustrated by the enigmatic character of the subject he taught, Adams wrote: "Scarcely half-a-dozen men in America could be named who were known to have looked a dozen years ahead; while any historian who means to keep his alignment with past and future must cover a horizon of two generations at least. If he seeks to align himself with the future, he must assume a condition of some sort for a world fifty years beyond his own." [1]

There are, of course, those who pretend to stand outside the history which has formed them and to observe the unfolding panorama. This spectator-view of history was stated by David Hume: ". . . to see all [the] human race, from the beginning of time, pass, as it were, in review before us, appearing in their true colors, without any of those disguises, which, during their lifetime, so much perplexed the judgment of the beholders—what spectacle can be imagined, so magnificent, so various, so interesting?" Historians, in Hume's description, have a wonderful knowledge and discernment: They "are sufficiently interested in the characters and events, to have a lively sentiment of blame or praise; and, at the same time, have no particular interest or concern to pervert their judgment." [2] One never knows when Hume has his tongue in his cheek, and one must be supercilious indeed

---

[1] *The Education of Henry Adams*, Chapters XXXII, XXVI.

[2] David Hume, "Of the Study of History." (Punctuation slightly modified.) In *Essays, Moral, Political, and Literary*, II, 388–91. (Ed. by T. H. Green and T. H. Grosse. London: Longmans, Green, 1875.)

to call this canny Scotsman naive; but if his words are to be taken at face value, we can only say that many a hack politician on congressional investigating committees knows better.

Hume was less positivistic than many historians of the following century, who omitted the "sentiment of blame or praise" and, considering history a science on the pattern of the natural sciences, set out simply to determine the facts. But increasingly the practice of historians is acknowledging different methods. Instead of memorizing the kings of England and the dates of their reigns, historians study the intricate and obscure relations between Elizabethan politics, Shakespearean drama, and the economic situation in England, Spain, and the New World— problems in which the historian's interests and assumptions loom large. The direction of the investigation is determined by the historian's concerns and the significance of a fact is often known before the fact is verified.

Are we then forced into the skepticism which sees the arbitrary and subjective aspects of history as so important that historical truth becomes meaningless? Must we say with Napoleon that "history is a fable agreed on," or with Voltaire that "history is after all only a pack of tricks we play on the dead"? No, skepticism must be more disciplined. There are facts and there are honest historians, and the discovery of facts about the past can change our conception of history. There are even canons of historiography which give at least some rough guidance for evaluation of significance of facts, though here we are on more slippery ground. We recognize, or think that we recognize, spurious accounts of history from propagandists of the political left or right, who sometimes falsify facts of which we have direct knowledge, and sometimes blow events out of all proportion to their importance. We recognize certain errors and distortions in records left by biblical historians who wrote with inadequate knowledge and for the purpose of illustrating doctrines.

Thus data and evidence combine with interpretation to make

the history we know. The evidence, though fragmentary at best, is overwhelming in quantity. Simply to record and catalogue it is hardly to write history; the result, says Karl Barth, "is not history: it is photographed and analysed chaos." In a similar predicament the natural scientist can proceed by concentration on uniformities and by the method of abstraction. But history loses its character when it ceases to be concrete. Historical method must be based on selection—and selection from variety. Since the selection will be influenced by the historian's point of view, he had best be honest and recognize that he has a point of view. The historian, writes Collingwood, "is not God, looking at the world from above and outside." He takes his viewpoint within history. "This point of view is valid only for him and people situated like him, but . . . unless he *has* a point of view he can see nothing at all."[3] Or as Karl Popper puts it, all knowledge requires a point of view, "and the naive attempt to avoid it can only lead to self-deception, and to the uncritical application of an unconscious point of view. All this is true, most emphatically, in the case of *historical description*, with its 'infinite subject matter,' as Schopenhauer calls it."[4]

In this situation the necessary and practical safeguards are honesty and critical methods, willingness to face whatever facts other viewpoints may disclose, and the attempt actually to take varying points of view upon occasion and so far as possible. But these devices do not evade the problem, which is reflected in the

---

[3] R. G. Collingwood, *The Idea of History* (Oxford: The Clarendon Press, 1946), p. 108. *Cf.* p. 236.
[4] *The Open Society and Its Enemies*, II, 248. I have cited Collingwood, an idealist, and Popper, a skeptical naturalist, because they represent two diverse philosophies, neither controlled by theological assumptions. The same insistence can be found in the naturalistic realist, Morris Cohen (see *The Meaning of Human History*) and in the theologian, Reinhold Niebuhr (see *Faith and History*). The subject has had extensive consideration in the American Historical Association and in professional journals of the historians and political scientists.

fact, pointed out by many thinkers since Hegel, that the very word *history* has an ambiguous nature. It may refer to a series of events, or to the record and interpretation of these events. A man may write a *history*, encompassing several ages; but his act of authorship is one minute event in a continuing *history*, of which he has recorded a part. The two meanings are inseparable, just as in human experience event and the understanding of it are inseparable.

II. VIEWPOINTS AND UNIVERSAL HISTORY

We are frequently told that there are as many histories as there are points of view. The sheer quantity of evidence and the innumerable perspectives of historians make the statement plausible. One may write a history (admittedly incomplete) of American politics, or of Renaissance art, or of navigation from ancient times to the present—or, as one writer has recently done, produce successively histories of plumbing and of beards. Yet history is more inclusive than any of these histories.

The writing of history has been described by Horace Friess in a sentence: "Some great action and the interests it arouses, like the wars between Greece and Persia, or the expansion of Rome, gives occasion for great historians to sweep many tales into a significant unity, as did Herodotus, Thucydides, and Polybius." [1] Without the "significant unity" the fragmentary data we may collect are not yet history. Here, then, is the problem of understanding history. The historical significance of a battle, for instance, is not that at such and such a date such and such armies met, so many men were made casualties, so much materiel destroyed. These facts get their importance only as they fit into a wider range of events; the question of who "won" the battle is a question of what possibilities were realized or destroyed. The historian must place the battle within a span of events that in-

---

[1] "On the History of the Philosophy of History in Western Culture." *Journal of Philosophy*, XXXIV (1937), 6. *Cf.* p. 14.

cludes, finally, himself—for it is he who decides that a "unity" is "significant."

But, as the historical pluralists point out, there are limits to the extent of the unity which any one mind can discern. Friess concludes: "But to construe all history in terms of one pattern or set of factors, to represent it as the unfolding of one inclusive plan, idea, purpose, being, or group, is to force a fictitious unity into it, an attempt which always does violence at many points to the real interplay of significant differences." A glance at the writers of history who have interpreted all human history in terms of its significance for their own national, racial, religious, or class concerns bears out the justice of this protest.

Nevertheless, the hunger for ever more inclusive unities persists. Lovejoy reminds us that the true historian is interested in historical problems beyond their solution to some particular problem he happens to face at the moment when he studies the past. "The historian's . . . general and perennial problem is . . . the problem of human nature and human behavior." [2] Here, it may seem, is the possibility for an understanding of *history,* beyond the diversity of *histories.* But how much continuity is there amid all the variations in human nature? Is there a common human quest, in any sense, for a city of mankind or a city of God?

In historical practice if not in theory we acknowledge some unity. Although men may "talk different languages" even while using the same syntax and vocabulary, we assume certain normative ways of thinking and talking. When a Hitler runs wild, we say he is wrong and organize the world to stop him. In doing so, we are no doubt guilty of pretension; we assume that our values are final and force a premature unity on history. A more humble recognition of the partial character of the values we absolutize may take the form, among others, of historical pluralism. But we do not go so far as to say that Hitler's interpretation of history is

[2] Arthur O. Lovejoy, "Present Standpoints and Past History," *Journal of Philosophy,* XXXVI (1939), 484.

one among many, all of which have their usefulness. Any concerted action on an ethical basis assumes some standards of truth and right which transcend the pluralisms of history.

This degree of unity, however, gives little help to the enterprise of a "philosophy of history" with the ambition "to sweep many tales into a significant unity" which includes the whole. For what can we say of anything so inclusive as human history? From the vast diversities of human experience, can any general conclusions be drawn? Any possible inductive results are extremely slight. On Toynbee's reckoning, which would be generally accepted, the history of civilizations has occupied about two per cent of human history thus far, and a far smaller fraction of the possible remaining period of human history on this planet.

Furthermore, no major historical event is completely past. Its influence lingers. A now forgotten deed may, generations hence, assume new importance. Whether we talk of the historical significance of Plato or Caesar, of the steam engine, or of the whole of history, only a fraction of the evidence is in. Theoretical judgments must be cautious and tentative. For example, historians of the New Deal or of the Second World War try now to select and record, from the limitless data, the significant events. But many of the events will have historical consequences yet unknown. So the historian must attempt an educated guess as to what future generations will consider significant. Thus the very recording of history, even with the best of evidence, is a precarious enterprise and depends in part on the future.

The birth of Lincoln was historically more important than dozens of other births on February 12, 1809, though many of them might have seemed a great deal more important at the time. On that day, or a few weeks or years later, no one could tell its importance for history. Even today no one knows what future importance it may have. To take a more controversial illustration, we might investigate the significance of the birth of Jesus of Nazareth and the sequence of events connected with his life.

There is general agreement that the events were historically more important than anyone in Rome guessed on the day when Jesus was executed. But beyond this agreement, the history connected with Jesus of Nazareth still baffles the historian. How can one compare him with the Caesars who were his contemporaries? Is ancient Rome or ancient Jerusalem more important to our history today?

The answer to the question must finally include the whole destiny of man. If man's destiny is superhistorical as St. Paul affirmed, if history is a province of the Kingdom of God as Toynbee says, the fact makes a major difference for our understanding of history. No historian simply *qua* historian can say so; he lacks evidence. Yet, if the belief be the truth, its omission vitiates the history which is written without it.

Thus the writing of universal history confronts the historian with an insoluble dilemma. The prerogatives of his vocation give him no right to claim a viewpoint from which he can interpret the whole of history. Yet the neglect of such a viewpoint—if there be one—falsifies his understanding. The historian usually goes about his work by assuming more modest tasks than a universal history. The religious or philosophical thinker who would try to interpret history cannot, however, avoid the problem.

III. PHILOSOPHY AND THEOLOGY OF HISTORY

Despite divergence in viewpoints, it is possible to suggest in a paragraph a history of the human race. Although obviously involving interpretation, it aims to be factually accurate in the judgment of practically anyone who accepts the general methods and conclusions of the sciences.

After a long period of cosmic evolution, of which we know almost nothing, and a shorter period of biological evolution, of which we know somewhat more, there appeared the being, perhaps misnamed, homo sapiens. After some millennia of an existence now described as primitive, men began to build societies which, because of their achievements in control of nature and social organization, are called civilizations. Numerous efforts had varying degrees of success, but none lasted very long on the time scale of history. Later ages may hope for better and more enduring achievements of their own. But whatever the probabilities for fairly long-range success, presumably history is destined to a final doom. Whether with a whimper or with a bang history may be expected to run out; the planet, perhaps the universe, will know human life and history no more.

Beyond these few facts and conjectures, there is little verifiable knowledge, except the addition of endless detail. But clearly our sketch of history has not answered many of the persistent questions men ask of history. Does this process in time accomplish anything? Does it mean anything that men have lived and died, loved and hated, triumphed and suffered? Shall we say that history is the one bedrock reality, beside which all the notions of religions and philosophic idealisms are ideological illusions, as the Marxist tells us? Or is history itself the realm of *Maya*, while reality is accessible only through the arduous discipline which culminates in the rational-mystical Nirvana? Must we believe that history tells its own tale; that there is nothing more; that when the last generation has finished its weary course and human history has ended, then the final word has been said and the works of man linger only like burnt-out volcanoes scarring a dreary waste? Or can it be that nothing of history is ever lost, that the kingdoms of this world gain their meaning through a Kingdom not of this world, yet ever present in this world to those who acknowledge its sovereignty?

These are questions the human race has asked again and again, and men cannot avoid them. Historiography, however, can do little to answer them. They are not likely to be answered by the additional evidence which a few more years—or millennia— will offer. Meanwhile, we must live on the basis of our answers to such questions, whether we formulate them or not.

A statement by Henry N. Wieman will illustrate the problem. "The bomb that fell on Hiroshimo cut history in two like a knife. Before and after are two different worlds. That cut is more abrupt, decisive, and revolutionary than the cut made by the star over Bethlehem." [1] Well, is it? Christian theology has often called Christ the "center of history." Have we here a new center? To St. Paul the bomb might have seemed the sort of thing one should expect from this age, while Christ was the power of victory over the age. Who is right—Paul or Wieman? Can any measuring of evidence, any calculating of consequences determine? Does not the answer depend rather upon the context within which history is seen? And is the context not determined by a decision of *faith*?

If the historian offers us answers, he does so not in the practice of his profession, but simply as a human being living in history and thinking in philosophical or theological ways. Philosophy and theology try to deal with the questions. They use the data of human experience—the experience disclosed by the specialists in anthropology and history, by the Churchills and Eisenhowers who have made and written history in our time, by the farmers and laborers who also make history and sometimes wonder why it is so baffling. Probing the data, they may gain some understanding, some insight. And they may—as Marx both insisted and illustrated—change history.

There are, however, hazards in the enterprise. The philosopher and theologian who deal with history must not claim to do too much. They must leave it to the historian to determine the events of the past, keeping the right, however, to criticize historians' viewpoints which may prevent knowledge of the past. Thus the philosopher will never allow the historian to have the sole word on the history of Greece in the time of Plato, nor will the theologian turn over the history of Palestine in the days of

---

[1] *The Source of Human Good* (Chicago: University of Chicago Press, 1946), p. 37.

Pontius Pilate exclusively to the historian. But the philosopher and theologian must not let their insights take the place of evidence about the events of history. We cannot say, for instance, that on the basis of a certain theory of history, society *had to* start with a primitive communism, which was disrupted by the emergence of private property throwing society into class conflict; we will instead let the anthropologist and historian tell us, as far as they have evidence to say, how societies have started and developed. We can no longer estimate, on the basis of documents of revelation, that history started about 4004 B.C.; again we will ask the historian, the paleontologist, the geologist what facts they have found. This lesson philosophy and theology have, on the whole, learned.

They have perhaps been more reluctant to admit that they must be equally cautious in forecasting the future. It is true that the past may give clues for understanding the present and for discerning tendencies which will affect the future. But seers of the future are notoriously inaccurate, perhaps never more so than in modern times. To read the political prophets of a few decades ago is to learn a lesson about the finitude of human knowledge. Clearly some were wiser than others. But history shows little respect for any who claim to discover its secrets in advance.

, There are other perils in philosophizing about history. Someone becomes fascinated by some influence upon history—perhaps geography and climate, or heroic personalities, or the role of ideals and ideas, or economic and technological developments, or religious movements, or subconscious psychological drives, or a particular pattern of progress or of cyclical recurrence. Whatever factor it be, if he studies it carefully, he is likely to find its influence extending into unexpected areas. He may become intoxicated by the idea and decide that it is the clue to the multiplex happenings of history. He may propound a new "philosophy of history" and claim to "understand" history.

There are dozens of such philosophies of history. And so extensive are the data of history, so intricate the net of historical causation, that evidence can be found to confirm any such theory for the mind who falls under its spell. But any single factor is one of many which enter into history. Some factors are far more important than others, some more comprehensive, more capable of synthesis with others. All, however, are factors, and the attempt to interpret history by any one is bound to mean a distortion.

Theology makes the same error if it tries to explain history in terms of religious, rather than political or cultural or physical factors. Theology's claim to give an inclusive interpretation of history can never mean that history is to be understood as a spiritual process rather than, e.g., a result of the hunger-drive. Rather it means that the hunger-drive cannot be understood apart from the distinctively human aspects of history. Human hunger is inseparable from the anxieties and hopes that lead men to build and destroy civilizations, to write love poetry, to thrill at the conquest of the air in aviation, to worship gods false and true. History, theologically understood, is the story of the being who yearns for salvation, and nothing is alien to its concerns.

IV. MEANING AND MYTHOLOGY

Inescapably this discussion has used the language of "meaning." The questions men ask of history are finally the questions, Does history have a meaning?, and if so, What is it? Religion, particularly, asks for the meaning and purpose of history—not for the partial meanings and purposes which we insert into history.

Positivistic philosophers, of course, will challenge the right even to talk about the "meaning" of history. The very phrase, they say, has no "meaning," because it has no reference either to a sense impression or to formal logic. Admittedly, if we try to answer the positivist, we cannot define *meaning* in its most meaningful usage. For *meaning* is an *Ur*-word; it is the basis, not the conclusion of thought and definition. The question of life's meaning lies in the background of most serious thought and imagination, whether of primitive peoples or of the great speculative philosophers. To cease to ask the question may be the mark, not of keenness but of emptiness.

To view the question negatively, few people have much doubt what Karl Popper means when he says, *"History has no meaning,"* or Spengler, when he says that *"The history of humanity has no meaning whatever."* [1] What these men deny is what most philosophy and theology seek. So able a logician as Morris Cohen entitles a book *The Meaning of Human History* and asks the question, "What is the significance or meaning of the human drama as it unfolds itself in the course of historic studies?" [2] Theological thinkers write of *The Meaning of History* or *Meaning in History* and recurrently discuss the questions of meaning.

It is true that not all men engaged in the quest for meaning are looking for the same thing. Naturalism—the richer naturalistic philosophies should not be confused with positivism or materialism—usually finds meaning when an experience is related to wider human experiences. Idealism—most recent idealisms should not be confused with subjectivism or rigid monism—usually finds meaning in the relation to the whole. The religious idea of meaning is usually somewhat more inclusive than naturalism's, somewhat less rationally ambitious than idealism's. For it seeks to relate human experience to an ultimate reality which is the source and end of all, but makes little or no claim to be able to comprehend the ultimate. It is more concerned

---

[1] Karl Popper, *The Open Society*, II, 256. Oswald Spengler, *The Decline of the West*, II, 44.
[2] P. 4. One might ask whether Cohen answers the question. At least his "tragic view of history" contains signs of an answer.

with purpose than with intellectual coherence, with the living relation to truth than with speculative appreciation. Its character is indicated by Paul Tillich's phrase, "ultimate concern."

Just this idea of *concern* is the key to the Christian attempts to answer the questions of meaning which, as we have seen, get little help from historiography. Some questions, men have found, are as much illuminated by intense participation in history and thought demanded by historical decision as by extensive musings over catalogues of facts. He who tries to be an observer removes himself from the turmoil, incompleteness, and agony of history, and thereby loses access to the data which are so important for history.

It is the Christian conviction that in certain crises of history insights are found—in the language of faith, are revealed—which offer a glimmer of understanding, which do something to make sense of the whole, or to offer men salvation through the struggles of history. Such insights do not, of course, do the work of the historian in ascertaining facts about events; they offer meaning for life in history.

Let us make clear what theology claims for faith and revelation. It may be stated in a proposition which is almost unanimously affirmed by contemporary Protestant theology, and almost unanimously ignored by those who attack theology. The proposition is that God reveals Himself, not facts about Himself or His conduct of affairs. Or as William Temple stated it, there are no "revealed truths" delivered to man; there are "truths of revelation," which give expression to man's understanding of his relation to God. God's self-disclosure is mediated, not through propositions but through historical events in which men are confronted with a responsibility and a demand for decision, with a judgment and a promise coming from the divine Lord. In the "divine-human encounter" men are confronted by the God who reveals something of His majesty and grace. Revelation, to be sure, has a content but its content is recognized in encounter and cannot be equated with the propositions in which men try to express it.

Thus the whole drama of history from Creation to Last Judgment, although related most intimately to the Christian apprehension of God's self-revelation and to the teachings of the historical Person in whom Christians find God disclosed, is not itself something revealed by God. It is rather the expression of certain convictions, whether of dread or assurance, which have come to men who have been confronted by God. The theologian does not defend his doctrines against opponents by claiming that they are revealed; he says instead that they give some expression to the experience of those who have stood in the situation of revelation—the situation of repentance and faith.

The Christian answer to the problem of viewpoints, then, is neither that of the pluralist nor that of the would-be spectator of universal history. It recognizes the limitations of any human viewpoint, thus insisting upon a provisional pluralism. But it seeks to relate such viewpoints to the infinite perspective which man cannot attain but which, he senses, is the source of and judgment upon such wisdom as he can realize.

Faith is embarrassed when it seeks language to express its convictions. It is not simply that faith requires interpretation; we have seen that while all history is interpretive, it may aim at factual accuracy. But the expression of faith takes the form of mythology—a form typical of most of the religions and irreligions by which men live.[3] It stands in a curious relation to fact. It talks of a future in fantastic terms that shock the rational imagination. Like a child baffled by the perspectival problems of drawing a picture on the flat dimensions of paper, faith struggles to put its

---

[3] The term "myth," used frequently in contemporary theology, encounters objection from some who fear that it may confuse the difference between Christian faith and the rather frivolous ideas sometimes connected with the word. Karl Barth's substitution of the word "saga" is hardly an improvement. Richard Kroner's suggestion of the phrase "dramatic image" is more appropriate. However, Christianity has never hesitated to use

intimations of eternity in the flat language of a more limited world. The greatest of thinkers run into difficulties when they try to fathom the depths of life with the incomplete tools, or mental categories, of the human mind. Human thought is confined within a horizon of finiteness, as Kant saw so clearly, though he expressed it in overly rigid ways. Beyond the range of temporal experience it cannot penetrate. Yet thought is driven by inner compulsion to discern its own place and significance against the backdrop of infinity.

> Our knowledge is a torch of smoky pine
> That lights the pathway but one step ahead
> Across a void of mystery and dread.
> Bid, then, the tender light of faith to shine . . .[4]

The light of faith does not, of course, replace the smoky pine torch with which we continue painstakingly to ferret out the facts of history. Nor does faith disclose factual information about the future. But it is a conviction of things unseen; and the conviction must express itself in the only language available.

It may offer some clarity to recall that not only religion requires non-literal thought. In what sense does a scientific theory literally represent fact? John Dewey said that it is obviously impossible to compare a scientific theory with facts; rather, one uses it like a pair of glasses. Neither the theory nor the glasses correspond to reality, but both enable us to meet the world more effectively.[5] And Ernest Nagel, precise logician, describing

---

the word "God," even while it disdained "false gods" and "idols." It seems to me appropriate to keep the word *myth*, like the word *God*, as a reminder of the relation between Christianity and the wider human intimations of the divine, emphasizing at the same time the distinctive character of the Hebrew-Christian "mythology."

[4] George Santayana, Sonnet III. One might question whether "tender" is the adjective to describe most historical faiths.

[5] It did not occur to Dewey that one may wear bifocals, or for certain purposes look through microscopic or telescopic lenses. Dewey offered the basis for a richer theory of knowledge than he developed in his exclusive reliance upon a purported "scientific method."

Dewey's idea of science, says that the "electrons postulated by a
theory are defined exclusively by that theory, and are defined in
such a way that they have none of the familiar qualities of objects
in daily experience." [6] Parallel language might be used of theological symbolism.

If some would dismiss these statements as evidence of
pragmatism's cavalier attitude toward truth, we may look at a
description of the universe attributed to Einstein, thoroughgoing realist. The four-dimensional universe is described as a
cylinder whose axis is the dimension of time, and whose spatial
dimensions are finite and whose temporal dimension is infinite.
Clearly we are at the limits of thought, where visual images
suggested by the language have no more literal accuracy than
the wood and wire models which once seemed to give a fairly
truthful picture of the inner life of the atom. Morris Cohen,
whose philosophic realism counters Dewey's instrumentalism,
says of the quantum theory that it "is purely symbolic and makes
no pretention to describe the hidden structure of things." [7]

However fantastic scientific imagery gets, we do not deny its
importance. And for all its strain upon credulity, we know that
it is not arbitrary. We may argue as to what constitutes its accuracy, but every element in a scientific theory has some relation
to specific elements in man's experience of the world. In the
mythological forms required by religious faith, the same may be
said.[8] We need not here, perhaps cannot ever, work out an ade-

[6] In The Philosopher of the Common Man: Essays in Honor of John
Dewey (New York: Putnam, 1940), pp. 78–79.
[7] Cohen, The Meaning of Human History, p. 251.
[8] In using analogies with scientific knowledge, I have no thought of en-
gaging in the enterprise, popular among some fundamentalists and modernists, of showing that the latest scientific discoveries confirm religious
beliefs. I am concerned solely to show the non-literal character of much
of human thought and the problem of the mind in dealing with a
reality not commensurable with our ordinary modes of thought.
Religious thought must always be willing to recognize scientifically
confirmed facts and to correct its own misconceptions. But I have no

quate theory of symbolism; but every element in theology's mythological representations must have specific relation to the realities
of historical experience. Admittedly religious symbolism does not
have the exactitude of scientific (although Whitehead has repeatedly reminded us that the exactness of most of our notions
is "phony"). And it can be confirmed only by its relevance to
faith's understanding of life and history, not by usefulness in
making verifiable predictions, or whatever it may be that confirms a scientific theory.

The appreciation of Christianity or almost any of the great
religions demands a willingness to acknowledge that a dramatic
representation may strike truth neglected by rigorous analysis—
that a bit of pre-scientific literature or an unsophisticated Negro
spiritual may reflect a more profound feeling for the relation of
time and eternity than the notions of many a technically brilliant
philosopher. This lesson learned, we may investigate the understanding of history in some of the faiths men live by.

V. THE RELEVANCE OF THE CHRISTIAN DRAMA

When we confront the problems of history and search for
meaning and purpose, the rivals of Christian belief are certain
other mythologies which claim to bring some unity or coherence
into the tangled thread of history. Something of the relevance of
Christian thinking may be seen by a quick comparison of it with
its principal modern alternative—the faith in progress. (Both
faiths will be considered in more detail later.)

Both the progressive and the Christian conceptions of history
are far from the brief, semi-positivistic sketch of the course of history which I have earlier suggested. On what basis, then, can we
assess the adequacy of the two interpretations? One would not

more expectation of seeing Christian faith confirmed by the evidence of
natural science than I have of seeing the greatness of Bach confirmed by
the experiments at Oak Ridge. Human life fortunately has a variety of
interests which are legitimate even though they may not all have a strict
theoretical relevance to each other.

compare portraits by taking a ruler and measuring correspond-
ences with the subject—particularly expressionistic portraits—and
both our interpretations of history have their expressionistic
aspects. The question is whether they catch the extra dimensions which portraits are meant to catch. Here is no absolute,
scientific criterion. Judgments are possible; we can make compari-
sons and criticisms. But finally we will say of one or another, as
Socrates said of a myth of judgment which others might dismiss
as an old wife's tale, "I am persuaded of the truth of these things."

The distinguishing feature of the progress mythology is not
that it affirms the fact of progress; almost any interpretation of
history may take account of certain progressive developments. It
is only when progress is understood as a central principle, as the
key to interpreting the facts and discerning the meaning of history, that it takes the all-embracing form of a mythology. As with
all mythologies, some adherents of the faith in progress do not
realize that it is a myth and a faith, but many clearly do. The
earlier Dewey apparently did not. While cautiously denying
many a theory of inevitable progress, he insisted that scientific
method was the guarantee of progress if men wanted it, and
made the amazing claim: "We have now a sure method. Whole-
sale permanent decays of civilization are impossible." [1] A later,
more chastened Dewey, asking whether there were grounds for
his own faith in "the potentialities of human nature," said: "I do
not attempt to give any answer, but the word *faith* is intentionally
used. For in the long run democracy will stand or fall with the
possibility of maintaining the faith and justifying it by works." [2]
Similarly recent representatives of progressivism, forced by events
to admit the inaccuracy of the extravagant expectations of recent
traditions, have replied, in effect, "No, it's not literally true. But
it is a great faith to live by."

Christian theology criticizes the hopes of the progress myth-

---

[1] "Progress," *International Journal of Ethics*, XXVI (1916), 314.
[2] *Freedom and Culture* (New York: Putnam, 1939), p. 126.

ology, partly because it often pretends to be factual when it is not. But more basically, theology criticizes progressivism, less because it is myth than because it is bad myth. It proposes as a more penetrating and a more realistic interpretation of man's historical situation the ancient Christian drama of redemption.

To generations habituated to the progress mythology, the Christian drama appears fantastic. It seems incredible that otherwise sane theologians should once again be speaking seriously of it. For it asserts that God created the world and man; that although man was granted freedom and used it to sin, God maintained a sovereignty over history and worked mighty acts of salvation within it; that God sent His Son to redeem history; and that God, after revealing His purposes in His Son, will in His own time end history with a Last Judgment and the establishment of His undisputed sovereignty in a Kingdom of God. These statements Christian theology makes, asserting them "seriously, but not literally," to use Niebuhr's well-known phrase.

Exactly what can be the relevance of this cosmic-historical drama? The mid-point of it is pinned to historical fact—the career of Jesus—though no one would claim that the fact would convince the objective observer of the Christian belief about the fact. The beginning and end of the drama do not purport to have the slightest empirical historical evidence in their favor.

To examine just one aspect of this Christian faith, let us consider a bit of Maxwell Anderson's *Joan of Lorraine*. The plot, it will be recalled, involves a play within a play. The director, Masters, in trying to make Joan comprehensible to his cast, explains that all people live by some sort of faith, and other characters are questioning him about the idea.

Elling. But how do you know a bad faith from a good one?
Masters. I can't tell you. Nobody can tell you. But you have to know, because you're held responsible if you follow a bad one. Those who followed Hitler are held responsible, you may have noticed.

Long. Those that aren't able to lie out of it.
Masters. Yes.
Tessie. But who holds us responsible?
Masters. We do. The human race. We hold each other responsible.
Tessie. It's a very imperfect system then.
Masters. Very. It just barely works. It might break down altogether.[3]

Anderson's observations are acute enough. But are they the last word? The eighteenth-century *philosophes,* enamoured of the myth of progress, would have said that posterity will hold men responsible for their acts.

O Posterity, holy and sacred! Support of the oppressed and unhappy, thou who art just, thou who art uncorruptible, thou who wilt revenge the good man and unmask the hypocrite, consoling and certain idea, do not abandon me! . . . Posterity is for the Philosopher what the other world is for the religious.[4]

In retrospect this idea seems rather puerile—and perhaps makes us (posterity) a bit ashamed of ourselves. Maxwell Anderson is surely wiser than the many people who elaborate doctrines to show that history holds men responsible for their acts. But are we to assume that when this imperfect system breaks down, as it sometimes does, we are not held responsible? Is the only judgment on our acts the distorted judgment of our fellows? The Christian idea of the Last Judgment expresses the conviction that men are responsible to God who is the Judge of history, that His judgment is the one absolute judgment, that it is ultimate, final, with no word beyond or after it, but that so long as history runs its course the judgment is incomplete and obscure. The doctrine is a vivid expression, perhaps the only possible expression, of certain fundamental Christian convictions. The depth

---

[3] Maxwell Anderson, *Joan of Lorraine* (New York: William Sloane Associates, Inc., 1947), pp. 85–86.
[4] Diderot, quoted by Carl Becker, *The Heavenly City of the Eighteenth-Century Philosophers*, p. 150. Becker has collected a great many statements illustrating this faith.

and importance of its meaning should be clear to those who believe and those who reject it; but exactly what is its literal and temporal meaning, no finite being can presume to know.

Similarly other aspects of the Christian drama express and illuminate man's awareness of his historical life and destiny under God's sovereignty. We may now move to a more careful analysis of some of the Christian perspectives upon history.

Part I: Perspectives From Tradition

CHAPTER II

SOME LEADING CHRISTIAN IDEAS—WITH

HELP FROM ST. AUGUSTINE

CHRISTIANITY is an avowedly *historical* religion. Its faith frankly stems, not from general philosophical truths, but from particular events in history. And it asserts that God is sovereign over history. To read the record of history with its cruelties, confusions, and absurdities is to wonder why any religion should want to claim to be a historical religion. Many a skeptic reports that it is hard enough to believe in God, harder to believe that He reigns over, and reveals Himself in, history. Yet Christianity stakes everything on claims which most religions consider an unwanted burden.

Why? The answer can be found only in examining a few of the leading ideas of the Christian tradition. The greatest help will come from St. Augustine's great work, *The City of God*. Its vivid relevance for contemporary thought has been noted by many a recent writer, secular as well as Christian. Often neglected and considered only waste lumber in the attic of Christian tradition, this book which came out of one of the last crises of the Roman empire has revealed powerful meanings to modern civilization in its time of troubles.

I. THE REINTERPRETATION OF BIBLICAL ESCHATOLOGY

From the beginning the faith of the church was *eschatological*.[1] That is, the Christian community believed that history's significance lay not merely in its obvious day-to-day course of events, but in its final destiny under God. Loyalty to God might plunge the believer into sufferings and confusions whose purpose he could not discern. But he was confident that in the last days (at the *Eschaton*), God would manifest Himself. This faith may also be called *apocalyptic*; for it looks forward to a revelation or manifestation (*apocalypse*) of God at the *End* of history. The apocalyptic writings of the Bible (and many more fantastic ones which did not get into the canon) are puzzling in their spectacular and imaginative language. But they express the conviction that God has the last word over history. His power, now dimly discernible and opposed by vicious evil, will assert itself in His Kingdom. The meaning of history, now hidden, will be revealed.

Many of the New Testament writers clearly expect history to come to an early end, when the Kingdom of God will supersede the kingdoms of this world. In the Gospel teaching the Last Judgment is so imminent as to give meaning to every moment of life. History stands immediately before its fulfillment. Numerous Gospel statements tell that the Kingdom is at hand, is al-

---

[1] As I finish writing this book the correspondence columns of the *Christian Century* carry a layman's protest, made in all sincerity, against *eschatology*. The writer says that he lived seventy-seven years without hearing the word and finds no need for it in the afternoon of life. The answer is that as long as he lived with the New Testament he has lived with eschatology. Of course, English translations of the New Testament do not suggest the exact word; but the idea is there, in all the Gospels and most of the other books. It is unfortunate that religious scholarship must so often use a technical vocabulary. But so must physics and law and baseball. Fortunately, faithful men can belong to God's eschatological Kingdom without knowing the word.

ready evident within history, or will come with sudden crisis. The day and the hour are unknown and do not matter; the important thing is that the Kingdom is imminent—in some sense actually present. The signs of the times are full of meaning.[2]

Such an interpretation may have a perennial religious relevance, as many a Christian has discovered in the recent holocausts of history. But it minimizes the ordinary questions of an understanding of history. It takes little account of the cultural and historical problems involved in the movements of kingdoms and empires. The state—symbol of so much of the stuff of history —is on the way to its end; the Christian may, like St. Paul, advocate acquiescence to it, or like the seer on Patmos, hurl defiance and judgment against it. In neither case is it, or the whole political-social order of secular life, of final importance.

As the years went on Christianity had to take more and more account of worldly history. The impatience of eschatological hopes had to be subdued—to some extent even in the New Testament, and increasingly through the years. Especially after Constantine's edict in 313 A.D., when the religion of a once persecuted minority became respectable and started the move toward dominance in Rome, Christianity had to come to an understanding of society and history in more general terms than before. Christian thought now had to assume a relative permanence and significance for a continuing history and to take a responsibility for the social order.

By the time of Augustine Christianity was the accepted religion of a great empire which was falling apart. The decline of empire, which would once have been the expected thing among

---

[2] New Testament scholars disagree widely in trying to establish exactly what Jesus taught. But all the above ideas are evident in the Synoptic Gospels. In the midst of the diversity of New Testament scholarship, I am assuming a point of view which is in general supported by a broad consensus of experts, ranging from Rudolf Bultmann, with his *Formgeschichte* and strong apocalyptic emphasis, to C. H. Dodd, with his much more conservative critical position and realized eschatology.

Christians, now presented serious problems and required restate-
ment of the Christian view of history. Augustine wrote his *De
Civitate Dei* between the years of 413, soon after Alaric's Goths
had stormed and sacked Rome, and 426, four years before he
died while the Vandals besieged his African city of Hippo. And
the work was written as the direct outcome of the challenge involved in the course of historical events.

Augustine's permanent importance lies in his adaptation of
New Testament eschatology to the expectation of a continuing
history. The materials for his reformulation he took largely
from the Bible itself. On this issue, in fact, he made little use of
the non-Christian philosophies (Stoic and Neo-Platonic) which
influenced other aspects of his thought. In Old Testament
prophecy history is a mighty drama with God the author, and
the New Testament does not forget its heritage. In prophetic
teaching the nations are as drops in a bucket before God, who
raises and destroys them according to His holy will. But though
God is judge of the nations, His judgment is not easy to discern.
His wrath and His patience are mingled. And each evidence of
judgment is found incomplete; wrong is crushed but new wrongs
appear. God's will is evident in the actual movements of history
but is never completely expressed in the particular event. There
has to be a future reference. Increasingly prophecy sounds the
eschatological note. In the perplexities of history more attention
is given to the individual; the books of Jeremiah, Ezekiel, the
Psalms, and Job record the result. But the problem of history
remains. What is the meaning of the judgments of history if
they are always incomplete? To answer the problem prophecy
must be transformed into apocalypse. A Last Judgment and a
Resurrection will see God's sovereignty clearly manifest. But
the prophetic insistence that God is the ruler of history is not
lost.

Augustine's Christian understanding of history unites prophecy and apocalypse. He sees the will of God effective in the long

sweep of history; but he finds that the story of history can be told only in view of its End.

II. THE BASIC MEANING IN ESCHATOLOGY, AND ITS ALTERNATIVES

The Hebrew-Christian faith, confident that history under God has meaning, rejects the two frequent alternatives: (1) the belief which finds the meaning of life in escape from history; (2) the belief that history creates and exhausts its own meaning. Instead the Bible expresses the conviction that history derives its meaning from a transcendent God. This God is not located at a point in space; He does not come alive, mature, and die in time like men. Yet God, superior to space and time, is concerned with history; He acts to reveal Himself at a particular place and date. Thus the eschatological understanding rejects both the non-historical and the completely historical alternatives.

It is the non-historical alternative which has probably dominated most philosophical thought, although it has not been prominent in the modern western "climate of opinion." As Christopher Dawson says, "This denial of the significance of history is the rule rather than the exception among philosophers and religious teachers throughout the ages from India to Greece and from China to Northern Europe." [1] It is basic to such widespread religions as most forms of Hinduism and Buddhism. It is the tendency of philosophies of idealism and mysticism, and entered much of Christian thought via Hellenism. If God—the ultimately real—is pure being, immutable in contrast to the changing temporal realm of experience, history with its obvious relativities and contingencies becomes finally insignificant. Hence comes the devaluation of history in Platonism, Neo-Platonism, and the host of mystical religions of ancient and modern times. Even Aristotle, rebelling against Platonic other-worldliness but just as non-

[1] In *The Kingdom of God and History* (Oxford Conference Book) (New York: Harpers), p. 198.

historical, wrote in his *Poetics* that "poetry is something more philosophic and of graver import than history, since its statements are of the nature rather of universals, whereas those of history are singulars" (1451b5).

Augustine, with his Neo-Platonic tendencies, had to come to terms with the non-historical points of view and sometimes came too close to a mystical negation of history. But the Bible restrained him. For eschatology, even at its most other-worldly, does not promise a mystical salvation; rather history moves forward toward its consummation, a consummation which is in the hands of the God who created history and rules it, even if from a distance. Further, salvation relates to historical communities— at the very least the community of the faithful. The Kingdom of God is in some sense a continuation of history, even though it be a new heaven and a new earth. Eschatological faith shares the conviction of most religions that there is more to reality than we see, that the obvious in history does not contain all of history's meaning. However, the meaning is not to be found by transcending the partialities of history to discover universals, but by living out the historical process to its End.

The second major alternative, in which the only meanings of history rest within the historical process, is likewise frequent. Its most common form finds the meaning of history in the success of a particular state or imperialism. Then a threat to the state undermines the philosophy of history and throws into question the entire religious significance of life. This was specifically the problem which occasioned Augustine's *City of God*.

State religions—whether overtly or subtly religious—really make impossible a philosophy of history. All states have the same right to claim that they embody the significance of history, so the result is an absurdity. The Roman empire could make the claim more plausibly than most others—certainly more so than the North European society in which Hegel was to imagine the culmination of history centuries later. It was a more logical candidate for the position than is any modern nationalism and probably than any of our theoretical schemes for world government. In what Cochrane calls the "Vergilian theology," the meaning of history is "fully disclosed only with the culmination of secular process in the evolution of Eternal Rome." [2] But Christianity had always been convinced that *Roma Aeterna* was not eternal and had rejected its pretensions to be the object of religious loyalty. Against all attempts to link the divine with any particular civilization, Augustine points to a succession of fallen empires and asks ironically what happened to their gods.

With equal vehemence Augustine opposed Epicureanism—a non-nationalistic representative of this-worldliness. In its original Greek form and in its transplanting to Rome in the verse of Lucretius it advanced materialism as an answer to the anxieties and dreads involved in religious superstition. As is so often true of materialism, its goal is as obviously salvation as that of other religions. Epicurus was sometimes called "Savior" (σωτήρ) by his followers. Like Cicero, Augustine knew Epicureanism in its more degenerate forms. But even at its best, its ideal of tranquillity would have affronted Augustine—both the passionate mystic and the ecclesiastical activist. More fundamental, it denied completely any place in history (or without) for the divine meaning which is essential to Christian apocalypse, and Augustine attacked its materialism as well as its ethics.[3]

These two opposing alternatives to the apocalyptic interpretation may not be so far apart as they appear. Whether divine significance be completely denied or utterly separated from history in remote transcendence, the result is to leave history the

---

[2] Charles N. Cochrane, *Christianity and Classical Culture*, p. 68. Cochrane points out the repeated attributions of eternity and finality to Rome in the cases of Vergil (pp. 27, 68–71), Suetonius (p. 1), Polybius (p. 93), and Livy (pp. 96 ff.). The whole education and discipline of citizenship involved the same claim (p. 151).

[3] *City of God*, V, 20; VIII, 5, 7; XI, 5; XIV, 2; XIX, 1; *Confessions*, VI, xvi, 26.

realm of the finite and contingent, and thus to deny it the meaning which Christian apocalypse affirms. Thus it is not remarkable that both of these alternatives showed tendencies toward the cyclical interpretation of history.

The modern western world, which has inherited from the Hebrews and gone on to develop the dynamic conception of time and of the historical process, seldom realizes how extensively cyclical interpretations of history have dominated human thought. The theme of world-cycles is repeated recurrently in the mythology and literature of the various religions of India.[4] Arnold Toynbee describes its appearance in China, developing partly from indigenous, partly from Indic or Babylonian origins; and in the quite independent Aztec mythology of successive world-ages.[5] The prevalence of cyclical conceptions in classical historians, philosophers, and dramatists has often been noticed. They had even, in the case of Ecclesiastes, got into the Old Testament where they called for all of Augustine's exegetical ingenuity to overcome them. Augustine knew the theory best in the weary cyclicism of the the Stoics, so evident in the writings of Marcus Aurelius. But the issue is not entirely an ancient one. The cyclic conceptions are found in Schopenhauer and Nietzsche, and more recently in Spengler. Shelley's Final Chorus of *Hellas* protests against the classicism which entrances him. Arnold Toynbee's thought constantly evidences both the classical and the Christian conceptions which have helped to form it.

All of these cyclical interpretations present a problem for a philosophy of history. Obviously, any empirical approach to history will find a succession of political orders, of cultures and civilizations, which have risen and fallen. It will find resemblances as well as differences in the courses of these various historical societies. But the problem of a philosophy of history is

---

[4] For an analysis of this tendency see Sir Charles Eliot, *Hinduism and Buddhism* (London: Arnold, 1921), I, lxvii f., 42–47.
[5] *A Study of History*, IV, 23–39.

the significant meaning of history. Thus Christian interpretations, in opposing cyclical philosophies of history, will not deny certain periodic characteristics of history. Insofar as classical views are supported by empirical evidence, they must be accepted. Augustine, for example, was aware of the long succession of empires which constitute history. In opposing classical views he did not argue so much about the evidence as about the meaning of the evidence. Empirical evidence, of course, is relevant; it can be used, as a matter of fact, to refute the rigid cyclical determinism of a Pythagorean, a Polybius, or a Spengler, and to show the variety of actual history. But the problem, except in the most extreme theories, is not one of detailed factual recurrence; the question is whether the meaning of history is exhausted in events which can only repeat old monotonous meaning or meaninglessness.

Influenced though he was at so many places by current secular philosophies, Augustine forcibly wrenched loose his Christian doctrine of history from opposing cyclical ones and refuted them vigorously. The idea of eternal recurrence is abhorrent to him. It shatters the entire meaning of life and history. Man's present life, with all its trials, is vibrant with significance as long as it is seen as moving, under God's plan, to its eschatological outcome. Cyclicism arises when the finite, human mind, unable to grasp the incomprehensible, tries to force the infinite into its own patterns of thought. Augustine may have little reticence before his opponents, but he has a deep humility before God; so he derides the futile attempts to grasp eternity quite inadequately in the form of a circle. His own positive utterance comes after a vigorous denunciation of cyclical conceptions, when he bursts out:

Far be it, I say, from us to believe this. For once Christ dies for our sins; and, rising from the dead, He dieth no more.[6]

---

[6] *Ibid.,* XII, 13. *Cf.* XII, 10, 13, 14, 17, 20; X, 30.

The quotation from Paul is quite to the point—more so than it seems at first glance. Augustine is not using a mere proof-text or bit of reasoning from authority. He is answering the question: Is there something about human decision in history which is irrevocable and unrepeatable, a unique act of freedom, which cannot be subsumed under the categories by which we interpret nature or "natural history"? Or does history simply illustrate the natural process, which can be interpreted in terms of natural laws and in which variations are not decisive events but accidents?

For Christianity historical events are unique, and God's act in Christ is the supreme such event. To some extent all human decisions are unique and unrepeatable, as is every human personality. But in Christ the Christian recognizes the sheer uniqueness of an event, the *Einmaligkeit* or once-for-all-ness, which modern theology stresses. A contemporary theologian's argument parallels Augustine's exactly at this point. "Only through this decisive event is it impossible to turn Time into a myth, and the idea of eternal cycles is eliminated. . . . In the event of Christ, as it is grasped by faith, the mythical cycle has been broken through, the idea of everlasting recurrence has been eliminated."[7]

Thus an apocalyptic interpretation of history, which is in part frankly other-worldly, can yet contribute to a dynamic conception of history. For it asserts divine activity in original, irreversible, unrepeatable events.

III. CHRISTIAN PARTICULARISM AND UNIVERSAL HISTORY

The emphasis upon a unique event like the Incarnation as a focal point for the interpretation of universal history raises a new

[7] Emil Brunner, *Man in Revolt*, pp. 442–43; *Revelation and Reason*, p. 406. *Cf.* Donald Baillie, *God Was in Christ* (New York: Scribners, 1948), pp. 76–77.

set of problems. How can history be given meaning by a historical character or event unknown to the majority of the human
race? Any culture, of course, can assume that history culminates
in itself. But this is merely to repeat the errors of Vergil and
Augustus and a host of others; and such errors, repeated through
the centuries, begin to appear ridiculous.

The problems of historical pluralism have been made obvious
by the writings of Troeltsch, Spengler, and Toynbee, who have
shown how entire cultures have come and gone with values,
world-views, and purposes quite different from ours. The problem was not unknown to the Mediterranean world, which was
the center of many cultural cross-currents. Augustine was
aware of a considerable history of political and religious diversity,
and deliberately aimed to meet the problems which it raised.
The interpretation of history could not depend solely upon
transitory movements.

Creation, the fall, and final salvation (or damnation)—these
for Augustine are clearly events in the history of mankind. They
are the most significant events for the human situation of any
man—regardless of race, geography, or time. By these events the
varieties of history are unified. As Figgis has stated it, "History is
a unity. No one before or since taught more plainly the solidarity
of man." [1] If mankind, united in sin, faces a universal need for
salvation, then the answer to that need is universal. There are
no detachable individuals or nations, who can be unrelated to
this historical heritage. We are all in Adam. The glory of the
Creator's image and the distortion of sin are ours, because we are
part of the history of the human race. We can separate ourselves
neither from our contemporaries nor from our ancestors.

Whatever difficulties there are in the idea, it is clear that
this is both universal and historical thinking. But how can so
universal a problem, requiring so universal an answer, be con-

[1] John Figgis, The Political Aspects of S. Augustine's 'City of God,' p.
43.

nected with the particular unique event which, judged by most historical criteria, is of minor importance? Christianity is often accused of an interpretation of history which haughtily disdains the non-Christian world.[2] Augustine meets the problem by an extensive use of the *logos* doctrine. The doctrine, of course, was fundamental to the Fourth Gospel and to some of Paul's epistles, notably Colossians: "all things were created through him and for him" (1:16). If all things are created for Him, He is the Christ of all men.

Developing this idea Augustine finds it not at all necessary— in some cases, at least—that men should have historical knowledge of Christ in order for God's grace to save them. The most far-reaching claims of Christian particularism are united with universalism, as Augustine says:

. . . the Lord Jesus may be understood to be our God who is before the worlds, because by Him the worlds were made, working our salvation in the midst of the earth, for the Word was made flesh and dwelt in an earthly body.[3]

The thought that Christ is the answer to man's universal predicament is expressed in the idea that He is the fulfillment of prophecy. Page after page Augustine enumerates pagan as well as Old Testament prophecies of the coming of Christ. Obviously he relies on a fantastic and obsolete exegesis, but his method cannot be dismissed so easily. For the thinker who found in man and all creation the *vestigia Dei* thus finds likewise in Christ the fulfillment of men's longings and needs throughout all history.

---

[2] Even if the charge were true, it would be no worse, as such, than the viewpoint of modern intellectuals who must write off the majority of history in which men had no sense of the salvation which can be wrought by our particular understanding of scientific method. See Arnold Toynbee, *Civilization on Trial*, p. 89.

[3] *City of God*, XVII, 4. Cf. *Ep.* 102, part 11.

Thus in a letter written in 409 Augustine expressed his Christology in very broad terms:

Therefore, from the beginning of the human race, whosoever believed in Him, and in any way knew Him, and lived in a pious and just manner according to His precepts, was undoubtedly saved by Him, in whatever time and places he may have lived. For as we believe in Him both as dwelling with the Father and as having come in the flesh, so the men of the former ages believed in Him both as dwelling with the Father and as destined to come in the flesh. . . . Wherefore the true religion, although formerly set forth and practised under other names and with other symbolical rites than it now has, and formerly more obscurely revealed and known to fewer persons than now in the time of clearer light and wider diffusion, is one and the same in both periods.[4]

One might turn even so universal an interpretation into a more subtle theological imperialism, but Augustine was aware of that danger and—at least sometimes—knew how to avoid it. On the whole his attitude toward Christian truth is humble, not possessive. He is ready to acknowledge a considerable degree of relativism in the historical forms which religion may take:

For since . . . the ages of the world do not roll on under the dominion of chance, but are controlled by divine Providence, what may be fitting and expedient in each successive age transcends the range of human understanding, and is determined by the same wisdom by which Providence cares for the universe.[5]

In the same spirit Augustine in the *City of God* recognizes, following St. Paul, a doctrine of "general revelation" (VIII, 11).

The concern for universal history makes necessary some shift in the emphasis of New Testament apocalypse. St. Paul, although obviously aware of a long and significant tradition, was more concerned with the intensity than the length and

---

[4] *Ep.* 102, part 12. Cf. *City of God*, X, 25, 32.
[5] *Ibid.*, 13.

breadth of history. His apocalyptic drama had two main foci: one past—the Cross and Resurrection, and one future—the return of Christ and the End. Augustine pushed the frontiers of significant history far forward into the future and far back into the past.

As for the future Augustine thinks that history may run on for an indefinite time. The millennium (which for Augustine started with Christ) is a symbol for an unknown length of time, and he makes the conjecture that history may be going on after six hundred thousand years. He has only disdain for those whose "audacious presumption" uses Scripture as a means to predict details of the future.

Similarly Augustine extends his interpretation of history into the distant past. In the setting of a vaster cosmic history he undertakes to survey the entire course of the human race. Within the variety of forms of historical life, Augustine discovers the two realities which unite, and divide, all history: the two historical societies or cities. The two start with the "foundations of the earth," with the first man and woman, and even before them with the angels. The sharp Pauline distinction between B.C. and A.D. becomes in one sense less important, as the two societies alike extend through the sweep of history. Since the entire *logos* of history—both in its unity and its division—is the *Logos* which was made flesh, it may be said that for Augustine, as for many another, Christ is the "center of history." [6] But this center has nothing to do with chronology. Augustine's intention was not to describe Jesus of Nazareth as the founder of the heavenly society.

The whole human race is divided into these two communi-

---

[6] Wilhelm Windelband writes that "all doctrines of Christianity, however widely they may otherwise diverge philosophically or mythically, are yet at one in seeking in him [Jesus] and his appearance the *centre of the world's history*." *A History of Philosophy* (New York: Macmillan, 1893), p. 256.

ties, which are now intermingled but are destined to be separated.[7] The distinction between them is the inner character which animates them—a difference of faith and of love:

Accordingly, two cities have been formed by two loves: the earthly by the love of self, even to the contempt of God; the heavenly by the love of God, even to the contempt of self. The former, in a word, glories in itself, the latter in the Lord. For the one seeks glory from men; but the greatest glory of the other is God, the witness of conscience.[8]

All other aspects or institutions of history—the various kingdoms and peoples with their historical achievements, the admirable insights of some of the philosophers, the institution of the Christian church—are subordinated to the central issue of history.[9] From this perspective Augustine surveys the whole of history, tracing the conflict of the two societies from its beginning to the present. Looking ahead, he expects no progressive transformation of society into the Kingdom of God, but continued conflict, with the church probably suffering more persecutions, until the end of history. Then will come the final battle, with Christ conquering Satan. After the resurrection and Last Judgment, the two cities will be finally separated. In a great con-

---

[7] Repeatedly Augustine emphasizes the universal character of the two societies in time and geography. See *City of God*, XI, 1; XLV, 1, 28; XV, 1, 2; XIX, 17. Also, *On the Catechizing of the Uninstructed*, XIX, 31; XX, 36; XXI, 37.

[8] *City of God*, XIV, 28.

[9] It is natural for Protestants to emphasize this non-institutional side of Augustine's thought, which often veered toward a more rigid ecclesiasticism. But Roman Catholic scholars usually agree in this interpretation. Among Protestants Heinrich Scholz has investigated the problem in great detail. He expresses the theme of the *City of God* in the title of his commentary on it, *Glaube und Unglaube in der Weltgeschichte*. Among Catholic scholars, Christopher Dawson finds the divine society "as wide as humanity." See "St. Augustine and His Age," in *A Monument to St. Augustine*, p. 66. *Cf.* Etienne Gilson, *Introduction a l'Etude de Saint Augustin*.

flagration this heaven and earth will pass away and there will
be a new heaven and a new earth.

Thus Christian particularism offers Augustine the opportunity to survey the whole of universal history, the establishment
of great empires and the problems of the individual human life.
At the beginning Christ is the *Logos* through which the world
is created. At the end Christ is the Judge of man. In the broad
expanse of history between beginning and end, Christ has been
revealed—in one manner or another—to all men of the divine
society. At one particular point in history, He was revealed in a
special manner, in the Incarnation. Here the meaning of history
and of life is brought into clear focus. But, though the devil
is chained, the struggle of history still goes on as before, awaiting
the final victory of the Christ who has already been made known
to men.

Any interpretation of history must deal with the significance
of the particular. Only non-historical religions—idealistic or
mystic—can insist that the general alone has ultimate significance.
But if a religious interpretation insists upon the final significance
of any single particular event to the extent of making much of
history irrelevant, it destroys the possibility of a philosophy of
history as decidedly as does its opposite. Augustine offers a possibility of relating the universal and the particular in such a way
that history may have a divine significance—with meaning in
every stage of the process, as it is seen in relation to God's supreme and unique revelation in Christ.

In Gilson's words, "The point of departure for Augustine is,
then, the revelation which, in conferring upon history the universality which our fragmentary experience cannot attain, un-
veiling especially its origin and its end, makes possible the
philosophy of history and confers upon the universe an intelli-
gibility within the temporal order." [10] Somewhat similarly a non-

---

[10] Etienne Gilson, *Introduction a l'Etude de Saint Augustin,* pp. 237–
38. (My translation.) *Cf.* Emil Brunner, *Revelation and Reason,* p. 405.

theological writer, R. G. Collingwood, has said that a history written on Christian principles is necessarily universal, having undergone the Copernican revolution which destroyed the particularistic centers characteristic of all previous Greek and Roman history.[11]

IV. THE SOVEREIGNTY OF GOD

The problem of history is the problem of the sovereignty of God, from which the meaning of history derives. Several possible religious attitudes on this issue are evident.

The first possibility is to assert the complete sovereignty of God in simple terms. This is to say that the whole of history is meaningful to the human mind—or at least that it will become meaningful if the mind is persistent and intelligent enough in trying to understand. It is to insist that the world and history are rational. Such a view, although most typical of idealism, may take naturalistic forms (as in Stoicism). It is the religion of reason. Whether or not it finds cosmic and historical meaning congenial to human desires, it insists that the whole of reality is, in some terms, meaningful, and that the sovereignty of God, however God be conceived, is complete.

Such a faith, from the viewpoint of Augustinian Christianity, does not take sufficient account of the limitations of the finite mind interpreting reality, or of the meaning defying elements of reality. It is extremely difficult to discern a rationale of history—a reason why rationalism has been more popular in metaphysics than in philosophies of history. A recent interpreter of Augustine, criticizing this religion of reason, says: "In point of fact, it constitutes an audacious anthropomorphism, a kind of sky-writing which projects upon the cosmos a merely human rationality and translates it into an account of nature and of God."[1]

---

[11] *The Idea of History*, pp. 49–50.
[1] Charles N. Cochrane, *Christianity and Classical Culture*, p. 167.

The most obvious alternative to such confident rationalism is to deny any over-all rationale of history—to discover areas of meaning in a history which is not entirely meaningful. The viewpoint may be expressed in polytheism or in the affirmation of a finite God. It takes seriously the irrational and capricious, the incoherent and purposeless, elements in history. It can say of cataclysmic natural events which influence history, like a disastrous drought or a freak of weather which decides a battle, that they are pure accident (or pure determinism) and have nothing to do with the meaning of life and history. It can say of historic events like the eruption of Nazism that they are the result of forces of human freedom which successfully defy the sovereignty of God.

The difficulty of this interpretation, from an Augustinian viewpoint, is that it makes all meaning in life precarious. If God is not fully sovereign, He is not really sovereign at all. If life and history do not take place within a total context of meaning, they are in the end hopeless. For the human mind to sketch out areas of meaning within a futile and senseless cosmic or historical context is to sit in a lifeboat which will at any moment be engulfed by the sea. The threat of meaninglessness makes all meaning insecure. If there is to be a religious interpretation of history, the meaning-defying elements must be finally subject to the meaning-affirming elements. In traditional language even Satan must exercise his power within the sovereignty of God.

In contrast to the two alternatives Augustine asserted that God is infinite and omnipotent but that finite man cannot comprehend all the ways of God. This is to insist that although man cannot puzzle out the meaning of all that happens, there is meaning in everything. It is the feeling of St. Paul—"to know God, or rather to be known by God" (Gal. 4:9). In the confidence that God is sovereign, Augustine did not worry that he could not discern the purpose of all that happened. He could say, as Santayana has said: ". . . a really naked spirit cannot assume that the world is thoroughly intelligible. There may be surds, there may be hard facts, there may be dark abysses before which intelligence must be silent, for fear of going mad." [2] But Augustine could accept the irrationalities of history without going mad because of his assurance that the surds and abysses were intelligible to God. He could acknowledge the mystery of existence, regarding the mystery as divine and not merely chaotic. He could be confident that "the Almighty does nothing without reason, though the frail mind of man cannot explain the reason." [3]

Obviously this Augustinian judgment must be that of faith. It cannot be empirically established or rationally deduced. But there is nothing inherently foolish or even improbable about it. If one accepts it as a principle, an *arche*, for interpreting history, it is at least as useful as the alternatives and may go farther than they in meeting the problems of a philosophy of history.

Augustine has no use for the pagan deities, *Tyche* and *Fortuna*. Nothing is sheer chance, meaninglessness. The appearance of chance in any event is due to our failure to see the reasons involved.[4] This does not mean that for Augustine, as for many moderns, the concept of accident is made obsolete by the recognition of undiscovered efficient causes. Augustine is not interested in efficient causality, but in ultimate meaning. The modern refinements of scientific analysis with their stress upon efficient causality do not make irrelevant this idea of the expression of God's sovereignty in all events. Frequently Augustine intimates the idea that Kant was to make explicit—that time and causality are human modes of apprehending and cannot be applied to the ultimate divine reality. Nor do his vivid anthropo-

---

[2] George Santayana, "Ultimate Religion," in *Obiter Scripta*, ed. by J. Buchler and B. Schwartz. (New York: Scribners, 1936), p. 290.
[3] *City of God*, XXI, 5. Cf. V, 21; *De Genesis contra Manichaeos*, I, xvi, 25.
[4] *Retractions*, I, 1–2. Migne, Vol. XXXII.

morphic descriptions of God endanger his reverence for the divine mystery, for he frequently warns against the danger of literalism.

Thus the all-encompassing sovereignty of God is expressed:

Therefore God supreme and true, with His Word and Holy Spirit (which three are one), one God omnipotent, creator and maker of every soul and of every body; by whose gift all are happy who are happy through verity and not through vanity; who made man a rational animal consisting of soul and body, who, when he sinned, neither permitted him to go unpunished nor left him without mercy; who has given to the good and to the evil, being in common with stones, vegetable life in common with trees, sensuous life in common with brutes, intellectual life in common with angels alone; from whom is every mode, every species, every order; from whom are measure, number, weight; from whom is everything which has an existence in nature, of whatever kind it be, and of whatever value; . . . —that God can never be believed to have left the kingdoms of men, their dominations and servitudes, outside of the laws of His providence.[5]

The insistence on the sovereignty of God did not beguile Augustine into a failure to take seriously the evil in the world. In his spiritual pilgrimage he had tried and rejected Manichean dualism and Neo-Platonic monism, in favor of a doctrine of creation. The peculiar relation of sin and evil to divine sovereignty is illustrated most vividly in the discussions of Satan and the demons. Ancient demonologies sometimes seem amusing to the twentieth-century mind; but in the twentieth century, more than in many another, it would seem foolhardy to deny the aspects of history which other ages have represented by demons. Certainly there are forces in history—whether in the subconscious workings of collective psychology or the entirely nonconscious historical processes—which turn human ignorance and

---

[5] *City of God*, V, 11. *Cf.* V, 21; VII, 30; X, 14.

sin to destructive consequences which men would never deliberately plan.

Augustine meets this problem by recognizing (in the demons)
the reality of evil as blunt defiance of God, not to be minimized
or explained away. But he insists that this defiance of God does
not defeat God, either in the whole of history or in the particular
event. No situation becomes so destructive or chaotic that it cannot serve to enhance faith. In Augustine's vivid language:

[The demons] have only that power which the secret decree of the
Almighty allots to them . . . : for as wicked men on earth cannot do
all they would, so neither can these demons, but only in so far as
they are permitted by the decree of Him whose judgments are fully
comprehensible, justly reprehensible, by none.[6]

If such reasoning may on occasion be apologetic sophistry, the
answer is that in Augustine's case it is not. The key to the issue
is in the insistence that one meets the issue of evil not by pro-
pitiating the demons, but by praying to the God who is stronger
than they.

On this basis the discussion of the rise and fall of empires in
human history becomes intelligible. As bitingly as any cynical
atheist might, Augustine ridicules the pagan ideas of a dispensation of providence by which the good are made to prosper and
the bad to suffer. But this is preliminary to the statement of his
own faith in providence:

Therefore that God, the author and giver of felicity, because He
alone is the true God, Himself gives earthly kingdoms both to good
and bad. Neither does He do this rashly and, as it were, fortuitously,
—because He is God not fortune,—but according to the order of
things and times, which is hidden from us, but thoroughly known to
Himself; which same order of times, however, he does not serve as
subject to it, but Himself rules as lord and appoints as governor.
Felicity He gives only to the good. Whether a man be subject or a

---

[6] *City of God*, II, 23. *Cf.* XVIII, 18; XX, 19; XXII, 2.

king makes no difference; he may equally either possess or not possess it. And it shall be full in that life where kings and subjects
exist no longer.[7]

Augustine, of course, does not argue that the bare facts of history reacting upon a bare human intelligence will show divine
providence. It is only the insight of faith that can perceive God's
action in events; but life and history are such as to grant this
insight to faith.

The Augustinian conception of the divine majesty makes
quite unnecessary, if not ridiculous or blasphemous, any detailed
justification of the ways of God to man. Yet the Christian seeks
to fit evil as intelligibly as possible into his interpretation of
history. Augustine suggests several theoretical answers to the
problem of evil. (1) The theory of evil as non-being, a deposit
of Augustine's early Neo-Platonism, is never entirely abandoned
even in the later insistence that sin is a dynamic perversion of
will. (2) The old Stoic aesthetic theodicy is echoed; evil, like
the shadows of a picture, contributes to a larger good. (3) Most
important, and most biblical, is the basic insistence, expressed
in the famous sentence: "For He judged it better to bring good
out of evil, than not to permit any evil to exist." [8] This is not to
say that all evil contributes to recognizable goods. It is to say that
when man adjusts his purposes to God's purposes within the
heavenly society, he can trust that evil has its place within the
scheme of salvation. The only alternative to this is impossible for
Augustine—the acknowledgment of areas of life and history
which are totally devoid of any possibility of meaning.

More important than this theoretical theodicy is the practical
counsel which Augustine gives, in his City of God, to Christians

---

[7] City of God, IV, 33. Throughout Books III–V Augustine gives his conjectures as to why God has granted dominion to various relatively worthy
or unworthy sovereignties, always granting that there are hidden reasons
beyond his knowledge.
[8] Enchiridion, 27. Cf. City of God, XXII, 1; XI, 17; XIV, 27.

troubled by their sufferings in the breakup of the Roman empire. There is the idea—offering little comfort in itself—that all men are deserving of punishment. There is the more helpful judgment that it is human sin which makes many events into suffering, for "in the same affliction the wicked detest God and blaspheme, while the good pray and praise." [9] There is the closely related idea that Christians, if they cannot find God's purpose in events, will nevertheless find an opportunity—an opportunity to demonstrate trust and love, patience and beneficence. Even death can be turned into the glory of man.

The final and all-important element in this practical theodicy is the assurance that God grants true blessedness only to the faithful. The cause of all blessedness is adherence to God, and the cause of misery, defection from God. Here is the real assurance of the sovereignty of God. Referring to the sufferings of the Christians in the sack of Rome, Augustine writes:

> But, say they, many Christians were even led away captive. This indeed were a most pitiable fate, if they could be led away to any place where they could not find their God.
> They lost all they had. Their faith? Their godliness? The possessions of the hidden man of the heart, which in the sight of God are of great price? Did they lose these? For these are the wealth of Christians. [10]

So the two societies move through history: "both alike enjoy temporal good things, or are afflicted with temporal evils, but with diverse faith, diverse hope, and diverse love" (XVIII, 54).

This whole theodicy draws its significance from its context— the eschatological interpretation of history. At the End of history there will be made plain the purposes of the divine will, which have been expressed so bafflingly in history. Then will be made

---

[9] *City of God*, I, 8. *Cf.* I, 10; V, 24. There are Stoic antecedents to this idea, but Augustine pointedly attacks the Stoic ideal of *apatheia* and turns his doctrine in a different direction. See XIV, 9.
[10] *Ibid.*, I, 14, 10. *Cf.* XII, 1, 6.

evident the justice in the mysterious and inscrutable will of God.[11]

To many this continuous appeal to an incomprehensible mystery will appear an evasion. As used by some Christian apologists, it is. If one presents a neat argument for theism as the most coherent explanation of the available data, then runs into the problem of evil, it is an evasion to take refuge in appeals to the inscrutable judgment of God. But for Augustine finite man's recognition of God's grandeur and infinity is the starting point as well as the conclusion of the argument. He does not appeal to God's inscrutability at the point of difficulty; he merely recalls that it is at the heart of his entire interpretation. Throughout his conception of history he insists that man cannot comprehend the meaning of everything, but can proceed with the faith that history and the universe have a meaning.

We shall return to the problem of the sovereignty of God. But any further developments of the idea will find their background in the Christianity of Augustine.

V. THE THREE-STRANDED THREAD

Henry Adams could not have found from Augustine the "spool on which to wind the thread of history without breaking it." The spool no man can find; God alone holds it. Man cannot discern with any clarity the direction the tangled thread takes. But if the man of faith seeks guidance for life in history, God has granted him a thread that he may hold as he gropes his way through the dimly lighted earthly pilgrimage. It is a thread, less of theoretical understanding of the scheme of history, than of practical assurance in historical life.

The thread which Augustine holds is twisted of three strands, and the breaking of any one leaves the thread precariously frayed. The first is the emphasis upon the ultimate eschatological fulfillment which gives meaning to an otherwise chaotic

---

[11] Ibid., XX, 2.

and incomplete history. The second is the significance within history of the divine society, conceived as the true church, in contrast to the earthly society. The third is the appreciation of history itself, including "secular" history and its dynamic possibilities of human achievement. Augustine did not give equal emphasis to the three strands, but he included them all. Subsequent Christian interpretations have re-evaluated the significance of the three, shifting the emphasis among them, sometimes omitting one or another.

A. THE ESCHATOLOGICAL FULFILLMENT

Traditional Christianity could not conceive history apart from the Last Judgment and the establishment of God's Kingdom in purity and power. This radical eschatological emphasis, so foreign to modern thought, becomes a live option when one considers the alternatives—as many of its critics refuse to do. From the Augustinian viewpoint the alternatives are utopianism and cynicism. Utopianism is the illusion of those who think history can fulfill itself. Cynicism and despair are the result of assuming that there can be no fulfillment of history. Many people, it would appear, avoid the sharp consequences of either alternative simply by mingling the two inconsistently and striking a happy average. In Augustine's conception the Christian finds blessedness by participation in the heavenly society, which is a pilgrim and sojourner on earth. So he is "happy in the present time by hope."

In attacking the illusions of secularism Augustine achieves a realistic view of temporal history. As Arthur Schlesinger, Jr., has said, "Whatever you may say about Augustine, at least he would not have been much surprised by the outcome of the Russian Revolution." [1]

It is easy to point out with some amusement how Augustine mingles the most eloquent descriptions of the goodness of the

[1] "Niebuhr's Vision of Our Time," *Nation*, CLXII (1946), 754.

created world with morbid accounts of the dangers and evils of life. But the inconsistencies are derived from a basically consistent position: Life is good, but its goodness comes from God. When men rely for security on their own plans and ideals, so obviously subject to accident and destruction, they become self-deceivers, victims of their own empty dreams. The undeniable blessings of health, intellect, political justice and peace, of friendship, of righteousness, of the visible church, of life itself are imperfect and precarious. So Augustine rejects the classical ideal of "the good life," with its goal of *virtus* or *arete*—the "art of living" or of regulating life so that all its good things contribute harmoniously to happiness. Christians use the goods and evils of historical life for the sake of the heavenly society, and thereby find healing and blessing in hope.

But does the realistic Augustine suddenly become thoroughly unrealistic in his beliefs about the ultimate future? Secular critics of modern Augustinian thinkers frequently agree with their political realism but reject their religious affirmations. "The Kingdom of God," it is said, may be a useful limiting concept, like that of infinity in mathematics, but any positive affirmations about it are illusory and perhaps absurd. Such criticisms have their place in warning the theologian against the dangers of using finite concepts to elaborate the infinite—a warning inherent in Christianity but sometimes forgotten by its apologists. Certainly Augustine's scriptural literalism—though at times he makes sophisticated criticisms of it—betrays him into crude and unwarranted descriptions of the future.[2]

But even with his errors Augustine's basic position stands out clearly enough. With searching realism he denies all historical illusions; then he insists that history is not simply a process

---

[2] However, in the conception of beatitude as the final peace of the divine society, and of hell as the violent warfare of passion and will, Augustine used ideas with both psychological and political relevance to historical life. *City of God*, XIX, 28.

of making the best of a miserable situation, but is the realm where God, who has the last word on history, gives meaning to the confused situation. This assurance of faith is hardly subject to empirical vindication or denial. To many it still appears to do justice to the experiences of human life and history, more truly than does either faith in history itself or despair about history.

The apocalyptic mythology, of course, may take an other-worldly direction which devalues history. If Harnack's criticism that Augustine "found this life in itself objectless" itself reflects a contrary prejudice, there are still elements in Augustine which threaten the very possibility of a meaningful interpretation of history. Remnants of Neo-Platonic depreciation of the temporal cling to his thought. The glorification of celibacy and monasticism, despite a high evaluation of family life, is essentially anti-historical in character. For instance, Augustine's praise of continence leads him to the thoroughly anti-historical wish that all people might with good conscience be continent and thus end history; but such a remark is not typical. We shall investigate in the next chapter the consequences for history of two other ideas: the conception of *totum simul* as against the significance of the time process, and the mystical idea of final beatitude as a contemplative *Visio Dei*.

Yet eschatology refuses to succumb to non-historical other-worldliness. The temporal world is no mere shadow world dimly mirroring some transcendental essences. Augustine reveals a sound psychology as well as the absence of an anti-physical, anti-historical bias when he insists upon the resurrection of the body instead of the immortality of the soul: "For the body is not an extraneous ornament or aid, but a part of man's very nature."[3] History is moving toward its fulfillment. Eternity, although it will destroy the sinful character of history, will fulfill the tem-

---

[3] *City of God*, I, 13. Cf. XXII, 4–5, 26. The idea is often misunderstood. Augustine has too much common sense to say that the body will be restored in its present form. XXII, 21.

poral process. "For when the judgment is finished, this heaven and earth shall cease to be, and there will be a new heaven and a new earth. For this world shall pass away by transformation, not by absolute destruction." [4] Thus the Kingdom of God is neither simply the denial nor simply the enhancing of history. To use the language of modern theology, the relation is dialectical. It involves both continuity and discontinuity.

The Christian thread of history falls apart without its eschatological strand. But this strand must be re-enforced by two others, lest it lose the Christian feeling for the *dynamis* of the Kingdom of God and retreat into other-worldliness.

B. THE CHURCH

The church in Christian thought may be significant both for the *meaning of history* and for the *government of history*. The latter emphasis has often led to the dangers of religious persecution but it may be derived from the former.

To find the clue to the meaning of history in a special constellation of events is not necessarily erroneous, provided the choice illumines rather than denies meaning to the rest of history. Any problem of interpretation involves a selective evaluation of evidence. Hebrew prophecy with its remnant, early Christianity with its communion of saints, Hegel with his peoples who are conscious of history and freedom, Marxism with its proletarian messianism—all find the significance of history focussed in certain groups. But all such claims are subject to the dangers of imperialistic pretension. If the historical group is an ecclesiastical institution, the additional danger arises of dividing history into secular and religious history and thus destroying the possibility of a philosophy of total history.

Augustine faced these problems directly. We have seen that the divine society, as it exists in history, is for him essentially a

---

[4] *City of God*, XX, 14.

community of faith and of love, drawn from all peoples and all times, whose hidden boundaries are known only to God. Thus far the conception raises no problems. If eschatology is to have any significance for history, it must make some difference in human community.

The difficulty comes when Augustine establishes a close relationship between the society of God and the church of Rome, and tends to apply the attributes of the invisible community to the ecclesiastical institution.[5] The issue of history is salvation, and the church offers two essentials of salvation: the authoritative truth and the sacraments.

Regarding the truth Augustine made the dramatic statement: "I should not believe the gospel except as moved by the authority of the Catholic Church."[6] Few would disagree that salvation— however conceived—demands some sort of assurance and security. But Augustine does not make clear the distinction between the assurance of religious confidence and trust, and the infallibility of particular moral judgments or theoretical statements. Contrary to his own better insights, he tries to contain the significance of divine infinity within the limits of finite authorities.

As important as the truth were the sacraments. One might wonder why the Augustinian doctrine of salvation by grace should be logically dependent upon a rigorous sacramental system. Augustine would simply insist that God ordained the sacraments. But his thought is confusing on the issue. Against his insistence that infants require baptism to be saved and his sometimes almost magical conception of the sacraments, he makes the statement that a dying confession of Christ has the same effect as

---

[5] We may pass by the issues of Augustinian exegesis which concern historical scholars. The details are controversial and obscure. The general thesis is fairly clear: Augustine does not equate the *civitas Dei* with the institutional church; he does frequently tend to attribute the character of the *communio sanctorum*, which is the *civitas Dei*, to the hierarchical church.

[6] *Against the Epistle of Manichaeus called Fundamental*, V, 6.

baptism, and preaches: "Only believe and thou hast already partaken of the sacrament." [7]

It is the broader view of the church, or of the heavenly city, which makes possible an interpretation of universal history. In general Augustine assumes that the elect are either within the visible church or will enter it before their deaths. But at least twice he suggests that exclusion from the church is not of ultimate significance, that nothing is finally important to a man "so long as a guilty conscience does not blot his name out of the Book of Life." [8] And repeatedly he distinguishes in the most emphatic way possible between the church as it is destined to be, without spot or wrinkle, and the church in its present state of pilgrimage.

It was a portentous day when Augustine, against his earlier judgment, advocated the use of the secular power against the Donatist schismatics. The provocation was great and religious leaders have often succumbed to the same temptation. Reluctant though he was, Augustine's doctrinal justification was far-reaching and opened the door for most of the extravagances of later ecclesiasticism.

The ecclesiastical strand in the thread of history is both a necessary and a dangerous one. It may offer a needed immediacy of experience by which the demands and the promises of the eschatological community become vivid in history. Or it may make impossible an understanding of universal history. Augustine's *civitas Dei* gives meaning to all of life and history, overcoming the various human divisions which would destroy the possibility of universal history. But when the *civitas Dei* is so closely associated with an ecclesiastical institution, it is subjected

---

[7] *City of God*, XIII, 7; Sermon 112, Ch. 5. The narrower view is found in *City of God*, XX, 8; *On the Merits and Forgiveness of Sins, and On the Baptism of Infants*, I, 21, 35, 70.

[8] *Ep.* 68, par. 4 (c. 404 A.D.). Cf. an earlier writing (c. 390), *De Vera Religione*, VI, 10–11, in Erich Przywara, *An Augustine Synthesis*, pp. 275–76.

to human error and sin—which may be magnified in ecclesiastical pride.

C. THE DYNAMIC CHARACTER OF HISTORY

Without the typically Hebrew sense of history as the sphere of God's dynamic activity, the preceding two strands of interpretation may take a non-historical direction. Apocalypse may turn other-worldly. And ecclesiasticism may turn static, trying to keep a sinful history under hierarchical control or to sanctify it sacramentally.

Augustinian Christianity, with its rejection of so many types of confidence in history, is not usually esteemed for its emphasis upon the creative character of history. Yet a comparison of Augustine with the Stoic Marcus Aurelius shows the former's much higher evaluation of history, though the latter was an emperor with a this-worldly philosophy.

Several Christian doctrines force Augustine to take history seriously. *First,* his tremendous emphasis upon God's creation of the world makes the whole of human life significant and filled with possibility. The man whose thoughts of self and nature led him directly to God found that his thoughts of history led him to the society of God. *Second,* the affirmation of God's sovereignty and providence makes secular history a significant realm. God's providence operated in granting dominion to the Roman empire, as well as in guiding His people to their heavenly destiny. *Third,* the doctrine of the Incarnation elevates the importance of history. Emphatically Augustine objects to Neo-Platonic doctrines of divine transcendence which make intercourse between God and man impossible. *Fourth,* the essential eschatological mythology insists that history has a direction and moves forward through time to the End which gives it final significance.

None of these doctrines means that Augustine approaches the modern faith in progress. Hasty critics assume that he was too ignorant to appreciate progress. However, the *City of God* repeatedly lists evidences of progress. Men become more "enlightened" through the passage of history (XXII, 7). Inventive genius has achieved marvels in the arts, invention, industry, medicine, weapons, navigation, mathematics and astronomy, music—even cooking (XXII, 24). History shows a development of religious understanding and perfection, as men's minds are drawn from the temporal and visible to the eternal and invisible (X, 14). But none of these is the final issue of history. The great conflict between the two societies moves toward its climax, not by gradual improvement but by a heightening of the tension until the return of Christ to battle His adversary, the devil.

The facts of cultural diversity and creativity, so impressive in a modern understanding of history, are not overlooked, but are given subordinate emphasis. The universal aspects of the *civitas Dei* are far more important than cultural diversity. However, there are hints that the different epochs of worldly history and the different cultural and linguistic groups have their distinctive contributions to make to the whole of history, according to God's plan.[9] Erich Frank writes: "St. Augustine in his *City of God* was the first to develop that Christian concept of history according to which mankind as a whole is to actualize a purpose in the world throughout the succession of generations. Thus history has a teleological structure: every nation may hope to fulfil its own mission through the development of its particular religious, political, or scientific faculties."[10]

It will not do to exaggerate this element in Augustine's thought or to read modern concepts back into him; yet there is more significance in his ideas than at first meets the eye. Colling-

---

[9] *City of God*, XIX, 17. *Ep.* 137, par. 15; 138, i, 5. Robert Flint, in his comprehensive study of philosophies of history, shows several schemes by which Augustine enumerates and lists the successive epochs of history, always implying an appreciation of development and accomplishment throughout history. *History of the Philosophy of History*, pp. 154–56.

[10] *Philosophical Understanding and Religious Truth*, p. 136, n. 9.

wood shows how Greek and Roman historiography was dominated by categories of *substance*. History did not describe the *development* of Rome, but rather the emergence of an eternal Rome which had been "ready-made and complete" from the beginning. Christian thought, in which the primary category is God's purpose, was much better able to understand historical process.

Just as the individual soul is a thing created in the fullness of time to have just those characteristics which the time requires if God's purpose is to be fulfilled, so a thing like Rome is not an eternal entity but a transient thing, that has come into existence at the appropriate time in history to fulfil a certain definite function and to pass away when that function has been fulfilled. This was a profound revolution in historical thinking; it meant that the process of historical change was no longer conceived as flowing, so to speak, over the surface of things, and affecting their accidents only, but as involving their very substance and thus entailing a real creation and a real destruction . . . the gain to history is immense, because the recognition that the historical process creates its own vehicles, so that entities like Rome or England are not the presuppositions but the products of that process, is the first step towards grasping the peculiar characteristics of history.[11]

Similarly Christopher Dawson says that to Augustine "we owe the characteristically Western ideal of the Church as a dynamic social power in contrast to the static and metaphysical conceptions which dominated Byzantine Christianity. . . . And thus the Western ideals of freedom and progress and social justice owe more than we realize to the thought of the great African who was himself indifferent to secular progress and to the transitory fortunes of the earthly state."[12]

It remains true that this dynamic aspect of history was less developed in Augustine's thought than the others. He was sure that the Christian had a social responsibility, that he must not

---

[11] R. G. Collingwood, *The Idea of History*, pp. 48–49. Cf. pp. 42–45.
[12] In *A Monument to St. Augustine*, pp. 76–77.

seek a perfectionist escape from history, but must take part in the wars and political processes by which human society makes its imperfect attempts at justice and peace. But he was never sure— though he wrote at length on the subject—how highly to evaluate the heroic virtues and the political achievements of men. Within the *civitas terrena* they have their valuable place; in the vision of the *civitas Dei* they are apparently useless.

Fifteen centuries of history have done little to change Augustine's judgment about the insecurity of earthly peace. But the modern Christian thinker would generally hope that the heavenly society might play a more creative role within the earthly one than Augustine conceives. Augustine esteems the peace of the earthly city primarily because the two cities must coexist; thus a *modus vivendi* which allows the city of God the possibility of development is to be valued, though intrinsically it has little worth.

Occasionally Augustine shifts from his pessimism with its tendency to devalue history and expresses a romantic strain of thought. He may conjecture what a wonderful state could be formed if the army—or the whole population—were made up of Christians, or if a Christian emperor should appear.[13] But the flights of imagination are brief. Augustine has no expectation that the world will become Christian or that the earthly city will achieve the peace of God.

In the thread which Augustine grasps to guide himself through the confusion of history, the apocalyptic strand is the heaviest, the ecclesiastical strand next heavy. But the strand of Christian dynamism is not lacking. Though nothing else in history is sure, this thread extending from God to man is sure. So long as his hand holds it, Augustine can walk confidently through the darkness of history on the route that leads to God.

---

[13] *Ep.* 138, ii, 15. Also *City of God*, V, 24–26. (*Epistles* 137 and 138 are parallel writings to the *City of God*, written as part of the same apologetic purpose which prompted the writing of the greater work.)

CHAPTER III

THREE THEMES:

THEIR INSIGHTS AND THEIR DANGERS

THROUGH the centuries the three-stranded thread has fascinated men. Thinker after thinker has worked with it, selecting some one strand or another for primary emphasis. The choice determines the whole temper of the resulting interpretation of history.

To change the metaphor, Christian conceptions of history develop around three themes and their intermingling. This chapter will examine one or two examples of the dominance of each theme. It will be convenient, without any pretense of recording the history of Christian thought on the subject, to take the examples in chronological order.

I. THE CHURCH AS THE KINGDOM OF GOD

The ecclesiastical theme dominates whenever history gains its meaning from a Kingdom of God which is identified with the institutional church. In the Middle Ages the interpretation of history was pushed farthest in this direction. The sacramental power of the church became a reality in the lives of men, whether they were peasants, knights, or kings. The church stirred the imaginations of half-pagan free-booters and of the devout, and the threat of an interdict made kingdoms tremble. Theory and historical fact reinforced each other, as churchmen developed their claims on the basis of the Bible and the writings of the Fathers—both authentic and occasionally spurious. The church actually became the unifying force in the feudal world which developed out of the chaos left by the fall of Rome.

It is not necessary to assert the exaggerated medieval unity sometimes claimed. There were obvious rifts and quarrels within empire and church and between the two. The spiritual and political prestige of the church was sometimes exalted, sometimes degraded. But the very controversies took place within the context of an attempt to institutionalize the Kingdom of God. Emperors and popes claimed to be God's delegates. A particularized Christian religion, taking the forms of a specifically Western medieval development and represented by a definite institution, was the focal light guiding and illumining history. The Kingdom of God was established and men could see it.

The other themes were subordinated to the ecclesiastical. The eschatological theme was taken for granted. But it took the form largely of other-worldliness. The vivid expectation of New Testament apocalypse was subordinated to the reality of an existing institution and a sacramental power available in the present.

Similarly, the emphasis upon this-worldly accomplishment was evident in the organizing genius and passion for realizing the Kingdom of God in a historical institution. No one can accuse characters like Hildebrand (Pope Gregory VII, 1073–85) of failing to be dynamic. But the conception of history which developed out of their efforts has less of the throb of dynamic expectation than of visible, realized achievement in the traditionally-given church, the hierarchical embodiment of the Kingdom of God.

The greatest thinker representing this strain of thought is St. Thomas Aquinas (1225–74). Some have made more extravagant claims for the ecclesiastical institution, and others have given more emphasis to history.[1] But none has matched his comprehensive thought.

---

[1] E.g., Bishop Otto of Friesing in the twelfth century wrote his extensive work, *The Two Cities: A Chronicle of Universal History*. Otto shows

A. HISTORY IN THE THOUGHT OF AQUINAS

Where Augustine desired to know nothing but the soul and God, Aquinas had a much wider interest in the world. Though contingent, the world is no shadowy, illusory realm; in the hierarchical structure the lower orders of being are taken with full seriousness. Nevertheless St. Thomas is in the end less concerned than Augustine with history.

To be sure, he accepts the outlines of Augustine's interpretation of history. He takes for granted the main events in the history of salvation—Creation, Fall, history of the chosen people, Incarnation, church, future judgment, and consummation of history. But though he writes on these in some detail, the interpretation of history is not a major concern. Sacred doctrine is for St. Thomas clearly a "science," to be developed systematically. History is not.[2]

Gilson writes that the Middle Ages, although not showing our modern conception of history, clearly had its own. Its conception provides "the totality of history with an intelligible explanation, which shall account for the origin of humanity and assign its end."[3] In this divinely ordained pattern, medieval Christendom

---

how the two cities have, in the course of history, become the one all-inclusive City of Christ. However, he is not deceived about the actual character of history. A strong ascetic tendency leads Otto to emphasize the insecurity, misery, and transitoriness of historical life; and although he justifies the power of the church, he is not sure that her "former humiliation" was not better (see Prologue, Bk. IV).

[2] One Roman Catholic writes: "St. Thomas knew nothing of a philosophy of culture in the modern and proper sense, and consequently he also did not recognize any epistemology of the cultural sciences." The writer continues by saying that Augustine had "displayed the material for building a true philosophy of history," but the Middle Ages followed Aristotle in its rational concern for universals rather than particulars. Hans Meyer, *The Philosophy of St. Thomas Aquinas* (St. Louis: Herder, 1945), pp. 365–66.

[3] *The Spirit of Mediaeval Philosophy*, p. 388.

of course has its distinctive place. It is the heir of all the past, the age in which the Incarnation has worked its result in the City of God, the final period of history before the establishing of the Eternal Kingdom. But it is worth noting that Gilson, in supporting this contention, relies more on Franciscans like Joachim of Floris, Bonaventura, and Roger Bacon than on St. Thomas.

Collingwood, who shows real appreciation for Christian contributions to historiography, makes a criticism of medieval historians which applies equally to the philosophers who developed explicitly the ideas which the historians simply presupposed:

. . . in their anxiety to detect the general plan of history, and their belief that this plan was God's and not man's, they tended to look for the essence of history outside history itself, by looking away from man's actions in order to detect the plan of God; and consequently the actual detail of human actions became for them relatively unimportant. . . . They did not want an accurate and scientific study of the actual facts of history; what they wanted was an accurate and scientific study of the divine attributes, a theology based securely on the double foundation of faith and reason, which should enable them to determine *a priori* what must have happened and what must be going to happen in the historical process.[4]

The same criticism applies to Augustine; but though he was certainly no accomplished historian, he had a stronger genuine interest than Aquinas in historical events and their meaning.

B. WHY HISTORY BECOMES UNIMPORTANT

If we ask why Aquinas, though more empirical than Augustine, gave a lesser significance to the actual stuff of history, we

---

[4] *The Idea of History*, pp. 55–56. Collingwood goes on to suggest that modern historiography has more similarity to medieval historiography than it recognizes.

can find the answer in his conceptions of God and of salvation, as well as of the church.

The Idea of God

The conception of God in St. Thomas is non-historical. Augustine had held together, however uneasily, two conceptions of God: the Neo-Platonic God of pure being and the Hebrew Lord of history. Aquinas combined instead the Neo-Platonic conception (perhaps retaining more of this than he realized) and the Aristotelian unmoved mover. The Hebrew conception was nominally retained; but the precise doctrine of "analogy of proportion" took the bite out of many biblical ideas by allowing them only metaphorical significance.

Thus the God of Aquinas, though the Be-All and End-All of history, is hardly a vibrant Lord of history. He is altogether immutable and impassive. He knows the created world only in His own self-knowledge. Indeed the question arises as to why there should be any creation or history at all, since God contains in Himself all possible perfections. The answer is the Neo-Platonic idea that all the grades of being should be filled. Such an explanation, whatever its use for metaphysics, does not lead to a dynamic conception of history.[5]

The difficulties are illustrated in the doctrine of the *totum simul*, already noted in Augustine. Aquinas elaborates the idea systematically. The whole of time, past and future, is envisioned by God as a total simultaneity; and all the events of history are caused by His same timeless act. But if the whole of the human and cosmic story is ultimately an everlasting now, what becomes of time? And what is history without time, without a genuine

---

[5] It is significant that despite his strong emphasis on creation *ex nihilo* as the unique prerogative of God, Aquinas often virtually equates creation and emanation. Thus he writes "de modo emanationis rerum a primo principio, qui dicitur creatio." (*ST*, I, Q. 45.) This idea of emanation, together with the privative theory of evil, brings him dangerously close to the pantheism which he takes pains to refute.

future? If in God's vision all has already taken place, how can history have creative significance? These questions, which are not easily answered, will be considered further in relation to Baron von Hügel (Ch. VI) and Karl Barth (Ch. VII).

The Hope of Salvation

Salvation for St. Thomas has nothing to do with the process of history, except for the bare fact that it is future. Final bliss is the contemplation of God, the *visio Dei*. The problems of history get a mystical rather than an eschatological solution. History is not thundering toward the realization of its destiny; rather the Christian, in the contemplative life, finds a foretaste of the heavenly vision of God.

It has been suggested that in contrast to the mystical hope of seeing God, characteristic of many religions, the typical biblical metaphor is that of hearing and obeying God.[6] And certainly obedience and activity are more historical categories than is contemplation. To be sure, Aquinas considers activity a useful discipline of preparation for contemplation, and regards the highest contemplation as that which issues in enlightenment of others. But the fulness of life, approached on earth in contemplation, is finally reached in a primarily individual and non-historical hope. The course of history is the prelude to salvation only in the sense of a preliminary discipline. The whole of non-Christian history, except for the few individuals possibly granted salvation, has little relation to the final meaning of life.

---

[6] John Hutchison, "The Biblical Idea of Vocation," *Christianity and Society*, XII (1948), No. 2.

When Hebrew writers do speak of visions of God, they are not likely to think in contemplative or aesthetic terms. J. S. Whale writes: "It is no accident that after St. Paul, the Hebrew, had seen a vision on the Damascus road, he could say, 'I was not disobedient unto the heavenly vision.' Only a Hebrew would talk of obeying a vision." *Christian Doctrine* (New York: Macmillan, 1946), p. 55.

The Kingdom of God Institutionalized

The purpose of history, as Thomas sees it, is not to be found in living through the turmoil of history and trying to find the destiny of men and nations under God's guiding hand. Nor is it to be found in future achievements of men on earth. It is already realized in a present historical institution, the church—save for the final beatitude of the *visio Dei*.

As with Augustine the church provides the two indispensables: the sacraments and divine authority. The sacraments are the present possession which anticipates the future vision of God. The "Eucharistic Doctor" found that through the central sacrament of his faith grace is given, man attains eternal life, sins are forgiven, and men are preserved from future sins. The Eucharist "is, as it were, the consummation of the spiritual life." [7] The sacraments in general cause grace, confer grace, contain grace, and thereby are necessary for salvation. It is clear that religious faith here comes to a focus, not in activity or in historical expectancy, but in an act in the life of an existing stable institution.

The church as divine authority gets no less emphasis from St. Thomas. Indeed the "sacrament of order" was Christ's establishing of the church and the ministry with the power to forgive sins. Just as God presides over the church triumphant, there must be one man to preside over the church militant. Christ would not have omitted to provide His church with a head. (St. Paul had said that Christ is head of the church; St. Thomas agrees, but says that the pope is, comparably, head of the church during the particular time of his pontificate.) [8] The statement on authority most significant for an interpretation of history comes in a political writing, where Thomas says that God has entrusted spiritual things to priests "and in the highest degree to the chief

[7] *ST*, III, Q. 73, art. 3.
[8] *ScG*, Bk. IV, Chs. 74, 76. *ST*, III, Q. 8, art. 6, 7.

priest, the successor of St. Peter, the Vicar of Christ, the Roman
Pontiff, to whom all the kings of Christian peoples are to be
subject as to our Lord Jesus Christ himself." [9]

Aquinas knows, of course, that the church is not now perfect,
that tares grow with the wheat. But what need is there for either
historical or vivid apocalyptic expectation when the church has,
as its present possession, the sacraments and a leader with power
comparable to Christ's? The great drama of history has passed its
climax; the denouement can be foreseen; the eagerness of the
Christian is no longer for a future act of God, but for the sacramental miracle performed in the church and for the eternal life
to which the church has the keys. Although God still performs
miracles, it is the church, not history, which is regarded as the
theater of His mighty acts.

C. SOME CONSEQUENCES OF THE THOMIST VIEW

So strong are the non-historical emphases in Thomism that
even the doctrine of providence is transformed from a historical
to a primarily metaphysical doctrine. Thomas discusses providence at length, but under categories of causality and agency,
substance, order and contingency, God's omnipotence and
human freedom.[10] The doctrine is complete, but it starts with
the attributes of God, not with the character of history. The
rather thorough discussions of providence say little about history.

Throughout the Thomist analysis the elevation of the ecclesiastical strand of interpretation submerges the other two strands
—the eschatological and the dynamic.

(1) Thomism, although nominally eschatological, loses the
urgent meaning of biblical eschatology: the idea of a divine
reality which invests every moment of history with meaning with-

---

[9] *The Governance of Rulers*, Bk. I, Ch. 14. With such a viewpoint the
Pope naturally has the right to absolve men from allegiance to kings by
the act of excommunication. *ST*, II–II, Q. 12, art. 2.
[10] See esp. *ST*, I, Qq. 19, 22, 103–104; *ScG*, Bk. III, Chs. 70–74, 88–
102.

out, however, becoming identified with or confined to historical institutions. For Thomas, although the "tares" in the church stand under judgment, the hierarchical institution with head-quarters at Rome does not.

Here again is the problem of finding the meaning of universal history in a particular institution. To be sure, the particularism of the Roman Church could not be so obvious to Aquinas as it became after the Age of Exploration. And the achievement of the Roman See was enough to dazzle any observer. Arnold Toynbee, who practically never is at a loss for a historical analogy, confesses himself baffled by the papacy. "In one respect after another, the Papal *Respublica Christiana* seems to defy classification and to reveal itself as something unique." [11] It is not surprising that Aquinas drew such conclusions as he did. Figgis points out that, although Thomas uses Augustine a great deal in the political sections of the *Summa Theologica*, "We do not hear of the doctrine of the two cities, for the obvious reason that it was no longer held to fit, now that the kingdom of this world had become the kingdom of our God and His Christ." [12]

It is the natural tendency of most peoples to regard their institutions as somehow the focus of the significance of history. St. Thomas was no exception, though his broad interests and intellectual calm saved him from the worst errors of fanaticism. He was ready to admit the possibility of salvation for some who might seem outside the pale. [13] He is rather generous, as these things go, in tolerating unbelievers. Worse than the unbeliever is the heretic. If he fails to respond after the church admonishes him

---

[11] *A Study of History*, IV, 515.

[12] *The Political Aspects of S. Augustine's 'City of God,'* pp. 94–95.

[13] "It is the common teaching that if a man born among the barbarous and infidel nations really does what lies in his power, God will reveal to him what is necessary for salvation, either by interior inspirations or by sending him a preacher of the Faith." *Sententiarum*, Lib. II, dist. 23, Q. viii, a. 4; as quoted by E. Portalie, "Augustine," *Catholic Encyclopedia*, Vol. II.

twice, the church should excommunicate him and turn him over to the secular authority for execution.[14]

However unfortunate such a position may be, it is not unusual. Human societies have seldom been tolerant of those whom they judged to threaten their very purpose and existence; and heresy was at least as serious to St. Thomas as deviation from the true faith is in a modern totalitarian state, or as sedition in a democracy. We might hope for a higher insight in a society calling itself "Christendom," but we should not be surprised if we do not find it. Nevertheless there is something peculiarly dangerous in the claim of a particular church to hold the powers of a transcendent God. The evidence of history would support the charge of contemporary theologians that this is a particularly perilous form of sin.

(2) The dynamic-historical strand is submerged but not entirely lost. Aquinas is aware of progress in history, of movement from the "Old Law" to the "New Law," of development "through an orderly succession of time," of the advance of human reason "gradually from the imperfect to the perfect." [15] More important is the interest in government, which implies a concern for history. Here, however, the reasoning is principally from given divine patterns, with arguments from the operations of the universe and of nature. Laws may be improved as man's imperfect reason better apprehends the eternal natural law, but only rarely. For "the mere change of law is of itself prejudicial to the common good." [16] Thus there is little or no sense that history will create new possibilities which were not envisioned in the old law, that new wine may burst the old feudal and ecclesiastical bottles,

---

[14] *ST*, II–II, Q. 10, art. 9; Q. 11, art. 3.
[15] The quotations are respectively from *ST*, I–II, Q. 106, art. 3 (*cf*. art. 4); and Q. 97, art. 1. See also Q. 98, art. 1, 6; Q. 97, art. 1; *ST*, I, Q. 1, art. 8. Martin Grabmann offers further evidence that Thomas had a real sense for the development of knowledge in history. See Thomas Aquinas (New York: Longmans, Green, 1928), pp. 41–43.
[16] *ST*, I–II, Q. 97, art. 1–2.

that the divinely ordained decrees which the church treasures may not be the last word. There are possibilities of change, but within the pattern of a static history.[17]

Here is a faith for which history's significance has been revealed, and the revelation is safely in the hands of a divinely ordained, hierarchically governed, traditionally inspired institution. The meaning of life is enclosed in the church. It is a broad ecclesiasticism, with room for the natural as well as the spiritual, the cardinal virtues of paganism as well as the Christian. In this mystical-hierarchical institution, the product of Christian spirituality and political ingenuity, the believer comes to God.

Here we have one of mankind's perennial solutions of its religious problem. Viewed as an interpretation of history, it is extremely dubious. If Toynbee's reading of history is at all correct and "the nemesis of creativity" is often the "idolization of an ephemeral institution," St. Thomas' interpretation of history would seem to be far more dangerous for today than it was for his age.

II. RADICAL ESCHATOLOGY

The eschatological theme dominates when Christians are especially impressed by the otherness of God, the radical divine

---

[17] See Ernst Troeltsch, *Social Teachings of the Christian Churches* (New York: Macmillan, 1931), I, 303–306. R. H. Tawney, who shows great appreciation for the ameliorative effects of the medieval church on economic abuses, nevertheless finds the same dominant conservatism and static ideal. See *Religion and the Rise of Capitalism* (New York: Harcourt, Brace, 1926), pp. 55–62. The great Roman Catholic historical philosopher, M. de Wulf, says that "the thirteenth century believed that it had realized a state of stable equilibrium, and . . . their extraordinary optimism led them to believe that they had arrived at a state close to perfection." Then, showing how St. Thomas justifies some changes in positive law, he writes: "On the basis of Thomistic principles, it is therefore possible to justify a series of progressive measures. The thirteenth century could of course not envisage them; but they are in the logic of its system." *Philosophy and Civilization in the Middle Ages* (Princeton: Princeton University Press, 1922), pp. 268–72.

judgment upon sin, and the fragmentary character of meaning in all human institutions. The most spectacular development of this strain of thought since apostolic times has been in the Reformation theology of Martin Luther (1483–1546).

Luther brought to the problem of history several insights capable of filling the gaps in Thomism. His attacks upon pretensions of ecclesiasticism and his insistence upon the holiness of all vocations opened the way to a new appreciation of the historical. His break with Rome stimulated historical investigations of the pre-papal church.[1] His activities as a reformer gave him a sense of historical destiny long lacking in Christendom. He feels the dynamic throb of meaningful time, and regards Renaissance learning as a sort of John the Baptist, preparing the way for renewed preaching of the Gospel.

This new enthusiasm for history is not entirely of the sort to make the historian cheer. Writing the preface to a translation of an Italian historical work, Luther emphasizes the value of knowledge of secular history, which shows God's judgments rewarding the good and punishing the wicked.[2] In the preface to his own translation of Aesop, Luther praises the fables for their moral value in terms very similar to those he uses to praise history. The naive philosophy of history here implied is not characteristic of Luther's more profound thought, but recurs occasionally in his writings.

More significant is Luther's revived interest in the dynamic aspects of Christian apocalypse. Here, as in so many of his emphases, Luther goes back to long obscured ideas of Augustine and the Bible. Throughout his writings he keeps the basic motif: history is the realm of conflict between the two cities, a conflict

---

[1] This historical interest was significant, for scholasticism despite all its traditionalism had almost ceased to write church history. See Ernst Schäfer, *Luther als Kirchenhistoriker*, p. 6.

[2] *Vorrede zu Galeatii Capellae Historie vom Herzog zu Mailand*, 1538. EA, LXIII, 353–57. Cf. *Letter to the Councilmen*, PE, IV, 128–29.

which will culminate in victory for the Kingdom of God. The eschatological urgency of the New Testament, long almost smothered, breathes again.

Yet Luther's interpretation of history finally breaks down. The other-worldly aspect of eschatology conquers the dynamic aspect. The Kingdom of God becomes separated, not from the individual Christian's life, but from history. We must investigate this demise of history in a theology which had promised to restore its significance.

A. LUTHER'S CONCEPTION OF THE KINGDOM OF GOD

While echoing the traditional conceptions of time and eternity (including the *totum simul,* or *ewiger Augenblick*), Luther heightened the significance of the historical and restored the vivid expectation of the future. Heaven, hell, and the Last Judgment might seem close enough to the medieval Christian, but the *historical events* which moved toward the new world were not highly significant. In Luther's teaching the Last Days became imminent. The "signs of the times" were evident everywhere. Luther saw them in actions of the pope, astronomical occurrences, and historical convulsions—especially the threats of the Turks. He saw them also in the rarity of true belief and the extent of hypocrisy and apostasy—the sort of "sign" that prophetic judgment has often seen in the times. In writings and preachings from 1520 until his death (as a check of the Weimar edition of his works will show) he makes frequent references to literal expectations of the End of history. His vivid forebodings were, however, combined with a common sense often lacking in extravagant apocalyptists. Luther refused to predict days and hours and frequently urged the duty of planning for posterity.

The End of history brings the Last Judgment—fearful and portentous for the sinner. But the man of faith may pray eagerly, "Thy kingdom come." In that day will be revealed the full purpose of God, which now is veiled and known only through faith in Christ and then but partially:

> God has reserved unto the last day the displaying of his greatness and majesty, his glory and effulgence. We behold him now in the Gospel and in faith—a narrow view of him. Here he is not great because but slightly comprehended. But in the last appearing he will permit us to behold him in his greatness and majesty.[3]

In the individual and cosmic apocalyptic transformation the Kingdom of God fulfills history.[4]

Although Luther's expectations were too literally conceived, they were the expression of a profound conception which has always been part of Christianity. For Luther recognized the contingencies of history and the inadequacy of history to solve its own problems:

> Thus we see that, over and above righteousness, wisdom, and power of this world, there is need for another kingdom, in which there is another righteousness, wisdom, and power. For the righteousness of this world has an end, but the righteousness of Christ and those who are in His Kingdom abide forever.[5]

Just as Luther rejects all tangible or measurable conceptions of individual salvation for a pure doctrine of justification by faith, so he rejects all promises of institutional historical security for a genuinely eschatological conception of the Kingdom of God. His reading of Scripture agrees with his experience. History, pregnant with meaning, moves toward its fulfillment.

This expectant futurism does not destroy the sense of the Kingdom of God as a living, present reality. In fact, the phrases

---

[3] Sermon, ME, VII, 131–32. Cf. sermon, WA, XVII, ii, 245.
[4] For a profound discussion of this entire aspect of Luther's thought, both as a historical study and as a contemporary theological issue, see Paul Althaus, Die Letzen Dinge.
[5] An Exposition of the 82nd Psalm, PE, IV, 323.

"Kingdom of God" and "Kingdom of Christ" usually refer to an immediate reality. Thinking of the End of history, Luther more often uses such expressions as "last days," "the judgment," "the coming of Christ." Consistently with Luther's typical conception of faith and works, the Kingdom of God is identified at times with faith and at times with the life flowing from faith:

> Nay, my dear friends, the kingdom of God consists not in outward things, which can be touched or perceived, but in faith.
> Dear friends, the kingdom of God,—and we are that kingdom,— consists not in speech or in words, but in deeds, in works and exercises. . . . For a faith without love is not enough—rather, it is no faith at all, but a counterfeit of faith.[6]

Again the Kingdom of God is identical with the Gospel—"nothing else than a state or government in which there is nothing but forgiveness of sins."[7]

The immediate and eschatological aspects of the Kingdom of God are nicely related in a comment on the petition, "Thy kingdom come":

> Grant that this Thy kingdom, now begun in us, may increase, and daily grow in power. . . . Help us that we may remain constant, and that Thy future kingdom may finish and complete this Thy kingdom which is here begun.[8]

B. THE SOVEREIGNTY OF GOD AND ITS EXECUTORS

Luther is sure that God is the sovereign Lord of History. Like Augustine he sees that the Christian faith demands that God's sovereignty be discernible even in the events that seem to defy

---

[6] See the fifth and first Wittenberg sermons of 1522, PE, II, 413, 392.
[7] Sermon, ME, XIV, 280. For a valuable analysis of Luther's conception of the Kingdom of God see Reinhold Seeberg, History of Doctrines (Philadelphia: Lutheran Publication Society, 1904), II, 277 ff.
[8] A Brief Explanation of the Lord's Prayer, PE, II, 377–78. Cf. Larger Catechism in Luther's Primary Works, pp. 116–17. Also sermon, ME, X, 80.

Him. But even more than Augustine, and far more than Aquinas, Luther emphasized the *hidden* character of God's sovereignty. He saw how baffling was the attempt to discover in history any rational or providential pattern. So he asserted that God's sovereignty is carried out in all events, but that His Lordship is concealed from our blind eyes until the last day when He will make Himself manifest.

But here Luther's thought raises a serious problem. How far are God's judgments actually carried out in history? On the one hand, the case seems clear. The devil can do no more than God will allow. God can punish Germany as He did Sodom and Jerusalem. History shows that those who rule unjustly and those who take the sword in rebellion are both punished by the wrath of God. Unjust princes fight futilely against God unless they fear Him and respect His wrath. Peasants will triumph if they have God's support; otherwise they will be destroyed. But on the other hand, there is an ambiguity about God's judgments in history. Finally the issue is not simply that of victory or justice in a historical struggle, but of the eternal destiny of body and soul. Even though one side may unjustly win a bloody struggle, its partisans will finally be destroyed and will lose their salvation.[9] To follow Luther's thought on this issue requires a look at his conception of the executors of God's will in history.

(1) *The Word of God.* The executor of God's will in its purest form in His own Word, which in Luther's conception has tremendous efficacy, both for salvation and for the course of history. Sometimes it seems that the Christian has no responsibility except to proclaim God's Word, since the Word will accomplish everything else. "Have I not with words alone, without any use of the sword whatever, done more injury to the pope, bishops, priests and monks than all emperors, kings and princes with all their power ever did before?" [10] Here is a magnificent—but hardly

---

[9] *An Admonition to Peace,* PE, IV, 223–25, 243.
[10] *An Earnest Exhortation,* PE, IV, 215. Cf. sermon, PE, II, 399–400.

historically adequate—indifference to the role of the German princes and many another historical factor in the German Reformation.

Luther makes a more historical analysis in writing *On War Against the Turk* (PE, IV). First, neither pope nor emperor has any right to take up the sword in behalf of faith against the infidel. The clear implication is that the only instrument of God's sovereignty in such a conflict is the Word, or such related weapons of the spirit as "repentance, tears, and prayer." However the emperor—whether or not he is a Christian emperor—has a duty to God to protect his subjects against an aggressor. Thus Luther usually regarded the Word as the sole justifiable instrument of God's sovereignty in spiritual affairs; he also recognized it as an instrument, but not God's only instrument, in temporal affairs.

(2) *The Christian Ministry.* The preachers who proclaim God's Word have two functions as executors of God's sovereignty over history. First, the preacher is the authorized critic of secular government. Rulers are subject to the judgment of God and of His Word, and it is the duty of the preacher to criticize the rulers boldly and openly. Ordinary men should not criticize their government, but Luther reviles the preachers who out of laziness, flattery, or fear fail to carry out this mission. Luther implies that this criticism has actual historical efficacy as the instrument of God's judgment upon rulers, who must "either listen to it or suffer all misfortune." [11]

Even more directly by the "work" and "word" of the preacher "the kingdom of God is maintained in the world." [12] This is a pastoral rather than a political task, but it affects the functioning of society in history.

---

[11] *Exposition of the 82nd Psalm,* PE, IV, 297.
[12] *Sermon on Keeping Children in School,* PE, IV, 149, 151. *Cf. Exposition of the 82nd Psalm,* PE, IV, 299–300.

(3) *The Rulers.* Over and over again, with references to Romans 13 and I Peter 2, Luther states that secular rulers are ordained of God. Their authority is not part of God's Kingdom, which as we have seen is spiritual in character, but they carry out His will. To despise earthly rulers is to despise God. Luther says: "I have written in such glorification of temporal government as no teacher has done since the days of the apostles, except, perhaps, St. Augustine." [13]

Luther has no illusions about the character of most rulers. Although the rulers are "usually the greatest fools or the worst knaves on earth," they "are God's jailers and hangmen and His divine wrath needs them to punish the wicked and preserve outward peace." [14] Wicked rulers are "the most harmful people on earth." But only if the ruler in his wickedness loses the support of God and passes away, does he cease to be an instrument ordained of God. As long as there are rulers, they are executors of God's sovereignty.

(4) *The Ordinary Man in His Vocation.* In God's providential scheme the common man in his daily work has an important place. Luther specifically discusses various vocations—those of the lawyer, teacher, soldier, scrub woman. The doctrine of "priesthood of all believers," though never denying the special office of the preacher, places the highest possible significance on the common man's Christian life: "we may be Christs to one another and Christ may be the same in all." [15] Ordinary men and women carry out God's will as truly as the mighty men; but their effect upon the events of history is obviously much less.

(5) *The Devil and His Allies.* The most intriguing of the executors of God's sovereignty is the devil, with his henchmen— the pope, the Turk, or any of a number of people whom Luther

---

[13] *On War Against the Turk,* PE, IV, 82. Cf. *Secular Authority,* PE, III, 232–33; *Exposition of the 82nd Psalm,* PE, IV, 290–306.
[14] *Secular Authority,* PE, III, 258.
[15] *On Christian Liberty,* PE, II, 338.

might have in mind at any moment. These are obviously God's foes, yet must be recognized as His instruments.

At times the devil appears as an enemy of God, whom God allows a little free reign but will check before he can do any severe wrong. At other times the power of the devil seems overwhelming. Men in their own strength cannot oppose him, but still he is powerless before God—as in the great hymn, *"Ein' feste Burg."*

But in all of this there is also the idea that the devil and his cohorts are tools of God, in their evil way doing God's will. There may be some useful advice for the present world struggle in Luther's analysis of his own times:

> For since the Turk is the rod of the wrath of the Lord our God and the servant of the raging devil, the first thing to be done is to smite the devil, his lord, and take the rod out of God's hand, so that the Turk may be found in his own strength only, all by himself, without the devil's help and without God's hand.[16]

Similarly in his most violent and justly-censured writings on the Peasants' Revolt, Luther frequently says that God has let the devil work among the people—perhaps in preparation for the last days. Hence come the bitter words calling the rulers to slaughter the rebellious peasants; but hence also come warnings to the princes to recognize the deserved punishment which God is allowing the devil to bring upon them.[17]

Luther's understanding of history has no place for a theodicy. The very idea is blasphemous, as he tells Erasmus in *The Bondage of the Will*. The need for a theodicy was largely removed by this conception of evil as God's instrument, calling us simultaneously to repentance and to battle against it.

---

16 *On War Against the Turk*, PE, IV, 88–89. *Cf.* p. 102.
17 *An Admonition to Peace*, PE, IV, 221–24; *Against the Robbing and Murdering Hordes*, PE, IV, 251.

C. SEPARATION AND CONFUSION OF THE TWO KINGDOMS

Luther's variety of incisive ideas on the exercise of God's sovereignty might have been brought together in a penetrating interpretation of history. But Luther never did this, because he could not decide clearly how the heavenly and earthly kingdoms might be related. The eschatological theme so dominated his understanding of history that he was unable to develop a constructive theology for a this-worldly social hope.

By comparison, Luther transformed, rather than submerged, the ecclesiastical theme. Although he yields little to Catholicism in his emphasis upon the church, he regards the church as a spiritual community built on Christ. In this sense, but not as a particular historical institution with a human head, the church is identifiable with the Kingdom of God and is of utmost importance for salvation.

Nations cannot be spiritualized and separated from militarism; hence Luther cannot deal with earthly kingdoms as he does with the church. The problem of history is that the Christian must live in two kingdoms which stand in the strongest contrast. They "must be sharply distinguished, and both be permitted to remain; the one to produce piety, the other to bring about external peace and prevent evil deeds; neither is sufficient in the world without the other . . ."[18]

We need not here join the critics who exaggerate Luther's ethical irresponsibility. The studies of Karl Holl and of contemporary Scandinavian Lutherans have refuted frequent unjust attacks. At many points Luther broke down the medieval separation between secular and sacred; he allowed the eschatological Kingdom to invade history in the personal and communal life of believers. His doctrines of vocation, of priesthood of all believers, of faith and love issuing in spontaneous good works on all levels of life were of great cultural significance. Unfortunately,

---
[18] Secular Authority, PE, III, 237.

Holl's investigations do not—as some seem to think—annul Luther's own political writings. Here Luther failed to carry his creative insights adequately into the area of politics. And history without politics after all is history with its skeleton removed.[19]

By so strongly contrasting the two kingdoms Luther let the pure Gospel ethic stand forth with no hedging or qualification and with none of the medieval devices for dulling its impact. But history's problems were left unsolved. A true Christian community would live in love, needing no law.[20] But in a world where only one man in thousands is a true Christian, the law is necessary to restrain men from evil. Christians and non-believers must live in subjection to the sword.

Instead of Augustine's complex interweaving of the two kingdoms, now in sharp conflict, now serving each other, Luther finds the Gospel completely irrelevant to the ugly realities of the earthly kingdom.

God's kingdom is a kingdom of grace and mercy, not of wrath and punishment. In it there is only forgiveness, consideration for one another, love, service, the doing of good, peace, joy, etc. But the kingdom of the world is a kingdom of wrath and severity. In it there is only punishment, repression, judgment, and condemnation, for the suppression of the wicked and the protection of the good.[21]

This attitude is tempered by many other considerations. Government benefits when Christians undertake civil or military office. Standards for positive law and political administration are

---

[19] Luther's economic ideas parallel his political ones. As R. H. Tawney observes, "He preaches a selfless charity, but he recoils with horror from every institution by which an attempt had been made to give it a concrete expression." *Religion and the Rise of Capitalism*, p. 96.

[20] Luther sometimes gives idyllic pictures of a world of true Christians. It might have been truer to his own insights to recognize that the justified Christian remains a sinner and that even "true believers" would scarcely fit his description. See *Secular Authority*, PE, III, 234; *On Trading and Usury*, PE, IV, 23.

[21] *An Open Letter Concerning the Hard Book*, PE, IV, 266. Cf. the still stronger words, *Commentary on Galatians* 2:14, p. 255.

rooted in natural law. (Luther's innumerable references to natural law—in which he includes the Golden Rule—make it impossible to ignore this element of his teaching, as some interpreters do.) Luther makes scathing criticisms of wicked rulers and often gives ethical directions to the just or Christian ruler— although sometimes with the qualification that he hardly expects to find one.

None of these references to political justice changes the fact that Luther does not expect to see it practiced. Hence he regards earthly authority as a severely repressive power with one purpose of keeping some kind of order in the wicked earthly kingdom. His deep pessimism about history made natural law almost as irrelevant as the Gospel.[22] The authoritarian view of the state is qualified by the belief that the Christian must obey God rather than men. This belief, though primarily relevant to matters of religion, has political application; it may authorize civil disobedience or demand martyrdom, but does not permit aggressive resistance. In fact Luther urges on the revolutionary peasants the Gospel ethic of non-resistance—a thoroughly incongruous stand in view of the repeated statements that the Gospel has nothing to do with civil law.[23]

---

[22] Luther's most radical statements are probably those in his *Commentary on Galatians*. (See esp. 1:4, where he paints so evil a picture of "the kingdom of the devil" as to make a Christian interpretation of history practically impossible.) This work is hardly typical, but many other statements are only slightly less pessimistic. See the opening remarks of two writings: *Secular Authority*, PE, III, 230; *On Trading and Usury*, PE, IV, 12, 35. Also *Exposition of the 82nd Psalm*, PE, IV, 322. An even more radical pessimism concerning *all historical life* is expressed in *Whether Soldiers Too Can Be Saved*, PE, V, 55. Luther's occasional hope for a "Christian government" is not at all typical. See *Letter to the Councilmen*, PE, IV, 130.

[23] The supreme inconsistency comes when the peasants are advised to practice non-resistance in the name of the Gospel, while the princes may "win heaven with bloodshed better than other men with prayer." *Admonition to Peace*, PE, IV, 237, 241. *Against the Robbing and Murdering Hordes*, PE, IV, 250.

All this relates curiously to the sovereignty of God. Wicked rulers are threatened with direst punishments, but who is to administer the punishment? The answer is that God will strike tyrants dead, raise up foreign rulers against them, *or unloose a rebellion*. But though the rebellion is by God's decree, Christian subjects will stay out of the fight. Since so few men arc Christians, the rebellion will achieve God's purpose anyway; then those who carried out the divine decree will suffer God's judgment!

Thus, as Luther sees history, God is sovereign Lord; but while the devil and his agents rage, the divine sovereignty is hidden, to be revealed only at the Last Day. Meanwhile Christians may in their personal faith, hope, and love live as members of God's Kingdom now. But the present Kingdom does not touch the earthly kingdom which carries the course of history on its evil way.

With incisive profundity unequalled since the New Testament, Luther stripped bare the religious issues of life from every pretense, every device that had been carefully wrought to dull the inner. Man reaches the Kingdom by the sheer vault of faith in response to God's love. All this is clear and beautiful. But with the discarded waste lumber goes too much of the stuff of history. The appreciation of the social possibilities of history on the grand scale is stultified. The heavenly city is neither a relevant model nor an inbreathing source of life for the earthly one—save in the social relations of the small group or the church.

The awareness of the radical character of Christian faith and of the sacredness of non-ecclesiastical life might have made possible a great interpretation of history. But the utter separation of the heavenly Kingdom of love from the earthly or devilish kingdom of secular power blocked such an interpretation.

III. THE HOPE FOR TRANSFORMING HISTORY

The development of the third strand in the thread of history neither identifies the Kingdom of God with a particular historical institution (like the ecclesiastical strand) nor separates it utterly from all historical institutions (like the radical eschatological strand). Instead it seeks the realization of God's sovereignty within an entire historical community, small or large.

This strand is harder to locate than the previous two. The Christian hope has never been entirely—and usually not primarily —for a development of the social-historical process. But if this strand sometimes seems lost, we need only follow the thread a little further to find it re-emerging.

The whole biblical-eschatological view of history contains at least the germ of the idea of dynamic realization. Augustine never quite forgot this side of biblical thought. In Charlemagne's eighth- and ninth-century ambitions—inspired in part by the *City of God*, especially V, 24–26—to establish a Christian empire, hopes for historical achievement glowed temporarily. And an emperor like the twelfth-century Frederick Barbarossa showed a curious mixture of ambition and Christian idealism. There were dynamic aspects in much of the ecclesiastical development.[1] Late medieval asceticism developed under St. Bernard, then under the Franciscans and Dominicans, along lines of increasing emphasis on active service in the world.

The Franciscans drew inspiration from the revised apocalypticism of Joachim of Floris (d. 1202), whose historic dynamism broke through conventional ecclesiasticism. Joachim revised the acts of the traditional drama, and saw three ages in history.

---

[1] A Protestant historian, quite critical of Romanism, can say: "The scope and audacity of the medieval effort claim Protestant homage as the first mighty expression of what is now often taken to be the peculiarly American Protestant ambition to mould all social and political life to the pattern of the Kingdom of God." James Hastings Nichols, *Primer for Protestants* (New York: Association Press, 1947), p. 43.

The age of the Father was that of the Old Testament and the law. The Gospel of Christ brought the second age, with law and gospel mingled. The dispensation of the spirit would bring true ascetic freedom, the regeneration which will spiritualize history. Here was a progressive motif: the succession of law, grace, and love; of slavery, filial service, and liberty; and—though the progress may seem less obvious to us—of the married, the clerics, and the monks. Joachim's idea of the three ages has had a long heritage in philosophical and political thought.[2]

The left-wing Franciscans envisioned St. Francis (d. 1226) as the messianic leader whom Joachim had predicted. The spirit of expectancy and perfectionist idealism was vivid and had strong repercussions within the more conventionalized church. Among the contemporaries of St. Thomas, Bonaventura (d. 1274) mingled apocalyptic expectation and mystical love, and Roger Bacon (d. 1294) combined the hope of progress through knowledge with predictions of the anti-Christ. Even the writings of Dante (d. 1321) were not without hints of a progressive motif and of messianism.

Non-empirical though such interpretations of history are, they represent no more of a superimposed pattern than the similar secularized version of the three ages presented in the nineteenth century by Auguste Comte in the name of science. They may be understood as a breaking out of an authentic but long stifled strain of Christian thought about history. They were not destined to have great influence in the Roman church, where Thomism became dominant. But, as Ernst Benz has shown, they merged into the heaven-storming spirit of Renaissance secularism and some of the Protestant sects. The visionary expectations of radical sects were then confronted by the disciplined realism of Calvinism. From these two movements, so different in character, the modern Christian world drew its impulse to transform history.

<hr>

[2] See Karl Löwith, *Meaning in History*, Appendix 1; Erich Frank, *Philosophical Understanding and Religious Truth*, pp. 169–71.

A. THE CALVINISTIC DYNAMIC

Calvin (1509–64), says one Roman Catholic historian, "inspired Protestantism with the will to dominate the world and to change society and culture." [3] To emphasize both the absolute sovereignty of God and the urgency of moral action might raise logical and metaphysical problems, but it was religiously effective. Predestination is not a matter of inevitable fate or of the working of law, but is God's unqualified will, which ordains the events of history and commands men to action. Calvin is scathing in his criticisms of those who excuse evil or laxity on grounds of divine determinism.

The sense of God's complete sovereignty does not in any way dim the insistence on man's sinful defiance. Obviously in some sense God's will is *not* done. Calvin passed off the problem of logical consistency here by finding the issue inscrutable to man's feeble eyes (in consistency with his whole doctrine), or made a stab at an explanation by differentiating God's *will*, which is always executed, and His *commands*, which are often defied. Evil is willed by God that He may overcome it for greater good and glory, and Christians are called to battle under God for the destruction of that evil.

The moral activism took form in the famous effort to establish a theocracy in Geneva, with the "Word of God"—in the form of biblical moral commandments—the absolute authority for public and private morality and for belief. Church and state were separate, but the two cooperated, subject to the will of God as set forth in Scripture. Since civil law was based on the Ten Commandments, the state punished violations of biblical law. The state had a specific mission to work with the church for the accomplishment of God's commands throughout the whole community including personal, political, and economic life.

The question arises as to why a social order, patterned on an

[3] Christopher Dawson, *The Judgment of the Nations*, p. 45.

unvarying legalism drawn from an ancient time, does not lead to a static conception of social order and morality. The answer lies partly in the sociological and economic situation of Reformation times. But there is a fundamental theological reason: Calvin's conception of the radical transcendence and righteousness of God as opposed to the iniquity of the world. Thomism had worked out its cautious gradations which blurred sharp contrast between God's will and the world: one could move from natural law to revealed law, from commands to counsels, from mortal sin to venial sin to sacramental righteousness, from world to Christendom to hierarchical church to Kingdom of God. Calvin, like Luther, wiped out the intermediate stages;[4] but then instead of despairing of the sinful world, he set out to conquer it. So McNeill writes:

> In Calvinism the world society is a definite object of hope and of ameliorative effort. Social optimism and idealism, emancipated not only, as in Aquinas, from apocalypticism, but also from subjection to the papal monarchy, emerge with fresh force. . . . Calvin probably allows himself more enjoyment of the future prospects of the mundane society than any writer before him. . . . This is because his view of the Christian society (*corpus Christianum*) is dynamic. It is the sphere of operation of God's efficient will through the enlisted will of man. Life is a combat, not only against inward temptation as for the monk, but against the satanic forces in human life.[5]

Further, Calvin's conception of God is so dynamic that the history which He governs must likewise be dynamic. God is no unmoved mover. "Calvin's God is the eternally creating, the eternally working, the ever acting God, the Almighty who *in*

---

[4] Calvin preserved medieval natural law, but for the most part subsumed it under biblical commands. His divine law, as Troeltsch shows, represents some accommodation to the world, but is strict and radical enough to create a real tension with the world.

[5] John T. McNeill, *Christian Hope for World Society* (New York: Harpers), p. 111.

this world and through this world builds his Kingdom. . . . All the power of the world, all the forces of the earth strive for the one great final purpose: the full realization of the glory of God." [6]

This same sense of God's transcendence, however, makes it impossible for Calvin to find the significance of history solely within history. He will tolerate no creature-worship, no idolatry of an ideal society. His aggressive ethical activity finds its spring in obedience to God rather than expectation of earthly achievement.[7] The Kingdom of God or the Kingdom of Christ is not to be confused with the Geneva attempt at a theocracy. The "spiritual kingdom of Christ and civil government are things very different and remote from each other." [8] Nor is the Kingdom identical with the church, though the relation is close. It is "of a spiritual nature"; it is "not of this world"; it consists not in earthly felicity but is "peculiar to the heavenly state"; yet it is "within us" as "righteousness, peace, and joy in the Holy Ghost." [9] With traditional eschatological emphasis Calvin asserts that Christ's kingship will not be consummated until the Last Judgment. But the knowledge of Christ's present, though concealed, kingship assures us of victory over the world, the devil, and evil.

Is the Kingdom of God then something for which we can labor? Clearly it is God's work, but God works through men. The petition, "Thy kingdom come," ought "to inflame us with an

---

[6] Karlfried Fröhlich, *Die Reichgottesidee Calvins*, p. 23. (My translation.)
[7] Calvin can talk of the world with as strong devaluation as Luther or Augustine. His "Meditation on the Future Life" is largely an almost morbid meditation on the miseries of this life. (*Institutes*, III, ix, 1–6; *cf.* x, 4.) However, he is capable also of enjoying life, granting that God "intended to provide not only for our necessity, but likewise for our pleasure and delight." (III, x, 2; *cf.* 1–6; ix, 2, 3.) Calvin's own life was not nearly so devoid of laughter, appreciation of beauty, hospitality, recreation, and sympathy as it is often represented. See James Mackinnon, *Calvin and the Reformation* (London: Longmans, Green, 1936), pp. 275–77.
[8] *Institutes*, IV, xx, 1.
[9] *Ibid.*, II, xv, 3–4.

ardent desire of mortifying the flesh, and finally to teach us to bear the cross; since these are the means which God chooses for the extension of his kingdom." [10] In personal life justification is followed by a sanctification through the Holy Ghost, in which man may make daily "progress." [11]

Fröhlich finds that Calvin stands "in the history of the idea of the Kingdom of God, midway between the primitive Christian eschatological expectancy and the modern dissolution of eschatology in the belief in progress." [12] We are still well within the traditional Christian understanding of history, which views earthly history as a pilgrimage within the vaster history of salvation. But in looking for concrete historical accomplishments, Calvin is developing one of the authentic themes in the Christian understanding of history.

B. SECTARIAN HOPES

The sectarian emphasis is a recurrent one throughout Christian history. Proclaiming the pure radical Gospel ethic, rejecting the churches' ethical compromises with the world, the sect is intentionally a minority group. It is formed of individuals who choose to enter its fellowship. Sharply critical of the world, says Troeltsch, "it always finally revives the eschatology of the Bible." [13]

By its very nature the sect would seem to have little hope of improving the world. But in those times when its eschatological expectancy becomes vivid, when in periods of change it feels a sense of historical destiny, or when it combines with a strain of romanticism in the prevailing *Zeitgeist*, the sect becomes imbued with a dynamic expectation for history. Such was the case with some of the Renaissance and Reformation sects.

---

[10] *Ibid.*, III, xx, 42.
[11] *Ibid.*, III, vi, 5. Cf. xiv, 9; xx, 42.
[12] *Gottesreich, Welt und Kirche bei Calvin*, p. 93.
[13] *Social Teachings of the Christian Churches*, p. 339.

Among the diversities of this "left wing of the Reformation," several common ideas prevailed. There was insistence upon a pure ethic, free from the compromises which Luther and Calvin had followed Catholicism in allowing. Usually the Sermon on the Mount replaced Calvin's use of the Ten Commandments. In contrast to the prevailing Protestant and Catholic state churches, the sect was to preserve its holiness in complete separation from the state. With these beliefs went a Christian primitivism, a glorification of the apostolic church with a hope for recovery of its spirit. The "fall" of the church from its primitive purity was set at various times—most often in the age of Constantine. This look to an idealized past was matched by a future anticipation, in what Toynbee might call a combination of archaism and futurism.

Setting themselves against the current of society, the sects found support in a heightened eschatology, derived from Scripture, sometimes with Joachimite overtones. The apocalyptic expectancy took two opposite forms: that of the revolutionaries (or "fighting sects") and that of the *Stille* (or "suffering sects"). In either case the difference from traditional eschatologies was that the sectarians felt that their own sects, whether military or pacifist, might be decisive for the establishing of God's reign. But it was still God, not man, who would bring in His Kingdom.

Recent investigations indicate that the radical sects have often been judged unfairly in church history. The famed Münster episode and a few other extravagances of the movement sometimes hide the fact that it was largely pacifist. Much of the traditional information about the sects has come from the accusations of their opponents. A different impression comes from the writings of the movements, consisting largely of obscure pamphlets or hand-written letters, often by laymen, expressing an unsophisticated faith and inner peace in the midst of persecution. The best of these documents have a simplicity and confidence reminiscent of early Christian writings.

In the small, holy community these Christians felt the power of rebirth as an anticipation of the imminent apocalyptic event. Their own martyrdom and non-resistance to persecution were their share in the work of God's triumph. True discipleship was interpreted in terms of the cross. It was said that Armageddon occurred whenever a Christian suffered persecution. One scholar writes:

Through all Anabaptist texts on martyrdom one perceives the one note: the present extremity is not just one stage on the path of martyrdom through history but it is its very last stage, it is the last act in the apocalyptic drama between God and Satan. . . . The martyr is the "true soldier of God" fighting against the power of darkness.[14]

The radical sectarian ethic leads to a strong spirit of separation from the world. At this point the community faces a choice in its historical outlook. Either it withdraws and puts its entire hope for history in the eschatological act of God; or it hopes to evangelize and transform the sinful world. Thus the sectarian may be more pessimistic, or more optimistic, than the rest of society. The former tendency has led to those communities, some still existing in Europe and the United States, with tendencies to cultural primitivism and abandonment of secular history. The latter tendency leads to missionary effort which overcomes cultural isolation and takes a far more exalted and dynamic hope for history than either Lutherans or Calvinists held. A letter of Jacob Hutter in 1538 says: "We say and wish that all the world would be as we are. It is our desire to bring and convert everybody to this faith; then, all warfare and all injustice would come to an end." [15] Such a conjecture was rare in the sectarian writings, but furnished a germ of optimism which flourished in later generations.

---

[14] Ethelbert Stauffer, "The Anabaptist Theology of Martyrdom," *Mennonite Quarterly Review*, XIX (1945), 197, 200.
[15] Quoted by Ethelbert Stauffer, "The Anabaptist Theology of Martyrdom," p. 214.

The eager spirit of world transformation came to flourish in the seventeenth-century English Diggers—a group interesting both as an example of the development of sectarianism and as a forerunner of Marxism. Their moving spirit and pamphleteer, Gerrard Winstanley, was originally a Baptist, but turned "Seeker." He revived imminent apocalyptic expectations, seeing in the events of the Puritan Revolution the signs of a vaster change in the character of history. Part of his faith was a glorification of the outcasts, midway between the Bible and Marxism in spirit. The opening words of his pamphlet, *The New Law of Righteousness* (printed 199 years before *The Communist Manifesto*), say: "Though you have been and yet are the despised ones of the world, yet the blessing of the most High (your King of Righteousness) is in you, and shall spread forth of you to fill the earth."

History and all creation, in Winstanley's view, labor under the curse of selfishness. There is no suggestion of a progressive view of history; rather the curse has been multiplied through the years. But the day of transformation is near. Sometimes this hope appears as a quite religious, apocalyptic hope, sometimes as an expectation of social reorganization. In either case the dynamic expectation for history and the emphasis on social responsibility are strong.

In the more apocalyptic expressions, Winstanley looks for mighty things from the army of the Lord, for a transformation of human nature, a society of Christian love, and a barren earth turned fertile and plentiful.[16] Though the hope is clearly for a miracle, it is for a transformation of history in this world.

In his more clearly sociological hopes Winstanley emphasizes the political and economic system. He calls upon Cromwell to give land to the oppressed commoners, and asks for a true "Commonwealth Government" under which there will be no "buying

---

[16] *Works of Gerrard Winstanley*, esp. pp. 153, 186.

and selling" and no oppression. Winstanley is not sure whether the spirit of covetousness leads to the institutions of property, or whether property and social conflict produce selfishness. In the former mood, Winstanley finds the covetousness of Adam (who is in every man) leading to the buying and selling by which he oppresses his fellowmen. In the latter mood the buying and selling constitute the fall, and all inward misery and sin is the result of outward inequality.[17]

In either case there is a dynamic hope for history. The spirit of covetousness can be overcome by the spirit of Christ. "There shall be no buying nor selling, no fairs nor market, but the whole earth shall be a common treasury for every man, for the earth is the Lord's."[18] In the Diggers the Christian hope for history has come into its own—and gone considerably beyond its own. Winstanley brings us to the doorway of many a tendency in modern secular philosophies of history.

C. THE MERGING OF CALVINISM AND SECTARIANISM

It was the combination of Calvinism and sectarianism which, as Troeltsch has shown, did so much (along with certain secular currents of thought) to mould the modern world. Despite the utter contrasts at so many points, there were tendencies which encouraged a considerable merging of thought—especially at the points determinative for an interpretation of history. Both movements understood the Bible as a revelation of God's demands— demands with strict relevance to historical life. Both placed great emphasis on moral activity, on holiness dominating all aspects of life. Both regarded the church as a disciplined community of God's servants. And both (with exceptions among the sects) had a tremendous sense of mission to remake the world according to a Christian pattern.

The interaction was most evident in England. Puritanism,

---

[17] *Ibid.* For the former, see pp. 157–58; for the latter, pp. 511, 520.
[18] *Ibid.*, p. 184.

uniting Calvinistic and sectarian impulses, is perhaps the most
vivid example. Christopher Dawson, the Roman Catholic historian, goes so far as to say: "Thus the modern Western belief in
progress, in the rights of man and the duty of conforming political
action to moral ideals, whatever they may owe to other influences, derive ultimately from the moral ideals of Puritanism and
its faith in the possibility of the realization of the Holy Community on earth by the efforts of the elect." [19]

We shall not pursue the story farther, because it merges into
the story of modern thought, where Christian humanitarianism
came to flow in streams formed largely by the banks of secularism.
Reformation and Renaissance produced curious combinations
even in the time of Luther. The sixteenth and seventeenth centuries saw a procession of utopian writings. The more famous
ones include Thomas More's *Utopia* (1516), Erasmus' *Instruction of a Christian Prince* (1516), Francis Bacon's *New Atlantis*
(1629), Campanella's *City of the Sun* (1623). Parallel with
these were a number of writings by Protestant theologians, with
Lutheran, Calvinist, and sectarian inspirations. The end of the
seventeenth century brought Quaker William Penn's *Essay
Toward the Present and Future Peace of Europe* (1693). Although the religious motivation in some of these writings is clear,
the mood of secularism is evident. Future interpretations of history were to take new turns.

The problem of the Christian interpretation of history is to
make its conception of the fulfillment of human life (the Kingdom of God) relevant to history without confusing it with historical accomplishments which are of ambiguous worth. The
dominance of the ecclesiastical strain errs doubly by confusing
the Kingdom of God with a particular institution and thereby
making it irrelevant to the vast areas of history which are not included in that institution. Complete dominance of the apoca-

---

[19] *Judgment of the Nations*, p. 51.

lyptic strain preserves the purity of the Kingdom of God, but leaves it irrelevant to history. What can we say of the dynamic strain?

On the whole, Calvin manages to secure a conception of the Kingdom of God which is relevant to, yet not confused with, history. Yet he fails partially on both counts. The relevance is too much a matter of hammering the world into subjection to a legalistic authority—which in turn confuses God's will with a historically-conditioned code of laws.

Sectarianism at its best has a grand vision. At its worst it falls into absurd errors and pretensions. The sect often claims too much. To define itself as a community of redeemed men, containing by virtue of its holiness a foretaste of the Kingdom of God, is its dangerous error. The sectarian, who frequently comes from the disinherited classes, sometimes appears as a repentant publican who gets religion, then thanks God that he is not as the Pharisee. Yet one must acknowledge the humility and love among some of the sectarians, whose patient suffering sometimes recovers a rare Gospel spirit. But isolated groups, keeping themselves spotless by avoiding political responsibility, offer a very partial and inadequate representation of the meaning of history. The sectarian outlook ignores too much of the historical life of mankind.

Part II: Modern Viewpoints

CHAPTER IV

THE IMPACT OF THE IDEA OF PROGRESS

CONTEMPORARY Christian interpretations of history develop in a different world from that of traditional Christianity. New ferments have been at work and have produced the variety of outlooks often labeled modern secularism. No contemporary interpreter of Christianity can ignore the challenge of these viewpoints, any more than Augustine could avoid meeting classicism and absorbing much of it even while he refuted it. Perhaps the contemporary Christian's task is more difficult, since the challenging viewpoints were born within Christendom and have there grown up to independence or rebellion. If they reject Christianity, it is not because they have never heard of it but because they disagree with it.

This chapter and the next will look at Christian thought as it has tried to come to terms with modern thought, particularly the dominant idea of progress and its most important variant, Marxism. Here Christian interpreters have modified or forsaken their traditional views to accept much of the new, sometimes taking the new as the real fulfillment of the old. Two more chapters will then look at contemporary Christianity, in revised Catholic and Protestant forms, reasserting itself against weaknesses in modern thought and laying down again the challenge of the faith of its fathers.

I. THE IDEA OF PROGRESS IN SECULAR THOUGHT

In modern Western civilization the idea of progress has taken the place of Christian eschatology. The ethos of progress has become so thoroughly a part of the climate of opinion that it has moulded the thought of people oblivious to it, just as the idea of the Kingdom of God did in former times.

Christian thinkers react variously to the idea of progress. Some accept it as the fruit of Christianity, as Christianity having come into its own. Others regard it as a Christian heresy, with a kernel of truth and a coating of falsehood. Still others see it as an outright foe, locked in conflict with Christian faith.

Non-theological writers show the same varieties of opinion. The Scottish philosopher John Macmurray holds that the idea conceives history as "a single action which is realizing an intention," and therefore assumes a universal agent whose intention and activity are carried out in history. "Thus it is clear," he says, "that the idea of progress can have no other origin than the Jewish one, and that it is an essentially Christian conception which can have no rational basis save in a religious consciousness of the world." [1]

At the other extreme is historian Charles A. Beard:

It was not until commerce, invention, and natural science emancipated humanity from thralldom to the cycle and to the Christian epic that it became possible to think of an immense future for mortal mankind, of the conquest of the material world in human interest, of providing the conditions for a good life on this planet without reference to any possible hereafter. [2]

Macmurray arrives at his viewpoint only by ignoring what have usually been the main features of biblical and Christian thought about history. But Beard ignores the element of truth in Macmurray's statement. Christian thought does show two inherent factors which are prerequisite to a thoroughgoing idea

---

[1] *The Clue to History*, p. 113.
[2] Introductiion to the American edition of Bury's *The Idea of Progress*, p. xi.

of progress: first, the insistence upon the unity of history; second, the assurance that history moves forward to a conclusion which enhances the meaning of all that has gone before. Separated from the religious convictions which gave them their life, these two ideas take the direction of a philosophy of progress.

Hence Morris Cohen, a famous philosopher who can hardly be accused of theological bias, wrote: "The modern conception of history has its roots in the Biblical story of Jahveh and of the world which He creates as the scene for the unfolding of a divine plan." [3] Almost uniquely among the religions and philosophies of the world, Judaism had the sense of a directed dynamic history. It was not a conception of progress, but it could be modified and secularized into a theory of progress.

The real significance of the idea of progress for Christianity becomes more evident when we see what it affirms. It is unimportant to state that history has shown development from primitive to more advanced stages. Few thinkers, whether Christian, pagan, or secular, have doubted that. In the ancient world Aristotle, Lucretius, and Seneca all pointed out advances in history, but none made progress the key to history. The distinguishing thing about the modern idea of progress is that it performs the religious function of offering a meaning for history. Thus Carl Becker writes significantly:

The modern idea of progress belongs in this category of answers to necessary but insoluble questions. Like the myths of primitive peoples and the religious and philosophical beliefs of more advanced societies, it springs from the nature of man as a conscious creature, who finds existence intolerable unless he can enlarge and enrich his otherwise futile activities by relating them to something more enduring and significant than himself. [4]

---

[3] *The Meaning of Human History*, p. 11.
[4] "Progress," *Encyclopaedia of the Social Sciences* (New York: Macmillan, 1934), XII, 495.

To follow Becker's analysis, the progressive interpretation of history was born out of the profound changes of the fourteenth to the nineteenth centuries, with their revolts against eccclesiastical and secular, political authority. Neither Renaissance nor Reformation were progressive in tone, the former glorifying the classical age and the latter, the early church. But in drifting away from the ecclesiastical-apocalyptic view, men could not return to the classical idea of history. In the first place, Christianity had accustomed men to look for a hopeful future destiny. (To this we may add that the Renaissance, despite its backward look toward classicism, had a tremendous confidence in the powers of man.) In the second place, the new developments of experimental science opened up possibilities for man to master his own destiny. Both physical and social scientists, with a disdain for the ignorance of the past, hastened to jump on the bandwagon of progress.

The apostles of progress were not all in agreement, but all contributed to a new world-view. The variety of faiths which opposed Christianity took, broadly speaking, three forms, which require brief analysis and illustration: (A) Faith in revolutionary rationalism; (B) faith in natural evolutionary development; (C) faith in technology.

A. REVOLUTIONARY RATIONALISM

In noisy outbursts of enthusiasm the worshippers of progress yearned to break with the past and create a new world. A man like Descartes with almost no feeling for history and no respect for historiography indulged in magnificent expectations. He was proud that he had forgotten his schoolboy Greek—a happy symbol of leaving the past behind. The first proposed title for his *Discourse on Method* was *The Project of a Universal Science Which Can Elevate Our Nature to Its Highest Degree of Perfection.*

The new historical hopes were quite unhistorical and non-

empirical in method. Bury has described the clash of two dog-
matic convictions—confidence in reason and veneration of classicism. The moderns argued from the dogma of the universality of
nature (e.g., lions are just as fierce as in ancient days, they said,
though no one tried or knew how to prove the point). If nature,
including human nature, is uniform, then increasing knowledge
means increasing superiority.

The new attitude came into full bloom in the eighteenth century's self-conscious assurance of its own "Enlightenment." With
glowing confidence men spurned encrusted traditions, gloried in
the promise of new methods, aimed to rewrite the human story
starting with a blank tablet. "It was," writes Whitehead, "the
age of reason, healthy, manly, upstanding reason; but, of one-
eyed reason, deficient in its vision of depth." [5]

Most dramatically in France, men disdained the past and
counted on their newly won rationality to work a radical change
in history. The *philosophes* gave past history a great deal of
attention, but only for the purpose of showing its crimes and
follies and pointing the way to a new future. Of learning from
the past or of understanding themselves better through study of
their past, they had little notion.

In their secular ardor few of the polemicists—Proudhon and,
later, Comte were exceptions—could be aware that they were
substituting a new religion for an old. But they were making
Progress their deity, Enlightenment rationality their *logos*, the
future their Kingdom of God, and posterity's appreciation their
vindication and Last Judgment. Becker describes their viewpoint:

As formulated by the *philosophes* the doctrine of progress was but a
modification, however important, of the Christian doctrine of redemption; what was new in it was faith in the goodness of man and

---

[5] A. N. Whitehead, *Science and the Modern World* (New York: Macmillan, 1947), p. 86.

the efficacy of conscious reason to create an earthly utopia . . . the *philosophes* demolished the Heavenly City of St. Augustine only to rebuild it with more up-to-date materials.[6]

Despising the superstition of the past, men looked to reason to create a new world, free from the machinations of priests and tyrants. So the Encyclopaedists organized to fight prejudice and spread knowledge. So men spun great dreams of a rational world of perpetual peace [7]—and worked a bloody revolution to destroy the grip of the past.

Certainly there was no uniform theory of progress in the Enlightenment. Cynics as well as utopians spun out their ideas. Deists might argue with materialists, physiocrats with literati. But the common strain was the proud confidence in newly realized powers of reason to reorder society. Hopes were centered in no eternal City of God, but in the cities enlightened man could build.

The most vivid example of the religious character of the faith of the French anti-clericals was Condorcet. Hiding from political enemies and the guillotine, he wrote his remarkable testimony of faith in history as an advance "towards knowledge and happiness." Although in early periods this progress was sporadic and unsure, now man, by studying this advance, could find the means

---

[6] "Progress," p. 497; *The Heavenly City of the Eighteenth-Century Philosophers*, p. 31. Cf. Bury, *The Idea of Progress*, p. 73: ". . . it was just the theory of an active Providence that the theory of Progress was to replace."

[7] Becker comments on the work of the Abbé de St. Pierre: "How industriously this priest labored in the secular vineyard of the Lord! How many 'projects' he wrote, helpful hints for the improvement of mankind —'Project for Making Roads Passable in Winter,' 'Project for the Reform of Begging,' 'Project for Making Dukes and Peers Useful.' And then one day, quite suddenly, so he tells us, 'there came into my mind a project which by its great beauty struck me with astonishment. It has occupied all my attention for fifteen days.' The result we know: *A Project for Making Peace Perpetual in Europe!*" *Heavenly City of the Eighteenth-Century Philosophers* (New Haven: Yale University Press, 1952), p. 70.

of securing and accelerating continuous progress. Thus Condorcet expressed his confidence that "the perfectibility of man is absolutely indefinite," that progress "may doubtless be more or less rapid, but it can never be retrograde." Thus he foresaw the day "in which the sun will observe in its course free nations only, acknowledging no other master than their reason; in which tyrants and slaves, priests and their stupid or hypocritical instruments, will no longer exist but in history and upon the stage."[8]

Here was a faith by which the victim of fanaticism could live and die. Here, as Condorcet makes clear in his ringing conclusion, is the vision which overcomes adversity, the consolation in the face of persecution, reward adequate for all effort.

In the actual writing of history the confidence in revolutionary reason is best illustrated by Edward Gibbon. British thought like the British revolution was less radical than French, but pervaded philosophy and politics (where Locke's self-styled "historical method" was aimed to clear away the underbrush of the past), the theater (where Shakespeare's plays were rewritten to conform to Enlightenment rationality), and historiography. Gibbon did not believe in universal progress; his great history of Rome was a story of degeneration from a past Golden Age. But Gibbon was confident that the intelligence of his day would prevent any such future "triumph of barbarism and religion." Among his reasons was the intelligence of civilized man which makes him superior in strength to any barbarians. Gibbon's crowning example is an ideal one to show what has come of his theory:

Europe is secure from any future irruption of barbarians; since, before they can conquer, they must cease to be barbarous. Their gradual advances in the science of war would always be accompanied, as we may learn from the example of Russia, with a proportionable

---

[8] *Outlines of an Historical View of the Progress of the Human Mind,* pp. 11, 258. Cf. pp. 266, 279.

improvement in the arts of peace and civil policy; and they themselves must deserve a place among the polished nations whom they
subdue.[9]

The idea of a revolutionary reason has been particularly influential in Americans' interpretation of their own history. Born
in the age of Enlightenment philosophy, America far more than
Europe could actually make the break with the past and build a
rational history. A religion of the frontier took the place of, or
was superimposed on, Christianity. In the self-confidence of a
growing nation, the lack of interest in any history more distant
than its own, the desire to avoid foreign entanglements, the
assurance that history could be freed from the weight of the
past with its kings and traditions, America has made this modern
faith peculiarly its own.

B. NATURAL EVOLUTION

Born later, expiring earlier, and altogether less important
than the faith in revolutionary reason was the faith in natural
evolutionary development. Here was the vision of a history
moving by a gradual natural process to steadily higher developments. Instead of seizing the bull of history by the horns and
changing its direction, men need only grab its tail and let it
carry them forward.

In part this attitude was typical of the British, with their
evolutionary politics, in contrast to the French. To a greater extent it was characteristic of the nineteenth, in contrast to the
eighteenth, century. The revolutionary fling had brought dis-
illusionment; and new scientific studies, especially in biology,

---

[9] *Decline and Fall of the Roman Empire,* end of Ch. XXXIX. Arnold
Toynbee used this illustration in his Bampton Lectures in America
(Columbia University, 1948) and has kindly helped me locate it. Toyn-
bee observes that Gibbon was uncannily half right: Russia did pick up
arts of civil policy from the West—the Marxist creed, as yet unborn in
Gibbon's day.

gave impetus to the idea of natural progress. To sum up, in Becker's epigram, "whereas the eighteenth century held that man can by taking thought add a cubit to his stature, the nineteenth century held that a cubit would be added to his stature whether he took thought or not."[10]

Comte (1798–1857) was one of several French figures who formulated a "fundamental law" of "progressive development of human intelligence." Diversities of race, climate, and political action can only speed or slow the basic movement of progress. Disdaining or ignoring a great deal of history, Comte confined his view to Europe. Mankind moves through three great periods —the theological, or fictitious; the metaphysical, or abstract; and the scientific, or positive. Each has its subdivisions, and progress through the three is not equal: astronomy, physics, chemistry, and physiology have in turn attained the positive stage, but "social physics" is just entering upon it. It is the final stage: "It can never again change its character, though it will be forever in course of development by additions of new knowledge."[11] In the age now dawning society will be authoritatively organized according to scientific social principles. Already Catholicism has lost its power and warfare will soon cease.

It is evident that Comte retains some of the rationalistic spirit of the earlier *philosophes,* but he has fitted it into a more sweeping conception of a universal law of progress. Herbert Spencer completely naturalized progress. No longer was it the work of a rationality struggling to establish itself, but a perfectly natural process needing no help on its upward route. Spencer's theory was given great impetus when Darwin added evidence for evolution in nature, instead of the uniformity on which the earlier French thinkers had built their case for progress. But the Spen-

---

[10] "Progress," p. 498. *Cf.* Collingwood, *The Idea of History,* pp. 99, 144–45. It should be noted that some of the eighteenth-century philosophers (*e.g.,* Diderot) had elements of an evolutionary concept of nature.
[11] *The Positive Philosophy,* p. 30.

cerian philosophy was already well developed and publicized by the date of the *Origin of Species* in 1859.

The law of progress in human affairs is the same law that governs the cosmos and the development of the earth, or the evolution of life, science, or language. Spencer aimed to formulate the law rather precisely in terms of organic development from the simple to the complex, from the homogeneous to the heterogeneous. That a bare physical principle of ever-increasing complexity should eventually produce the "perfect" man may not be entirely clear; but Spencer was satisfied in his own mind that "Evolution can end only in the establishment of the greatest perfection and the most complete happiness." "Progress is not . . . a thing within human control, but a beneficent necessity." [12]

Evil for Spencer was lack of adaptation; historical evil is lack of adaptation to the social state. In a typical purple passage Spencer assures us that "evil perpetually tends to disappear," that "man will eventually become completely suited to his mode of life." The development of the ideal man is as logically certain as that all men will die. [13]

It may seem strange that in the name of science men should be so gullible. But as Collingwood says, "In the later nineteenth century the idea of progress became almost an article of faith. This conception was a piece of sheer metaphysics derived from evolutionary naturalism and foisted upon history by the temper of the age." [14]

C. TECHNOLOGY

Philosophers were more likely to place their faith in reason or nature than in technology, but whole populations experienced at first hand the advances in applied science. The face of the

---

[12] *First Principles*, p. 517. *Illustrations of Universal Progress*, p. 58.
[13] *Social Statics*, pp. 74, 78–80. In the revision of 1892 (forty-two years after the original) Spencer adds a note making some qualifications.
[14] *The Idea of History*, p. 144.

earth and the habits of centuries changed and men began to conceive of the power of science and industry as unlimited.

At the beginning of the seventeenth century Francis Bacon was evaluating knowledge in terms of its utility. In that century and the next, as Bury tells us, there were writers ready to accord the inventor of the mariner's compass a more important place in history than any number of rulers or philosophers, to rank an ingenious artisan above a Newton or Leibnitz, or to rate the value of a road far above that of a cathedral. By the nineteenth century Comte was able to figure, by some process of reasoning, that firearms were making warfare less murderous.

It was the industrial revolution which brought out the real possibilities of technology. Reaching its main phase in England between 1830 and 1870 it caught the imagination of Europe and America and showed the reality of progress, or at least of change, in history. If God had not created the universe for man, then man could recreate it for himself. For any who were stirred by Wordsworth's feeling that

> The world is too much with us

there were many more to respond to Tennyson's line suggested by his trip on the first train from Liverpool to Manchester:

> Let the great world spin for ever down the
> ringing grooves of change.

Technology had its grand opportunity in America, a land of rich resources and vast areas. Its creative aspect was made evident as it spanned a continent and drew together into the political unity of the United States a variety of peoples who, in earlier ages, would almost certainly have let their parochial interests keep them apart. Even in recent years Charles A. Beard found technology the key to future history. For "technology is the fundamental basis of modern civilization, supplies a dynamic force of inexorable drive, and indicates the methods by which the progressive conquest of nature can be effected." Its dynamic character is its new significance. "What was once Utopian becomes actuality. What appears to be impossible may be surmounted." [15] Its drive is unlikely ever to fail, since each achievement opens new possibilities.

Further, said Beard, technology subordinates "the warrior, priest, and political leader" and elevates the masses. We are reminded of the hope suggested by Bacon, Descartes, and Condorcet that education would equalize men's intelligence and thus end injustice. Modern means of disseminating information made it inconceivable to Beard that we could ever return to the mass ignorance of past ages. In all this, of course, there are obvious elements of truth, or at least of probability; and Beard, writing in now remote 1931, could not know how effective modern means would become for disseminating misinformation.

Many a scientist took up the theme. In 1930 Robert A. Millikan, rejecting all forebodings about history as unsupported by sufficient evidence, added: "the conditions in the past that permitted periods of decline to occur have been so changed by the modern multiplication of agencies for both the spread and the preservation of science and of art that if there is anything that is certain it is that the Cassandras of the present merely represent a class that . . . in the language of Job 'multiplies words without knowledge.'" [16]

Thus in three general ways, with innumerable variations, the theme of progress took control of the modern mind. It served

---

[15] Introduction to the American edition of Bury's *The Idea of Progress* (pp. xx, xxiii), publication of which was stimulated by Chicago's "Century of Progress Exposition." Beard praised Bury for his appreciation of progress, but criticized his neglect of technology. He might have added that Bury was a great deal more circumspect than Beard, for Bury regarded belief in progress as an act of faith bearing upon the "mystery" of life.

[16] Charles A. Beard (editor), *Toward Civilization* (New York: Longmans, Green, 1930), p. 40.

and was served by the most contradictory ideologies—ranging from sweeping doctrines of *laisser faire* to the tightest ideals of social control. Rationalists and romanticists, idealists and materialists, determinists and voluntarists joined the chorus. The occasional Nietzsche or Schopenhauer who rose to challenge the theme only demonstrated the dominance of the majority who opposed him.

II. THE EFFECT ON CHRISTIANITY

The idea of progress posed new problems for Christian thinkers. The theological issue is not, as sometimes represented, whether historical progress is inevitable. Nor is it whether progress is a possibility. Most Christian thinkers, like most secular thinkers since the wane of Spencer's influence, would deny the former and affirm the latter. The issue is whether progress can be made into a religion. Does historical progress offer the solution to the religious quest for salvation?

Progress is only one aspect of the whole modern world view which has confronted Christianity. Much more disconcerting to most Christian thinkers was the picture of the universe which resulted from Newtonian physics. The question arises: Did Christian thought struggle to maintain its integrity against new philosophies of physical science, only to be taken into camp unwittingly by the new idea of history?

The temptation was subtle. Supposedly scientific philosophies of deism so clearly lost the values of Christianity that, despite some apostasies and compromises, Christian thought saw the issue and fought back—sometimes deftly, sometimes clumsily. But the idea of progress had some affinities with Christianity, and often seemed a plausible interpretation of providence. Further, it so captured the modern ethos that many a thinker accepted it unconsciously. Finally, those who questioned it were likely to find themselves in impossible company. Intellectual obscurantists argued against science and evolution and predicted the day of the Last Judgment, describing it in woodenly literal fashion. Social reactionaries blocked any attempt to cure the evils of war and rampant capitalism with the slogan, "You can't change human nature." So responsible Christian thinkers were frequently pushed unaware under the sway of the new doctrine.

Perhaps the key point came with Immanuel Kant. Lessing had already drawn the picture of a progressive education and revelation by God throughout history. And Kant's pupil, Herder, theologian and poet, had preceded his teacher in working out a philosophy of universal development in nature and history. But Kant met boldly the whole problem in the relations between religion and the scientific spirit. Satisfied neither with French positivism nor with English compromise, Kant broke a doorway through the solid wall of physical determinism which seemed to confine religion unbearably. And though he remained rather deistic in his own religious philosophy, he made it possible for some of his successors in German thought to develop creative theologies without opposing physical science. But on the issues of history, Kant reinterpreted Christian eschatology along progressive lines, and his followers were inclined to go along with him.

Kant was no wide-eyed optimist, but his writings on universal history and on perpetual peace contain ideas of a rationality to be achieved progressively in history. In *Religion Within the Limits of Reason Alone* (1791) he applies these ideas to the Kingdom of God and history. His acute doctrine of "radical evil" is much like a Christian doctrine of "original sin." Man's selfishness drives him out of the primitive harmony of nature, launches him into history, and sets the problem of history. After driving the argument to the point where a Lutheran doctrine of justification by grace seems inevitable, Kant suddenly recovers his rationalism and decides that the human will can set man on the path of moral progress. But the individual can conquer evil only as part of an "ethical commonwealth," a "people of God."

Here Kant carefully treads the border between Christian and Enlightenment eschatology:

To found a moral people of God is therefore a task whose consummation can be looked for not from men but only from God Himself. Yet man is not entitled on this account to be idle in this business and to let Providence rule. . . . Rather must man proceed as though everything depended upon him; only on this condition dare he hope that higher wisdom will grant the completion of his well-intentioned endeavors.[1]

Then the Koenigsburg professor, who could not stand hymn-singing and who avoided church even on academic occasions, surprisingly identifies the ethical commonwealth with the church. But the true church will be a universal church, founded on a pure and rational religious faith, avoiding most characteristics of the existing church. So Kant establishes the proposition: *"The Gradual Transition of Ecclesiastical Faith to the Exclusive Sovereignty of Pure Religious Faith is the Coming of the Kingdom of God."* [2] The Kingdom of God then takes the form of a gradual development within history, sometimes delayed but never completely interrupted.

The influence on Protestant theology, via Ritschl, is obvious. Ritschl defines the Kingdom of God in very Kantian language as "the association of mankind—an association both extensively and intensively the most comprehensive possible—through the reciprocal moral action of its members, action which transcends all merely natural and particular considerations." This conception of Jesus, says Ritschl, was quickly confined by the apostles to "the limited sense of the redemptive consummation expected

---

[1] *Religion Within the Limits of Reason Alone*, Bk. Three, Div. I, Pt. III, p. 92. In his essay on *Perpetual Peace* Kant sees a process of nature or providence which uses man's evil propensities for good ends and *guarantees* the arrival of a peaceful world.
[2] *Ibid.*, Pt. VII, p. 105.

in the future." [3] Ritschl avoids Kant's sometimes wooden legalism by usually stressing the bond of Christian love rather than
"reciprocal moral action," and he regards such love as supramun-
dane. Further "Justification and Reconciliation" are the work of
God, not of the historical process. But Ritschl's theology has
gone a considerable distance in absorbing a secular progressivism. The church, not in respect to its organization but insofar
as it is realizing the community of love, is progressively realizing
the Kingdom of God.

It was Hegel who managed to absorb God into the historical
process and still call the result Christianity. Far more sophisticated than most of the apostles of progress, Hegel was able to do
at least some justice to the infinite variety of history in a system
that was a combination of genius and effrontery. History for
Hegel is rational, but Reason is no closed, rigid thing; it moves
with thrust and counterthrust through dialectical patterns in a
constant development. History, says Hegel, "has constituted the
rational necessary course of the World-Spirit—that Spirit whose
nature is always one and the same, but which unfolds this its
one nature in the phenomena of the World's existence." [4]

In the process Reason becomes self-conscious, the Idea
achieves freedom. Thus though Spirit is the author of history,
Spirit in the full sense is the result and the achievement of history. For the essence of Spirit is freedom, self-contained existence,
self-consciousness, and these emerge only as history goes through
the dialectical developmental process. The system is thus progressive, not merely in detail, but in its fullest religious significance. Hegel was too radical here to suit Protestant theology,
which was much more inclined to develop Ritschl's milder ideas
of progress. But he wielded great influence over philosophy of
religion in Germany, Britain, and America, and thereby con-

---

[3] *Justification and Reconciliation*, Vol. III (Eng. tr. ed. by H. R. Mack-
intosh and A. B. Macaulay. New York: Scribners, 1900), Sec. 35, p.
284.   [4] *The Philosophy of History*, p. 10.

tributed to theology's increasing emphasis on divine immanence and on progress.

Ernst Troeltsch in 1912 looked at the pervasive change that had come over Protestantism since its formulation in Reformation days and analyzed the continuities and differences. He judged that the belief in progress, along with other features of the modern world-view, would be impossible without the background of "religious Personalism" which had come out of Christianity and had been enhanced by Protestantism. And he noted, as others have done, that the modern revolutions and Enlightenment had been carried through in Protestant countries like Britain, Germany, and the United States, without the violent break with religion that had occurred in France. But he recognized too that a great change had come over Protestantism. A "modern religious temper" had emerged, which, said Troeltsch, "in a thousand various modifications, has been so thoroughly absorbed by larger portions of modern Protestantism, that the latter can scarcely be distinguished from the former."[5]

Sometimes the permeation of secular and Christian sectarian influences was gradual and all but unnoticed. Germany, though it had two sharply opposed Lutheran orthodoxy and secularism, was able to draw from a tradition including Lutheran, pietist, and Ritschlian elements, and thus frame theologies in the modern liberal temper without putting all eggs in the basket of progress. Harnack, a liberal Ritschlian, saw the Kingdom of God in terms of inner spiritual growth; thus he could interpret away or subordinate most of Christian eschatology, view history as an upward development, and still not base his faith on historical progress. English traditionalism absorbed much of the spirit of progress while retaining qualifying emphases in theology and worship.[6]

---

[5] *Protestantism and Progress*, p. 183.

[6] I remember the startling effect when in Westminster Abbey during the Second World War I unexpectedly came upon the tablet to Charles Darwin. It is symbolic of the Church of England that the man who so challenged its faith should lie within its walls.

In the United States, however, the issues often seemed to force Christians to choose between clinging to stubborn fundamentalism or interpreting the whole Christian view of history in terms of progress. Thus we find Lyman Abbott, fighting the necessary battle for acceptance of evolution, carrying his convictions to the point of interpreting "the laws of spiritual life" by "the great laws of life which natural science has elucidated from a study of natural phenomena." With many others, he interpreted sin as the lingering animal nature in man and preached "Redemption by Evolution." History, along with everything else in life, he found best understood in terms of evolution, for "God has but one way of doing things"—"the way of growth, or development, or evolution."[7] Henry Drummond, once an associate and always a friend of Dwight L. Moody, declared enthusiastically that evolution and Christianity were identical—a method of creation, working through love, to make more perfect beings and complete *"The Ascent of Man."*

As Christian thought gradually absorbed the idea of evolution, it was better able to do it justice without making it the key to the whole understanding of history. Yet even such prominent thinkers as A. C. McGiffert and William Adams Brown, who stood near the center of the development of liberal theology, interpreted history almost entirely in evolutionary terms. McGiffert saw existence as "progress, in some degree at least, definite and constant."[8] Brown pointed to the "ethical progress of society" and defined God's method as a "method of progress." Proof of God's truthfulness and justice, he wrote, "is to be found less in individual examples, however striking, than in the entire course of his government, with its evidence of the growing supremacy of the rational and the moral in the life of man."[9]

---

[7] *The Theology of an Evolutionist.* See esp. pp. 8–9, 180.
[8] *The Rise of Modern Religious Ideas,* p. 186.
[9] *Christian Theology in Outline* (New York: Scribners, 1906), pp. 269, 109. Cf. pp. 218–19.

Both these theologians interpreted the Kingdom of God as the result of long historical growth. Brown, for example, saw the Kingdom of God as the result of God's gradual unfolding plan, recognized in part by science but seen more fully by religion. "As the appointed means for realizing the kingdom of God, Christianity is a progressive religion. Growth is the law of its life, and this along all lines,—doctrinal, institutional, practical." [10]

It would be easy to record examples from early twentieth-century writing and preaching which, in their confidence in progress, their ridicule of anything they could call "pessimism," and their assurance of an early achievement of utopia, rival the statements of Condorcet or Spencer. But the influence of the idea is better illustrated from the normative Christian thought of the period.

Harry Emerson Fosdick is often used as a whipping boy by current critics of liberalism, who should be grateful for some of the battles he won. Actually his *Christianity and Progress* (1922), though sharing the ethos of the first quarter of the century, criticizes the extravagances of the doctrine and gives a more balanced viewpoint than that of many more academic theologians. He finds that "the central problem which Christianity faces in adjusting her thought and practice to the modern age is the problem of coming to intelligent terms with this dominant idea." [11] Fosdick accepts whatever evidence of progress can be found, characterizes Christianity as a progressive religion, and looks for progress in religious understanding and in the influence of the Gospel on social life. But he furnishes many an idea or phrase which has since been used by the critics of "liberal" theology, as he attacks the "idol" of progress, "sentimental optimism," romantic expectations from education, the refusal to take

---

[10] *Ibid.*, p. 39. *Cf.* p. 219. *Cf.* McGiffert, *The Rise of Modern Religious Ideas*, p. 183.
[11] *Christianity and Progress*, pp. 41–42.

sin seriously, the "soft gospel of inevitable progress." He is aware
that history is a mixture of progress and regress. On the central
issue of whether progress can become religion, Fosdick is absolutely clear: ". . . a stumbling and uneven progress, precarious
and easily frustrated, taking place upon a transient planet, goes
but a little way to meet those elemental human needs with
which religious faith has dealt." [12] Fosdick represents one of the
more sober of those who give dominance to the progressive strand
in the Christian thread of history. He ends his discussion with a
ringing confidence in further progress which was peculiarly that
of the time in which he was writing.

Even today other writers are more confident than was Fosdick. America's best-known church historian still writes in terms
of the purest progressivism. He is confident that in actual fact
the community of love is "growing" and that its progress is the
"true meaning" of history.[13]

Only rarely during the first quarter of the present century did
a prominent Christian attack the doctrine of progress severely.
One of the exceptions was Dean Inge, who regarded it as a
superstitious distortion of Christianity and returned to a Platonic
belief in ultimate values and a historical doctrine of recurrence.
But Inge in his view of history seems neither modern nor biblical
and remains something of a stranger in recent Christian thought.
He has been dubbed "the gloomy dean" and left to the side as
the main currents of Christian thought have swept on.

III. THE SOCIAL GOSPEL AND ITS HEIRS

The Christianized doctrine of progress achieved its most
creative effects in the Social Gospel, whose influence is evident
in some of the thinkers already mentioned. From Calvinism

---

[12] *Ibid.*, pp. 49–50.
[13] Kenneth Scott Latourette, *The Emergence of a World Christian Community* (New Haven: Yale University Press, 1949).

came the stern determination of the Social Gospel to reshape the world in obedience to God.[1] From the sects came its emphasis on Gospel, its hope for a real sanctification of the community, its practice of tolerance, part of its impulse to economic reforms, and its hope that human efforts and human suffering might hasten the advent of God's Kingdom. This Christian stream of thought, formed by sectarian and Calvinist influences, merged with the secular faith in progress to form the Social Gospel's interpretation of history.

Numerous other landmarks lie in the background of the American Social Gospel. The eighteenth, nineteenth, and twentieth centuries have seen innumerable attempts to transform society along Christian lines. We have noted the strong ethical emphasis of Ritschl's nineteenth-century teaching of the Kingdom of God. Before Ritschl the Wesleyan movement in England stressed industry and philanthropy, exhorted men to sanctification, and preached love as the only answer to the evils of the world. In quite different vein Saint Simon (1760–1858) renounced Christianity (though influenced by Quaker thought) for a theistic religion of benevolence and social concern. Clearly Christian in motivation were the efforts of F. D. Maurice and Charles Kingsley, who in 1848, the year of Marx's *Communist Manifesto*, launched a movement for "Christian Socialism." Although not directly very effective, their work gave the impetus to many socializing and cooperative tendencies in Britain and America. In France the following year Louis Blanc's *Socialist*

---

[1] Those accustomed to associating Calvinism with encouragement of middle-class virtues and the "spirit of capitalism" may not regard it as a source of the Social Gospel. Without other influences it would not have produced the Social Gospel. But its strong ethical motivation led it to the regulation of economic evils, especially the evils of greed. Tawney writes: "Calvinism had little pity for poverty; but it distrusted wealth, as it distrusted all influences that distract the aim or relax the fibers of the soul, and, in the first flush of its youthful austerity, it did its best to make life unbearable for the rich." *Religion and the Rise of Capitalism*, p. 132.

Catechism described socialism as the Gospel in action. Christian Socialism in Europe, with sectarian motivation and zeal, transferred the apocalyptic hope to a desire to transform social conditions in this world. The result of these various movements for the Christian interpretation of history may be seen in McGiffert's statement in 1915:

The Kingdom of God, which has usually in Christian history been identified with the heavenly kingdom lying in another world beyond the grave, or with the Christian church itself—an institution in the world but not of it—is now widely interpreted as the reign of the Christian spirit on this earth, or the control of all human relationships and institutions by the spirit of human sympathy, love and service.[2]

The Social Gospel of Rauschenbusch and His Era

The most notable leader of the American Social Gospel was Walter Rauschenbusch, whose vivid devotion stirred many a churchman to deeper realization of Christian responsibility. In his *Theology for the Social Gospel*, Rauschenbusch made the Kingdom of God the center of Christianity, the focus of all other doctrines. Although not inclined to formulating definitions, Rauschenbusch frequently described the Kingdom of God as "the true human society," "the lost social ideal of Christendom," "a fellowship of righteousness," "humanity organized according to the will of God." God's Kingdom may not be identified with the church or any social system, but it is not merely an ideal. It is rather a vital power at work in history, energizing humanity to activity in behalf of human brotherhood.

Many biblical elements separate Rauschenbusch from the secular faith in progress. The Kingdom of God, he says, is "divine in its origin, progress and consummation." It is "miracu-

---

[2] *The Rise of Modern Religious Ideas*, p. 275.

lous all the way." God has the initiative in history. "Where others see blind forces working dumb agony, we must see moral will working toward redemption and education." [3]

His acute concern with the evils in social life gave Rauschenbusch a far more powerful doctrine of sin than had many of his contemporaries. Just here he mingles interestingly his biblical heritage with modernism. He wrote chapters on "The Super-Personal Forces of Evil" and "The Kingdom of Evil." He even took up the doctrine of "original sin," reinterpreting it to emphasize that the individual cannot detach himself from the stream of evil which corrupts social and historical life. But although he emphasized the grip of evil, he was remarkably confident that it could be shaken off. Evil was not the dynamic fury and vicious lust for power which later decades were to see. Rather, "The most important and persistent obstacle of progress is the conservative stupidity and stolidity of human nature." [4] So Rauschenbusch hoped, through certain social processes (for example, the movement from capitalism to economic democracy), to Christianize the social order. Theologically he urged a conception of salvation, not as primarily forgiveness, but as realization of the Kingdom of God.

Thus biblical concern merges with the progressivism of the epoch. Rauschenbusch sees the foolishness of some of the faiths in progress. He knows that history is a record of civilizations which have come and gone. "History laughs at the optimistic illusion that 'nothing can stand in the way of human progress.'" [5] Our responsibility is to see the causes of regress and so act that civilization may advance. In his enthusiasm for social advance, his buoyant spirit pronounces progress "divine" and calls men to a "revolutionary mission . . . lasting till organized wrong has

---

[3] The Theology of the Social Gospel, pp. 139, 223–24.
[4] Christianizing the Social Order, p. 30.
[5] Christianity and the Social Crisis, p. 279.

ceased." The Kingdom of God "implies a progressive reign of love in human affairs." [6]

In this interpretation of history the Social Gospel clearly gives primacy to the hope of historical accomplishment, decisively subordinating but not eliminating the other two strands in the thread of history. It sees all the pretenses and irrelevancies of sterile ecclesiasticism, the contrasts between church and Kingdom of God. The ideal is for humanity, not for a church. Yet there is a real place for the church as an instrument of the Kingdom of God, as one of the social institutions through which that Kingdom may be realized. And the church, insofar as it has the Kingdom of God within it, has saving power.

Similarly there is room for a reinterpreted eschatology. Rauschenbusch sought to strip away apocalypticism from the conception of the Kingdom of God, lest fanaticism or slothful quiescence be encouraged. Now that the fog of literalistic misconceptions which he fought has been cleared away, certain likenesses appear between his idea of the Kingdom of God, both present and future, and the New Testament eschatological

---

[6] *Christianity and the Social Order*, pp. 30, 324. *A Theology for the Social Gospel*, p. 142.

Rauschenbusch, although always energetically working for progress, varies in his expectations. Looking at history in 1907, he says, "It is either a revival of social religion or the deluge." (*Christianity and the Social Crisis*, p. 286.) In 1912, more confident of the social awakening of the American church, he sees Christian progress "in streaks and strata, with baffling inconsistencies and hypocrisies." But in many ways he far overestimated the progress that had been made: "The largest and hardest part of the work of Christianizing the social order has been done." (*Christianizing the Social Order*, pp. 123–24.) In his final book, written after the start of the World War, he sees no smooth road to the Kingdom of God. Catastrophes have their reality and their value. The Kingdom of God comes by conflict with the Kingdom of Evil. Nevertheless Rauschenbusch regards it as of the utmost importance to shift from catastrophic to developmental thinking. (*A Theology for the Social Gospel*, pp. 225–26.)

spirit. Although the intellectual context is vastly different, the mood is similar: "It is for us to see the Kingdom of God as always coming, always pressing in on the present, always big with possibility, and always inviting immediate action." [7] Rauschenbusch was quite aware of the incapacity of any ideal future social order to give meaning to millions of lives that had been stunted by the circumstances of history. Although he found the reward of Christian service in "every fractional realization" of the Kingdom of God, he did not say that efforts have meaning only insofar as they achieve concrete historical gains. His soaring idealism was not chained to the history whose evils he well knew.

There is little excuse for our generation, though it may have learned some things that the Social Gospel did not know, to sneer or condescend to Rauschenbusch. His purposes were so unquestionably generous and his enthusiasm so genuine that we would be foolish and ungrateful to forget his message. But since we have experienced a fury and intensity of history which he did not expect, and have found a persistent and demonic power in evil which he barely guessed at, we can recover powerful aspects of the Christian tradition and faith which he ignored.

So it is with others who have interpreted history in the general spirit of the Social Gospel. To recall their eager hopes is not to ridicule them, but simply to understand how suddenly history betrayed those who trusted it. Shailer Mathews, whose life span extended both before and after Rauschenbusch's, claimed to reject any single principle of interpretation of history in favor of an inductive approach doing justice to all factors. Yet he decided that in the expanse of history "we see the operation of many forces but only one tendency. And that is spiritual." Examination of the available data, he held, shows human progress which corroborates Jesus' philosophy of life and which, if con-

---

[7] A Theology for the Social Gospel, p. 141.

tinued, "will bring the world under the sway of the ideals of Jesus himself."[8]

Charles Clayton Morrison was typical of many Christian leaders when in 1927 he saw the assurance of world peace in the "outlawry of war." History he read as a record of an advance in which institutions once respected, like slavery and dueling, were overcome. War was to be overcome by the same process. The Senate, by passing the Borah resolution, would break the spell of war and inaugurate "the most stirring and glorious chapter in the upward progress of man," an age in which the voice of the people "would be indeed the voice of God!"[9] Morrison found a modern reawakening of the Christian eschatological hope in this-worldly terms: "It is the emergence of the social sciences that is now quickening a revival of the pristine social vision which the early Christians conceived under eschatological and supernatural categories."[10]

More recently (1943) Shirley Jackson Case has attempted to revive a thoroughly progressive view of history in Christian terms. Insisting on a completely "observational" rather than a "philosophical" approach, he would avoid completely the dark area of metaphysics and simply examine the evidence. Here he finds unquestioned assurance of progress in man's physical well-being and intellectual life. Social progress may at first glance seem more doubtful, but "if the history of social growth is viewed realistically, in terms of the actual developments of even the past century, no other area of civilization will exhibit clearer evidence of progress." Political progress lags behind, but is never-

---

[8] *The Spiritual Interpretation of History*, pp. 192, 210. Cf. pp. 67–68.
[9] *The Outlawry of War*, pp. 97–98, 280–81. John Dewey, in a fore-word to Morrison's book, saw the outlawry of war as a completion of the historic experience of mankind. It was not, indeed, a step-by-step process, but involved a right-about-face, and as such was typical of "all social progress." Pp. xx–xxi.
[10] *The Social Gospel and the Christian Cultus* (New York: Harpers, 1933), p. 151.

theless evident; and Case finally "has no difficulty in persuading himself that never before have so many men been capable of aesthetic appreciation, moral idealism, and spiritual striving."[11]

Case offers a clear illustration of the religious character which Bury and Becker pointed out in the idea of progress. For he not only insists upon the facts of progress. He also concludes (even while insisting upon purely empirical method) that "the ultimate meaning of history" is to be sought in its "strange recuperative power that ultimately negates every mood of discouragement and fear," in its "vitality that refuses to bow before the decrees of our most ardent pessimists." The "religious meaning" of history he finds in the human conquest of material nature and the self-improvement of men's spiritual nature. He rejects any attempt to recapture the meaning of apocalyptic mythology, which is out of place in a world "where catastrophe is no longer in vogue as a philosophy of history."[12]

Critical Appreciation of the Social Gospel

Far more typical of recent thought than a lone writer like Case are those who have tried seriously to rethink the doctrine of progress, criticizing it severely but holding on to certain aspects of the Social Gospel and its drive for historical accomplishment. Among these Walter Marshall Horton represents a notable heir of the Social Gospel, who is critical of the dogma of progress but

---

[11] *The Christian Philosophy of History*, pp. 83–86. Case throws considerable doubt on the purely empirical character of his judgments by his practice of constantly refuting more "pessimistic" interpretations of history by attributing them to particular historical experiences of individuals, especially in Europe. The criticism of an idea on the basis of its sociological genesis is always a two-edged sword which can be turned back on the critics. When Case asserts that "History to date is . . . reassuring" (p. 217), he invites the reply from those he attacks that perhaps his statement could appear only in a book that was sent to press from a home in Florida.

[12] *Ibid.*, pp. 153–54, 156, 184.

interprets Christian hope and confidence with reference to social gains.

Horton's intellectual career spans the period between the high influence and the severe criticism of the gospel of progress. He has moved from a youthful belief that progress and providence were the same to a faith in a providence which is largely inscrutable, but which may often be better recognized in the overthrow of corrupt institutions than in smooth progress. From an early enthusiasm for Henry Drummond's evolutionary theism, he came to wince at the once-thrilling phrases. After early devotion to an explicit Social Gospel, he has called it a thing of the past. Where once (under the influence of Shailer Mathews) he regarded history as the stronghold of rational faith, he came to see it as a problem for faith, though certainly not an insurmountable one.[13]

Horton's most thorough study of the problems of history comes in his volume, *Can Christianity Save Civilization?* (1940). Here he discerns a frequent cyclical pattern of history, but finds that religious faith has often formed the new center of life for declining cultures. A Christianity, enriched by contributions from the other religions of the world, might perform that function for our world and lead to the dawn of a world civilization. All this is no simple program for social change. Christianity is primarily a Gospel, offering a creative spirit—the spirit of Christ, of sacrificial love. And the Kingdom of God is not to be confused with a "Christian world civilization," though such an achievement would clearly be "another step in the earthly manifestation and triumph of that Heavenly Kingdom."[14]

---

[13] For these various changes see *Realistic Theology,* in *Theology in Transition,* pp. 87 n., 93–94. "Rough Sketch of a Half-Formed Mind," in V. Ferm (ed.), *Contemporary American Theology* (New York: Round Table, 1932), I, 169, 177–78, 185. *Theism and the Scientific Spirit* (New York: Harpers, 1933), p. 160. *Theism and the Modern Mood* (New York: Harpers, 1930), pp. 2, 31.

[14] *Can Christianity Save Civilization?*, p. 250.

Increasingly Horton emphasizes the Kingdom of God. Like Augustine he sees it as eternal, as present, and as yet to come.[15] But in keeping with the Social Gospel heritage it always has a reference for the social-historical task.

The Kingdom of God has both eschatological and contemporary social significance. It poses Christians a task, for "here 'on earth,' the coming of God's kingdom is largely contingent upon human willingness to do God's will."[16] But God's reign is not thereby jeopardized. For it is still certain that men cannot defy God with impunity. Only dedicated human activity can extend God's Kingdom. But God's judgment, operating through the moral order of the universe, puts limits on the power of evil. And God's grace, seen especially in the Cross, is able to triumph over all defeats.

The Social Gospel's stress on activity and its hope for genuine progress in history continue in Horton. He points to activities, inspired by Christian faith, for the abolition of infanticide and slavery, and establishment of socially creative institutions. These are victories of God in history. But the meaning of history—and this is the crucial point—is not to be found in these advances, certainly not in them alone. For there will be further defeats in history, perhaps disastrous defeats. The final assurance is that God can redeem them. For "whether in history or in his own ample eternity, we trust that God will in the end do what mortal creatures can never do if they work for a million years—give meaning to the world process as a whole and guide all the creatures that have issued from his hands back to their final destination in his eternal kingdom."[17]

The faith in progress has refuted itself by undergoing the cyclical process of rise and fall which it had denied. But this

<hr>

[15] "The Kingdom of God and the Church," *Christendom*, VI (1941), p. 163. *Cf. Our Christian Faith*, pp. 29–37.
[16] *Our Christian Faith*, p. 29.
[17] *Ibid.*, p. 122.

faith, born out of the biblical attitude toward time and history, then developing into a secularism, may have helped Christianity recover part of its birthright—a sense of the possibilities under God for historical action. Social Gospel optimism is now attacked on every hand. Yet influential Christians are retaining aspects of the Social Gospel. Their hopefulness is chastened and subdued, tempered with critical realism, but not blasted. It is probable that wherever historical conditions give opportunity for progressive actions, the influence of a Christian progressivism will remain. But it is doubtful that men will so eagerly seek in it the meaning of history. Final trust and security must rest on firmer grounds than the assurance that history means progress.

CHAPTER V

MARXIST AND CHRISTIAN ESCHATOLOGIES

THE most important variation on modern progressive faiths is Marxism. The snarling hostility between bourgeois liberalism and Marxism cannot conceal the presence of common assumptions. Both affirm the major idea that history moves toward its own redemption. No supernatural forces, no heaven-sent salvation are required. Human efforts—or often the inexorable process of history—will answer the problems of history.

The progress of history, as the Marxist sees it, is not smooth. Against the generally comfortable progressive view of the nineteenth century, Marx reacted with his message of conflict, crisis, and violence. Finding the Hegelian dialectical philosophy of history "standing on its head," as he put it, Marx turned it "right side up" and made it a "dialectical materialism." Instead of a gradual historical evolution Marx shows us a history driven by economic forces through the determined sequence of conflicts to the final classless society. From the viewpoint of twentieth-century man, harassed by a history that is too much for him, Marx's optimism would be decidedly comforting, if it could be believed:

Therefore, mankind always takes up only such problems as it can solve; since, looking at the matter more closely, we will always find that the problem itself arises only when the material conditions necessary for its solution already exist or are at least in the process of formation.[1]

[1] Preface to *A Contribution to the Critique of Political Economy*, pp. 12–13.

The question which immediately arises is why a creed so blatantly atheistic, so explicitly anti-Christian, so infused with strife and hostility, should lead to so many Christian attempts to appropriate some of its ideas. The only answer is that there are certain inherent likenesses or points of contact. Thus such a diversity of Christian thinkers as William Temple, Jacques Maritain, Reinhold Niebuhr, and Arnold Toynbee, among many others, have called Marxism a "Christian heresy." The designation carries the realization that a heresy is often a more insidious and dangerous foe than an alien enemy.

I. A FEW RELEVANT MARXIST IDEAS

Heresies typically seize upon specific elements of the mother faith and, by rearranging them and shifting the emphasis, work their distortions. Or they rebelliously revolt against the original faith, only to end with a hostile system which unknowingly takes over much of the framework of the rejected creed. Or they place an idea in a language and context so different from its original form that they blind themselves and their foes to the resemblance. Usually unwittingly, Marxism has used all these tactics. It will be useful to examine a few significant Marxist ideas in this light.

A. THE HISTORICAL IDEAL

However much Marx ridiculed Christian idealism, many of his phrases have a familiar Christian ring. Indeed, some of his anti-Christian fanaticism is best understandable as the jealousy of a would-be originator who dares not admit that his ideas have long been proclaimed by others. Although Christian thought has seldom shared Marxism's romantic view of historical possibilities, we have seen sectarian visions of a future much like the Marxist dream. The radical criticism of society and conventional morals, the drive toward historical realization of an ideal social order with an end of warfare and injustice, even the analysis of property as the source of discord—all these appear in the Christian development well in advance of Marx. So do the rigorous ethic, the severe discipline, the occasional specifically communistic practices.[2]

Of course these emphases are typical of fringe groups. But biblical and Christian tradition abound in exhortations which support social justice, classless society, ideals of freedom and community, internationalism and interracialism. There is an abundance of Christian polemic against greed and love of money, against individualism and competitive spirit, against will to power of race, class, nation, or individual.

The summit of the Marxist hope comes in its expectation of the day when "society will inscribe on its banner: 'From each according to his capacity, to each according to his need.'"[3] Marx might have found, though he probably did not, the basic idea in somewhat different language in Winstanley. In fact from New Testament times onward Christian faith has repeatedly given birth to communities which have practiced on a small and voluntary scale what Marx urged for vast economics. Nor is the Marxist aim a totally materialistic one. What Christian could take exception to the ideal of a society in which "the free development of each is the condition of the free development of all"?[4] Or to the objective of "the free-development, intellectual and social, of the individual"?[5] Christians might have their doubts as to the possibility of attaining so unqualified a utopia as Marx foresaw; but it has seemed to many that Marx, if only in his

---

[2] In addition to the examples cited in Ch. IV above, see R. Pascal, "Communism in the Middle Ages and Reformation" in *Christianity and the Social Revolution*. Also Toynbee, *A Study of History*, V, 581–87.

[3] Karl Marx, *Critique of the Gotha Programme* (New York: International Publishers, 1933), p. 31.

[4] *The Communist Manifesto*, II.

[5] *Capital*, I, 581. Cf. pp. 534, 649; *The German Ideology*, pp. 27–28, 70–78; *Anti-Dühring*, pp. 309–10.

vision of the future ideal, stood in the inheritance of the Hebrew prophets and of the New Testament.

B. THE ESCHATOLOGICAL FRAMEWORK

Even more significant is the parallel between Marxist and Christian eschatological frameworks. Both assume a genuinely historical outlook—in which a situation can be understood only in terms of its past and its future. And both find history driving toward its grand culmination. Increasingly modern analysts— Bertrand Russell, Arnold Toynbee, Reinhold Niebuhr, to mention a few—find the clue to Marxism in its secularization of the Christian apocalyptic drama.

History starts, in the Marxist interpretation, with a "primitive communism" analogous to the Christian paradise. Communal ownership and labor is the original spontaneous form of social organization. There are no private property, no private labor, no products of private labor to disrupt the primitive harmony and to send society careening through its history of class struggle.

But the idyllic harmony cannot go on forever. In such a society man is dominated by nature, "still attached to the navel string of the primitive community." [6] Like the paradise of Eden, this stage must end. However evil, the "fall of man" has to occur if there is to be a real history. Developing history, with all its evils, is in some sense a progress over innocent primitivism; salvation can come only if mankind moves through the tumult of the ages. As the Bible finds wicked imperialisms the agents of God's sovereignty (if only the "rod of His anger"), so Marx and Engels find all movements of history contributing to the

---

[6] Engels, quoting Marx, in *Origin of the Family*, p. 88. This book, in which Engels generalizes expansively on small bits of anthropological information, is the most detailed of the basic Marxist descriptions of primitive communism. But references are frequent in other Marxist writings, e.g., *The Communist Manifesto, Capital, Critique of Political Economy, Anti-Dühring*.

ultimate goal. Even the bitter polemic of the *Communist Manifesto* pays tribute to the accomplishments of the bourgeoisie. (Marx is doubtful that a country—Russia is the example—can achieve final communism without passing through capitalism, unless aided by a revolution outside the country.)

But the "fall" is thoroughly wicked. Through "theft, violence, fraud, treason," the class society of exploitation and oppression is established. The serpent in the garden is private property. An institution once despised becomes sacred. And to perpetuate the class division, to guarantee the exploitation, the state develops.

Henceforth history is the story of conflict and estrangement (*Entfremdung*). By the division of labor, by the development of private property and its exchange, by the class society, man is estranged from society, from the work of his own hands, from himself.[7] In his analysis of estrangement or alienation Marx comes closest to echoing Christian religious (as distinct from moral) ideas:

The possessing class and the class of the proletariat represent the same human self-estrangement. But the former is comfortable in this self-estrangement and finds therein its own confirmation, knows that this self-estrangement is its own power, and possesses in it the semblance of a human existence. The latter feels itself annihilated in this self-estrangement, sees in it its impotence and the reality of an inhuman existence.[8]

The history of "fallen" mankind now moves through various dispensations toward its culmination. The main stages are those of ancient slavery, medieval feudalism, and modern capitalism.

---

[7] *The German Ideology*, pp. 24–27. *Capital*, pp. 81 ff., discusses the enigmatic, mystical fetish-character of commodities in their separation from labor and use, a separation which warps the natural social relations of mankind.

[8] From *The Holy Family*. Quoted in notes to *The German Ideology*, pp. 202–203, n. 23. See also Karl Löwith, *Meaning in History*, pp. 35–36.

In the climactic age of capitalism, the bearers of the future are the persecuted, chosen people—the proletariat. The mantle of destiny has descended upon this class, now the disinherited, but soon to be the executors of the dialectic of history as it goes through its final "negation of the negation" and expropriates the expropriators.

History has prepared this chosen people for its task. They are in a position to see the truth which is invisible to others because of ideological blindness. But within the chosen people is the saving remnant, the *ecclesiola* within the *ecclesia*. What the proletariat as a whole knows only dimly and instinctively, the communists know and implement explicitly.

Like eschatological thinkers from the Bible on through the centuries, Marx tends to foreshorten the future and see the *Eschaton* as imminent. Typically he reads the signs of the times and thinks that the great judgment on history must be near. Again and again he and Engels see in historical events the crisis which they expect to touch off an early proletarian revolution.[9]

As in Christian teaching, the meaning of history is realized in the eschatological event. In Christianity the Kingdom of God fulfills history; in Marxism with its changed vocabulary pre-history gives way to history. Society makes "the leap from the realm of necessity to the realm of freedom."[10] The first shall be last and the last shall be first. History will move through the temporary dictatorship of the proletariat (a sort of millennium) to the final classless society (the Kingdom of God). Marx usually is wisely reluctant to make specific descriptions of this future state of affairs. But at times he describes it in the glowing terms suitable for an apocalyptic vision. It is the complete answer, not only to class conflict and poverty, but to man's basic *Entfremdung*. The end of private property will mean the solution of the conflict of man with nature, and of man with man; it will solve

---

[9] See Bober, *Karl Marx's Interpretation of History*, pp. 267, 387–88.
[10] Engels, *Anti-Dühring*, p. 310; cf. p. 125.

the opposition of freedom and necessity. "Universal dependence will be transformed by the communist revolution into the control and conscious mastery of these powers, which, born of the action of men on one another, have till now overawed and governed men as powers completely alien to them."[11] In this ideal future coercion, political power, the state will be unnecessary. When classes are abolished there will be no more political power, for political power is merely the means of class oppression. Engels writes: "The state is not 'abolished.' It *dies out*."[12]

C. IDEOLOGY AND SIN

Not only in his idea of estrangement does Marx parallel Christian anthropology; his doctrine of ideology bears a curious likeness to Christian thought. Despite modern criticism of the Christian doctrine of sin, both capitalistic and Marxist theory assume that self-interest rather than altruism is the mainspring of the economic machine. Far more profound than this commonplace assumption is Marx's conception of ideology, a conception suspiciously like the idea of sin—though many a modern who assumes the ideological character of human thought would never condescend to investigate the doctrine of sin.

In the Christian analysis man tries to overcome his finitude by acting as though he were the center of the universe, by pretending to be God. Or he makes gods in his own image reflecting his peculiar interest, then falls down and worships them instead of the truly universal God. In Marxist thought man tries to deny his finite class character by assuming that his class embodies the total welfare of society. Then, in his ideologies, he objectifies his

[11] *The German Ideology*, pp. 27–28.
[12] *Socialism, Utopian and Scientific*, p. 70. Lenin took up the words and in his *State and Revolution* laid great emphasis on this "withering away" of the state. It is ironical that the dictatorial politician of Marxism should be so much more precise in his speculations at this point than the original theoretician.

class interest in a system of thought by which he guides his life. In either case, the taint of ideology or of original sin pervades all man's activities, until he is incapable of thinking honestly and objectively. In his deluded, fallen state he believes that his tortured, biased reasoning is the truth.

Marx is caustic in his castigation of human nature as it exists in the class struggle. The "Furies of private interest," he says, are "the most violent, mean and malignant passions of the human breast." This self-interest is so dominant that Marx views individuals only as "the personifications of economic categories, embodiments of particular class-relations and class-interests."[13] Moral ideals are the expression of the interest of the dominant classes, and thus the direct reflection of ideological taint. Law, politics, religion, art, and philosophy are all ideological forms in which men become conscious of the more basic conflicts produced by economic conditions.

It is in tracing the origin of evil solely to economic factors, primarily to the means of production, that Marx differs sharply with Christianity. Often it would seem that for Marx "sin" is not at all a spiritual factor. We are not to judge social conflict and transformation in terms of the consciousness of those involved; "one must rather explain this consciousness by the contradictions in the material life, the conflict at hand between the social forces of production and the relations in which production is carried on."[14]

But Marx often belies his own words, in his moral indignation over exploitation. And he makes at least one seldom-noticed admission that nearly punctures his whole case. In discussing the acquisitive passion of the capitalist, he says that "the love of

---

[13] *Capital*, I, 15. (Author's preface to first edition.)
[14] Marx, *Critique of Political Economy*, p. 12. See pp. 11–13, 309–12; *Eighteenth Brumaire*, in *Selected Works* (New York: International Publishers, 1947), II, 344; *The German Ideology*, Part I; *Capital*, Preface to second edition, pp. 19–20; *Communist Manifesto*, Parts I, II.

power is an element in the desire to get rich." To support this contention he quotes at length Martin Luther's attack upon the usurer who "wants to be God over all men," "so that he may have all to himself, and every one may receive from him as from a God, and be his serf forever." Then Marx comments that "original sin is at work everywhere." [15]

Had Marx thought further on this remark, it might have blasted his theory of history. If "love of power is an element in the desire to get rich," one may assume that when men can no longer get rich (or at least no longer become capitalists) they may find other outlets for their love of power. They may learn that commissars can "be God over all men" as effectively as capitalists. If so, the removal of private property will not mean the end of exploitation and self-interest. In Christian terms the problems of human history lie deeper than changes in the modes of production, and communist revolutions show little promise of bringing history to its final synthesis.

The radical use of the ideological argument has other weaknesses. If all thought is ideology, determined by a particular social condition, what becomes of the omniscience of the Marxian analysts? How can we avoid writing them off, like everyone else, as victims of the circumstances which determined their thought?

Nevertheless, a considerable part of Marx's analysis is assumed by anyone who tries to understand political life. Theologians, whether of the Social Gospel or of more traditional persuasion, are justified in finding facets of Marxism helpful in their interpretation of human nature and sin. In his protests against idealism, against the belief that men view history from some detached position, Marx shares the existential bent of thought typical of Christianity. And there are real likenesses in the understanding of the existential situation.

---

[15] *Capital*, I, 649–50.

D. HISTORICAL DETERMINISM AND FREEDOM

Christianity and Marxism share an appreciation for the providential (or deterministic) character of history, combined with a radical call to men to exercise their freedom. Proud though Marx was to call himself a dialectical materialist, he was one of the most passionate voluntarists of history. In this respect Marx secularizes the providential viewpoint of Calvinism, where the conviction of divine determinism is an incentive to vigorous action. Marx makes the most of the hortatory value of both determinism and voluntarism. In the *Communist Manifesto* he and Engels on the one hand assert: "What the bourgeoisie therefore produces, above all, are its own grave diggers. Its fall and the victory of the proletariat are equally inevitable." [16] On the other hand they exhort voluntaristically in the closing words of the *Manifesto*: "The proletarians have nothing to lose but their chains. They have a world to win. Working men of all countries, unite!"

Engels shows that the analogy with Christianity is not a forced one: "It is still true that man proposes and God (that is, the extraneous force of the capitalistic mode of production) disposes." [17] The significance of the doctrine of providence for Christianity must be discussed later. For the time being it is enough to point out a practical consequence for historiography, clearly stated by Engels:

That which is willed happens but rarely; in the majority of instances the numerous desired ends cross and conflict with one another. . . . The ends of the actions are intended, but the results which actually follow from these actions are not intended; or when they do seem to correspond to the end intended, they ultimately have consequences quite other than those intended. [18]

---

[16] Part I. Similarly in *Capital* Marx claims to be dealing with "natural laws," with "tendencies working with iron necessity toward inevitable results." P. 13; *cf.* p. 837.

[17] *Anti-Dühring*, p. 345. Engels looks forward to the day when man will both propose and dispose. See p. 346.

[18] *Ludwig Feuerbach* (New York: International Publishers, 1939), p. 48.

We must not, of course, overlook the great difference between
the Christian God who works His purposes in history and the
Marxian dialectical process. The two interpretations of history
move in different realms of thought; but their paths are often
parallel and their answers analogous.

II. THE ATTEMPT AT A CHRISTIAN-MARXIST
SYNTHESIS

Clearly there are several places in Marxism where Christian
thought might attempt to take hold. It is no wonder, then, that
many Christian thinkers have found in Marx a help to their
understanding of history. The few who have tried to go the
length of a Christian-Marxist synthesis have also run into the
inevitable difficulties.

Probably the most notable philosopher to attempt such a
synthesis is John Macmurray. For many years Macmurray was
the prophet of the British group which called itself "The Christian Left" and regarded a communistic economic system as the
proper expression of Christianity. Out of Macmurray's writings,
two main grounds for the proposed synthesis emerge recurrently.

The first is the belief that the Christian ethic, taken seriously,
leads to the same form of social organization which communism
seeks. Throughout its history, Macmurray shows, Christianity
has repeatedly given birth to communal living. However, Christian hypocrisy has too often distorted its faith to evade the demands of the Gospel, and communism has rightly attacked the
false Christianity which has resulted. A synthesis of Christianity
and communism then simply calls Christians back to the original
and true version of their faith; it demands a great revolution in
Christian thought and practice, but not in Christianity's real
essence. The synthesis calls communism to take account of aspects
of human life which it has ignored—the truly "personal" aspects

of our nature.[1] For in prophetically rejecting institutionalized Christianity, communism has also rejected the creative core of faith. So an incomplete communism and a distorted Christianity demand synthesis with each other for mutual enlargement and purification.

This synthesis of objectives, although it has its historical precedents, raises its problems. To baptize Marx into a religion he so hated is a dubious undertaking. And to Marxianize the Christian Gospel is equally difficult. Macmurray's New Testament interpretation finds little support among recent biblical scholars who deny, practically unanimously, that Jesus was primarily a social reformer—or that he ever thought in terms of reorganizing the means of production. Nevertheless, few deny that a serious response to Jesus' ethical demands would have a transforming effect upon society.

More original than this idea that Christianity and communism share certain common aims is Macmurray's second basis for a synthesis—his contention that the two take a similar view of the process of history. Jesus was a dialectical thinker. "The meek shall inherit the earth" is not a moral glorification of meekness, but a factual statement about who shall inherit the earth in the dialectical process.[2] And Jesus applied the dialectic especially in economic terms.

Once again the interpretation of New Testament Christianity is strained. To say that Jesus reversed—and expected the Kingdom of God to reverse—accepted values and standards of prestige

[1] The theme of "personality" pervades all Macmurray's philosophical writings, including his non-political ones. His primary social concern is for the realization of a society in which persons may live in spontaneous creative relationships. So far as possible he interprets Marx along such lines. This same personal concern makes him urge a more pluralistic social organization with greater stress on personal rights than the Soviet Union exhibits.

[2] Macmurray emphasizes the theme repeatedly. See esp. *Creative Society*, pp. 66–67; *The Clue to History*, pp. 50, 104, 99–100, 237. Karl Popper criticizes Macmurray's stand in *The Open Society*, II, 260–61.

is clear enough. But the Marxist dialectic aims to be a specific description, or law, of the movement of history through a series of stages. If we are to find some non-biblical category for the understanding of the familiar New Testament motif, Macmurray's Marxian dialectic is less apt than Toynbee's "reversal of roles," so evident both in the Bible and in Greek tragedy. We can do full justice to the Gospel promise of redemption for the lowly and judgment upon the mighty, without regarding Jesus as a sort of proto-Marx.

Macmurray's difficulties become clear when he tries to apply the dialectic to a complete interpretation of Western history in *The Clue to History*. Here the dialectic, while avoiding Marxist rigidity, becomes so broad and loose as to be puzzling. Any historical event is explained either as a natural outgrowth of, or as a reversal of, something that went before. Both growth and defeat contribute to the dialectical progress of God's intention of a universal community of mankind, partly through and partly in spite of human intentions. So Macmurray tries to show how each of the great shifts of Western history—the rise of Rome, the fall of Rome, the organization of medieval society, the rise of the national states, the Soviet revolution, even the fascist states— marks a dialectical transition in which the Christian intention progresses. At the one point where the dialectic offers anything precise, its contribution is extremely dubious if not obviously false:

The essential truth of Christianity prevents Europe from destroying itself, and at the same time forces it through a series of revolutions which mark stages in the progress both of the acceptance and of the rejection of Christianity; and all these stages lead progressively towards the destruction of dualism and the achievement of equality, freedom and universal community.[3]

---

[3] *The Clue to History*, p. 149.

The dialectical concept has real values for understanding history. It rightly shows that historical development is not strictly linear, but often

Thus Macmurray reaches a confidently utopian understanding of the dialectic. Utopianism is a curious issue in Marxism. Marx and Engels attacked utopian socialism, only to fall into the most utopian—though purportedly "scientific"—dreams of a classless, stateless society. Macmurray similarly attacks idealism as a philosophy of utopian dreams, then accepts nearly all of Marx's utopianism. But he finally criticizes Marx's utopianism because Marx expects the classless society to solve all human problems, doing away with man's religious needs. Although he discerns quite profoundly some of the problems of personality and community, Macmurray conceives a romantic utopia in a classless society which is also a religious society, built on friendship and love.

This utopianism is the direct result of neglecting the doctrine of sin and naturalizing the idea of providence into a dialectical law. "The accomplishment of the Christian intention of a universal community of freedom and equality is inevitable." Every negative force runs into a negation of the negation which advanced God's purpose. But might not man destroy himself? The answer is direct: "No. This is impossible. The negative will can never destroy the positive will, since it is sustained by the positive." [4]

Here empiricism is forsaken for a confident prediction based upon dogma. Christian-Marxism seems to result in a worse utopianism (if possible) than either liberal theology or communism alone can achieve. Harry F. Ward, whose social analysis is

---

takes the form of development through actions and reactions, through struggles and their resolution on a different plane. It also shows how men's intentions, though sometimes effective, often are turned by the processes of history in unintended directions. But history is pluralistic in its processes. To reduce everything to a single dialectic—whether Marx's or Macmurray's—is to ignore too much evidence.

[4] *The Clue to History*, pp. 206, 101. Cf. pp. 58, 219–21. A decade later Macmurray was far more gloomy than in his major work on history. See *A Crisis of Culture* (Peace Aims Pamphlet No. 42).

more tough-minded than Macmurray's, returned from Russia in the 1930's with an equally utopian romanticism, expressed in his book, *In Place of Profit*. Macmurray's synthesis of Christianity and Marxism led him to an understanding of history no less mistaken than his understanding of Christian theology. A profounder conception of the transcendence of God might have allowed him not only a truer reading of the Bible but also a less fettered empiricism in analyzing history.

Thus both aspects of Macmurray's synthesis run into difficulty. Whether in the conception of the social-religious goal or in the understanding of the structure of history, the effort must be regarded as a *tour de force*, brilliant in many specific insights but unconvincing as a whole.[5]

III. CHRISTIANITY TAKING ACCOUNT OF MARXISM

More influential than Christian-Marxists are a number of contemporary thinkers who stand far more centrally in the tradition of Christian theology and still make incisive but critical use of the Marxist analysis of history. Typical of their approach is Reinhold Niebuhr's famous statement of 1936, urging "a more radical political orientation and more conservative religious convictions than are comprehended in the culture of our era."[1] In the succeeding years Niebuhr has developed his "more conservative religious convictions" into a full-blown interpretation of history in the biblical-Augustinian tradition, with a sophisticated appreciation and criticism of prevalent modern interpretations. During the same time the "more radical political orientation" has come to place less emphasis on Marx and more emphasis on the virtues of a pragmatic democratic liberalism. But Marx and the

---

[5] Such has been the reaction of a great variety of thinkers. See the extensive symposium on *The Clue to History* in *Adelphi* (Series 3), XV (1939), 223–37. Also C. E. M. Joad, "Dualism and Dialectic," *New Statesman and Nation*, XVII (1939), 370. Also Reinhold Niebuhr, "The Clue to History," *The Modern Churchman*, XXIX (1939), 75–81.
[1] *Reflections on the End of an Era*, p. ix.

Bible still contribute to Niebuhr's thought a biting quality not found in most liberal political analysis.

Many distinguished Christian thinkers combine appreciation with rigorous criticism of Marxism's conception of history. Nicolas Berdyaev, the creative Russian Orthodox theologian who was once a Marxist but who spent the last years of his life in exile in France, attacked Marxism severely but accepted many of its ideas. Paul Tillich—philosopher, theologian, leader in the German Christian Socialist party following the First World War, then foe of Hitler and exile from Germany—makes extensive use of Marxist philosophic conceptions, anthropology, and social analysis in his brilliantly original interpretation of history. Eduard Heimann, social and economic philosopher and a colleague of Tillich in German Christian Socialism, finds affinities between Marxist and Christian interpretations of history and regards Marx as an indispensable educator of the bourgeois world; but he finds that Marxism ignores or does violence to many of the most important forces in history and is unable to interpret recent history.

All these thinkers, despite widely varying ideas, agree on a few basic convictions. They regard Christian faith as the ground of their apprehension of the meaning of history and the Christian God as the Lord and Judge of history. But they reject the various legalisms and sentimentalisms which have tried to find in the Christian faith the tools for precise sociological and political analysis. In varying ways and degrees they find Marxism useful for just such analysis. But they resist utterly the pretension of Marxism to furnish a meaning for life and an understanding of the religious significance of history.

Thus these thinkers are able to use Marxist criticisms of bourgeois society without seeing any finality in Marxism. In many respects they can out-do the Marxists on their own grounds. For they can accept the Marxist analysis of ideologies, whether political, religious, national, or economic; they can then turn the same weapon against Marxist absolutism in a way that the communist dares not do. No human absolutism (again including religious ones) is so holy that it does not stand under the judgment of God—a judgment which may be clarified at points by the Marxist criticism of conventional pretensions, but which judges Marxism too.

This modern development in Christian thought may be analyzed in terms of three critical issues between Marxism and Christianity: (A) Marxist materialism. (B) The emphasis upon class conflict. (C) Marxism's religious pretensions.

A. MARXIST MATERIALISM

The issue of "atheistic materialism" is handled far too superficially in popular pulpit and political oratory. Marxism is atheistic only in a formal sense, not in its concrete religious character. And its dialectical or historical materialism is not completely materialistic, as a reading of Marx's furious denunciations of bourgeois morality will show. Marxists may revel in the language of materialism, but they also slip into phrases promising a "really human morality which transcends class antagonisms and their legacies in thought."[2]

Furthermore authentic Christianity has not been one of the many religions which draw a striking opposition between the physical and the spiritual. It comes as a shock to the unwary to learn that a great Archbishop of Canterbury has called Christianity "the most avowedly materialist of all the great religions."[3]

---

[2] Engels, *Anti-Dühring*, p. 105. Karl Popper is able to argue that Marx, far from being a consistent materialist, exhibited a "practical dualism" and actually sought for society to be lifted from the materialistic to the spiritual level, from the realm of necessity to the realm of freedom. See *The Open Society and Its Enemies*, II, 95–99. Cf. *Anti-Dühring*, pp. 309–10.

[3] William Temple, *Nature, Man and God* (London: Macmillan, 1934), p. 478. Temple was not "soft" toward communism; he regarded it as the most serious menace of recent centuries to Christianity.

By this he meant that Christianity neither denies nor ignores the material, but sets out to direct it to worthy uses.

The Christian-Marxist synthesis of Macmurray goes so far as to welcome communist materialism as the recapturing of a Christian insight lost in popular pseudo-Christianity. Materialism stands for the union of thought and action, of belief and conduct, against all dualisms which separate them and against all idealisms which assign a low worth to practical life and its obligations. The origin of philosophic idealism and dualism is social class dualism.[4] The Christian church betrayed its inheritance when it became the religion of the Roman empire and linked its destiny with the ruling classes. Simultaneously its theology developed under the influence of Graeco-Roman philosophies, reflecting the prejudices of thinkers who idealized contemplation. Henceforth it was easy to take the path of all false religions—to transfer beliefs to the realm of the ideal, letting the course of material life go its unredeemable way.

Christian thinkers who reject this Christian-Marxist synthesis find that it misinterprets both Marx and the Bible. Marx's materialism—however it must be qualified—certainly meant some things that Macmurray does not. And although Jesus' Hebraic thought allows little place for some of the conceptions which the Hellenistic ethos foisted upon it, the Gospel message cannot utterly give up the meaning of the "kingdom not of this world."

It is possible to find valid elements in Marxist materialism without bringing the whole into an inconsistent synthesis with Christianity. Marxism points to incontrovertible facts about the economic basis of life. And, as Niebuhr writes, "Its materialism is, on the whole, a justified reaction to pietistic religions which do not understand the social character of life and to 'spiritual' versions of Christianity which do not understand the unity of

---

[4] *The Clue to History*, pp. 121–22, 147. John Dewey frequently described the social origin of dualism similarly.

individual and collective man in the material and spiritual dimensions of his life." [5] Tillich's analysis avoids the glibness of either Macmurray's acceptance of materialism or popular propaganda against it:

The demand of the unity of theory and practice, or, in more recent terms, of "existential thinking" is a lasting insight that Marx has discovered in his fight against theoretical idealism and materialism. But the distortion of this insight into a sceptical relativism according to which all thinking is only the expression of a special kind of being (psychological or sociological) must be considered not only as a corruption, but also as the negation of existential thinking. In the same way . . . Marx is right in emphasizing the material reproduction of mankind as the foundation of the whole historical process. But the distortion of this insight into a mechanistic economics or into a metaphysical materialism must be rejected. [6]

Marxist materialism presents a further problem in its attitude toward personality. Christianity usually recognizes that personality is impossible apart from community; yet it cannot regard individuals simply as "personifications of economic categories." [7] Berdyaev, with his tremendous emphasis on personality and freedom, insists that both personality and society are stronger realities than class, while Marx makes almost a metaphysical substance out of class. Hence Marx indulges the contradictory hope that a materialistic process of history will result in a free society. But, says Berdyaev, a " 'class-ape' can never evolve into a human man." There is deep irony for Berdyaev in the fact that Marx,

---

[5] Faith and History, p. 211.
[6] "Marxism and Christian Socialism," Christianity and Society, VII (1942), No. 2, p. 17.
[7] Marx accused "liberal democracy" of taking over "that illusion, dream and postulate of Christianity, namely, man as a sovereign soul," of asserting that "each man has value as a sovereign being." Quoted by N. H. Alexeiev, in The Christian Understanding of Man (Oxford Conference Book. Chicago: Willett, Clark, 1938), p. 104, from an article by Marx on the Jewish question.

who saw so clearly the depersonalizing effect of capitalism, came to a like result in his emphasis on class and conformity.

However, says Berdyaev, the Marxist error was taken over from the capitalism which Marx attacked. The bourgeois is the original materialist; "homo economicus is precisely the bourgeois man." So "Marxism is a revolt against capitalism, but it has been bred by it and carries the fatal mark of its materialist spirit."[8] The Christian responsibility in history is to aim for realization of personality in society. This aim, Berdyaev finds, is shared by Marx the utopian dreamer, but is scorned by Marx the materialist.

B. CLASS CONFLICT

Like the issue of materialism, the issue of class warfare is often stated deceptively. Marxism believes in violent revolution; Christianity believes in peaceful change. So we are told in an antithesis partially false in both premises.

First, we must remember that Marx's own attitude on violent revolution was ambiguous. For the most part he clearly insisted that class conflict could be resolved only by bloody rebellion, because the existing expropriators would yield to nothing less. But especially in later years he and Engels recognized the possibilities of peaceful change through the ballot, especially in countries like England and America.[9]

Second, the Christian tradition has seldom rejected completely the use of arms as a means of dealing with oppressors. No Christian who has justified armed resistance against tyranny— whether in the German peasants' revolt, the American Revolution or Civil War, the overthrow of Hitler, or present armament measures to resist Stalin—can satisfy himself with the glib remark

---

[8] *Christianity and Class War*, pp. 39-40, 97. *Cf.* "Marx vs. Man," *Religion in Life*, VIII (1948), 483ff.

[9] For a well-documented statement of this position, see M. M. Bober, *Karl Marx's Interpretation of History*, pp. 262-67.

that communism believes in use of force. The problem of means and ends is a highly difficult one in any conception of history.

The critical analysts of Marxism,[10] while not acquiescing in the Marxist philosophy of violence, do not find it the principal issue separating them from Marx. They point out that most Christian ethical theories, while centering in the love-ethic of Jesus, offer grounds for evaluating social conflicts and making choices between better and worse when—as in most history—the best is not a political option. Hence Christian thought, outside of pacifist strains, must grant a possible justification for struggle against oppression when democratic means are forcibly stifled.

"Nothing is more unchristian than the 'idealization' of reality," writes Berdyaev. Therefore he finds the recognition of class conflict in history nearer to a Christian understanding than the optimistic bourgeois belief "in the natural harmony of contradictory interests." The latter merely disguises the "secret, camouflaged, and elusive warfare that goes on among the banks, stock-exchanges, parliamentary parties, and newspapers of capitalist society."[11] However, in agreement with most Christian observers, Berdyaev finds social conflict with all its rivalries of race and caste a far more complex phenomenon than Marx thought, when he derived it from problems concerned with modes of production.

---

[10] The Christian-Marxists, investigated above, handle the problem of revolution rather easily. Harry F. Ward sees violence as necessary and justifiable in behalf of the masses against reactionary fascist forces which will not yield to the democratic will. See *Democracy and Social Change*, pp. 140–48. Macmurray would modify Marxism by showing the limitations of revolutionary methods and the possibility of other methods of social change. Force is sometimes, but not always, inevitable. On the prospects for peaceable change in our own society, his answer varies. Clearly he has moved far from Marxism (and biblical thought) in the direction of an evolutionary progressive interpretation of history. See *Creative Society*, Ch. IX; *Marxism*, pp. 74–75; *The Clue to History*, pp. 113, 171–72, 176.

[11] *Christianity and Class War*, pp. 11–13. In American writings this point has been particularly evident in Niebuhr's *Moral Man and Immoral Society* and *Reflections on the End of an Era*.

Similarly Christian interpreters usually see more evidence than Marx admitted of forces making for community in any going society.

Many writers have pointed out how Marxism and Christian apocalypse share the sense of historic conflict and anticipation of a new world that will rise out of destruction. Significantly the breakdown of Christian progressivism has led to increased appreciation of both Marxism and traditional Christian eschatology— often by the same thinkers. But the question remains: To what extent can Christian faith, which finds the ultimate meaning of history revealed in an act of redemptive love, endorse class struggle or find it basic to the meaning of history? Christian perfectionism has sometimes been inclined to view political pacifism as a means to the redemption of history. But more typically the Christian tradition has seen God's victory in the Cross as an eschatological triumph, to some extent accomplished, yet awaiting fulfillment. Meanwhile men live in history, and the withdrawal from struggle, instead of ending struggle, may merely assure victory to the stronger or more ruthless powers. So Berdyaev can say: "Christians are living in this sinful world and must bear its burden, they may not steal away from the battle field." [12]

Similarly most Christian interpretations of history will share the Marxist viewpoint that openly rebellious classes may be no more guilty of class conflict than classes in power which piously defend an existing order in terms of peace and harmony. There can be as much force or threat of force in maintenance of an unjust *status quo* as in the more obviously violent attempts to overthrow it. The conventional bias in favor of law and order may often be, as the Marxist says, simply the ideological bias of the well-to-do.

It is clear, however, that Christianity must put a double qualification on the Marxist view of class conflict. First, it will

[12] *Christianity and Class War*, p. 50.

not make messianic claims for any one class. It will not hold that the proletariat is beyond sin. With the prophets and Jesus it may see a greater virtue in the cause of the poor and outcast, and a greater insight into truth among the disinherited. Lack of privilege may enable a class to see through the dominant ideologies of a society. But no class is automatically free from its own ideological bias.

Second, the Christian concern for history will seek peaceful methods of social change. In its doctrine of sin Christianity shares with Marx a realization of the difficulty of unseating the proud and rejects illusions of automatic harmony and good will. But it does not glory in violence. It knows aspects of the human spirit beyond the economic impulse and sees various possibilities for affecting the course of history. It knows the difficulty of redeeming historical clashes of interest, but it knows too a hope beyond conflict and a judgment upon all struggles.

C. MARXISM'S RELIGIOUS PRETENSIONS

The deepest point of opposition between Marxism and Christianity comes from the fact that both are finally religions. An intelligent Christianity is quite willing to take account of whatever the geographer, the sociologist, the industrial scientist, the economist discover about the processes of history. It cannot so easily make peace with hostile religions. The Marxist, for all the talk of materialism and science, is finally concerned with *Heilsgeschichte*. Marxism and Christianity alike are gospels of salvation.

Only from this point of view does Marxism's militant atheism make sense. Too much Christian polemic has implied that a formal acknowledgment of belief in God is the crucial point of faith. With far greater insight Jacques Maritain has transcended a common judgment of issues between a church which is holy and Christian and a communism which is atheistic and materialistic. The radical atheist, says Maritain, is a rebel against the conventional idolatries of society. Only the true saint is more radical in his protest.[13]

If Marx had simply wished to protest against conventional religion in the name of a radical demand for social justice, he could have found authoritative Christian support. The prophet Amos exhibits radical anti-clericalism based on the divine demand for justice. Jeremiah knew as clearly as Marx that religion could be an "opium of the people," and the same insight was not lacking in the church of Marx's own time. There is even good Christian precedent for a sort of "atheism," the word used by the Roman Emperor Julian to characterize the Christians, whose profound faith in God he did not understand. Such evidence from Christian history makes it preposterous to reject a rival philosophy glibly on the basis of its protests against ecclesiasticism or currently respectable beliefs.

Marx's hostility to Christianity was, however, a far deeper thing than a protest against conservatism. It is evident at points which have little to do with economics. Marx rejects the religious idea of creation, because it assumes that man is dependent, deriving his being from the grace of a Creator. The mystery of ultimate origins, of creatureliness, must be swept out of the way so that the socialist man can glory in his autonomy.[14] The Marxist, we have already noted, looks for the end of religion in the epoch when "man no longer merely proposes, but also disposes."

It is clear then that Marxism has its own scheme of redemption. Hence the renunciation of Marxism has so often in recent

---

[13] "The Meaning of Contemporary Atheism," *The Range of Reason* (New York: Scribners, 1952).

[14] See N. H. Alexeiev, in *The Christian Understanding of Man*, pp. 112–13. Cf. Emil Brunner, *Christianity and Civilisation*, I, 134, 151. Cf. Karl Löwith, *Meaning in History*, p. 47: Marx's "whole enterprise of changing the world by a world revolution has as its negative presupposition the denial of man's dependence on an existing order of creation."

years been clearly a religious conversion.[15] "Like all vital religion," says Niebuhr of communism, "it engages the entire human psyche and offers its interpretation of life and the world in order that it may challenge to action in conformity with its 'truth.' " Berdyaev draws the conclusion from his own past experience that "a Christian may, and in my opinion must, be a Socialist, but he can hardly be a Communist since he cannot accept Communism's pretense to being a complete and all-embracing world-view."[16] For the Marxist *Heilsgeschichte* there can be no transcendent judgment upon communism itself, no City of God beyond the city being fashioned by the movement itself.

This elevation of any movement or factor of history to the center of ultimate loyalty and the focus of history is exactly what Christianity means by idolatry. Its consequence is to localize evil in certain specific historical forces and to assume that the messianic revolutionary movement can do no wrong. It is natural for Marxism to result in fanaticism—a fanaticism which cannot be explained simply on the basis of Marx's indigestion or the despotic tradition of Russia. For as history moves to its final conflict between good and evil there can be no quarter. No one expects leniency toward Satan at Armageddon. In the new communist absolutism all conventional moral codes become entirely relative. Anything can be justified in the name of the

---

[15] For a penetrating story of such a conversion see Will Herberg, "From Marxism to Judaism," *Commentary*, III (1947), No. 1. Herberg has attained a greater perspective upon his experience than has the more spectacular Whittaker Chambers. (See Chambers' *Witness*, Random House, 1952.)

[16] Niebuhr, "Christian Politics and Communist Religion," in *Christianity and the Social Revolution*, p. 461. Berdyaev, "Marx Versus Man," *Religion in Life*, VIII (1938), 496.

The same point is obvious in C. L. Sulzberger's dispatch to the New York *Times* (March 10, 1949): "Moscow regards any 'international' religion—and heaven clearly is included as a non-Marxist domain—as 'dangerous.' "

156   MARXIST AND CHRISTIAN ESCHATOLOGIES

cause. The point of the transvaluation of values has been found.[17]

When confronted with communist (or nationalist, or scientific, or ecclesiastical) absolutisms which promise the answer to history's problems, the meaning of Christian eschatology becomes most clear. The mythological ideas of apocalypse appear, not as mere wild imagination, but as expressions of a sense of history with the most serious implications. Thus John Bennett writes:

This belief in Communism as an absolute movement of redemption in history, in the Communist society as a substitute for God, is not only false from the Christian point of view and incompatible with the Christian's understanding of man's dependence upon God; it has at least two other consequences that should be emphasized. One is that it precludes a transcendent judgment upon every society. A nation or a social order that acknowledges that it stands under God is open to criticism and correction and growth. . . . The second consequence of this belief . . . is that it creates a false optimism that leaves people unprepared for the new forms of evil that will appear in a Communist society.[18]

It is ironic that Marx, who was so harsh in his attacks upon "utopian socialism," should be criticized for his own utopianism by almost all the Christian thinkers who have learned from him. And it is instructive that the theologians, whom Marx regarded as peddlers of opium, should outdo him in the realism of their social analysis. This curious situation can be explained in part by the lessons of time. The theologians have the benefit of three decades of observation of a state which calls itself Marxist. They

[17] A wise modern philosopher has observed that "the ideal" begets superstition as easily as "the supernatural": "The ideal can lead to killing men for the glory of the Good in the expectation that the Good will be served and will appropriately bless the killer with a crown of glory." F. J. E. Woodbridge, An Essay on Nature (New York: Columbia University, 1940), p. 337.
[18] Christianity and Communism (New York: Association Press, 1948), pp. 51–52.

have seen Marx's idea of international proletarian solidarity repeatedly shattered by resurgent nationalism. They have seen history, influenced by the tenacity of institutions and by surprising new contingencies, move ahead with little respect for *a priori* guide lines. But behind these empirical advantages, the theologians have had the heritage of a Christian interpretation of the human situation which, except when entirely diluted by theories of progressivism, stood as a constant criticism of premature solutions and historical utopias.

The Marxist philosophy of history is the most modern and most thoroughgoing of the declarations that *Weltgeschichte* is *Weltgericht*. The counter affirmation of Christianity is that the history of the world is subject to the Judgment of the world. The consequent difference in interpretation of history and of human responsibility in history is immense. The significance for history of the belief in God's transcendence over history has been stated well by Alexander Miller:

. . . the man who serves God may find himself, not in line with the historic process which is the Marxist's only sanity, but against it, even to the point of historically fruitless martyrdom. In other words, while on the Marxist view the only sane and valid action is action which accepts the logic of the historic process and conforms to it, the Christian, who serves not the historic process but the living will of God, may be compelled to stand against the stream of history, even as a forlorn and protesting voice.[19]

The irreconcilable opposition between two contrary gospels of the redemption of history prevents any easy synthesis between Marxism and Christianity. It does not prevent the Christian from accepting insight and criticism from the Marxist. Any contemporary Christian attempt to understand history must take account of those aspects of history which Marx made into a complete philosophy and a religion. It will not regard Marxism as the law and the prophets.

---

[19] *The Christian Significance of Karl Marx*, p. 73.

CHAPTER VI

MODERN CATHOLIC INTERPRETATIONS

OF HISTORY

CATHOLIC thought does not often produce startling changes. In all its forms it emphasizes tradition; and in its Roman form it relies on infallible authority. Although through many centuries the church of Rome showed great variety in philosophy and doctrine, the tendency since the Protestant Reformation has been to solidify its teaching and to define more carefully its authority. In view of some of the narrowing tendencies of the papacy, it was actually a liberalizing move when Pope Leo XIII in 1879 made Thomas Aquinas the authoritative philosopher of the church. This honor to St. Thomas, confirmed by Canon Law in 1917, gave the church a philosophy of broad outlook and high esteem for reason. But it meant also that Roman Catholic thought was henceforth to move in a philosophic tradition of the Middle Ages.

The majority of contemporary Catholic writings are clearly in the Thomist tradition. Their main emphasis is on ethics and metaphysics, and when they deal with history it is essentially along the Thomist lines discussed in Chapter III above. Thus the most massive systematic thought in contemporary Catholicism, that of the German Jesuit Erich Przywara, is a development of scholastic rationalism on the basis of the *analogia entis*. Nevertheless Thomism is a canopy capable of covering a great diversity of interests and viewpoints, and appearances of uniformity may be deceptive. On many issues Roman Catholics may still disagree, and there is room for creative thought. From this rich and diverse development we may here discuss and illustrate a few ideas about history as they appear interesting to an outsider.

I. CREATIVE THINKERS AND OFFICIAL CONSERVATISM

The reaction of the Roman church to the changes in intellectual temper which have swept the modern world has necessarily differed from that of Protestantism. After its brush with Galileo the church was usually cautious about rejecting scientific findings; but it never accepted the general outlook of a secular, scientific age. Protestantism was too often inclined either to cling tenaciously to scriptural literalism or to revise its attitudes and accept uncritically most of the assumptions of the modern world. But the ecclesiastical and doctrinal system of Rome acted as a bulwark against the changed spirit of modern times. Her more creative thinkers were able, without the rigidity of Protestant fundamentalism, to conserve the essential content of their faith. Her central development has been stanchly conservative—so conservative as often to surprise even her own laymen when they unexpectedly learn of it. After the enthusiasm of the "religion of progress," writes a Catholic historian, Europe "was divided in two camps, on the one side the adherents of the Liberal revolutionary principles, on the other the followers of the Catholic and Conservative tradition."[1] As always in human affairs, institutional interests and personal traits affected the course of thought and sometimes formed a bizarre combination of new attitudes and old claims.

Issues within Catholicism came to a head after eighteenth-century rationalism and nineteenth-century developmental thought led Pius IX (Pope, 1846–78) to take a stand. This was

---

[1] Christopher Dawson, *Progress and Religion*, p. 205.

the pope who in 1869 convened the Vatican Council, which produced the doctrine of papal infallibility. In his earlier *Syllabus of Errors* (1864) he condemned eighty current popular opinions. The *Syllabus* is most famous for its rejection of religious liberty and separation of church and state. More important for the understanding of history is the denial of a progressive revelation corresponding with "the progress of human reason" (Error No. 5)—a doctrine which was making headway in both Catholic and Protestant circles. The *Syllabus* denies that "the demands of the age and the progress of science" required a change in the methods or principles of scholastic theology (Nos. 12, 13). A ringing conclusion denounced the final error, that "The Roman Pontiff can and ought to reconcile himself to, and agree with, progress, liberalism, and civilization as lately introduced." The wording is subject to rather broad interpretation; but it is clear that the pope was not accepting the popular evolutionary understanding of history.

Under the papacy of Leo XIII (1878–1903) both Thomist scholarship and a modernist movement flourished. The conception of *historical development* marked modernist thought at two critical points: its biblical criticism and its ideas on the evolution of dogma. The movement was disciplined under the pontificate of Pius X (1903–1914). Two of its leaders, Father George Tyrrell and the more radical Abbé Loisy, were excommunicated. One loyal Catholic believer commented on "the rapid succession of almost numberless condemnations and restrictions of every kind and of almost every degree of solemnity and precision."[2] The Pope and the inquisition in the decree *Lamentabile Sane Exitu* (1907) condemned belief in the progressive development of dogma and in Jesus' expectation of an early end of history. The document insisted that Jesus himself taught "a determinate body of doctrine applicable to all times," including the dogmas of

---

[2] Baron Friedrich von Hügel, *Essays and Addresses*, Second Series, p. 104.

Nicea and Chalcedon (Props. 59, 52). In the same year a papal encyclical, *Pascendi Gregis*, ordered teachers tainted with modernism to be removed from the schools and books to be severely censored. Particular criticism was levelled against the philosophy of evolution applied to religion—to "dogma, Church, worship, the Books we revere as sacred, even faith itself."

Clearly the modernists had enthusiastically accepted some dubious assumptions, and the papal policy thwarted some errors which Protestantism is now repenting of. But this forced doctrinaire conservatism was achieved at the cost of rejecting many insights for which evidence has continued to accumulate. Catholicism avoided the extravagant faith in progress as the clue to history; but it thereby failed to understand the relation of historical development and contingency to Christian institutions and beliefs.

Biblical criticism is clearly a case in point. "Progressive revelation" was a theory involving evolutionary assumptions; continued study of biblical records has led recent scholarship to abandon many features of this once popular interpretation. But scholarship is none the less aware of varied historical influences upon the biblical sources. Official Romanism, however, rejected the historical critical approach. In the time of Leo XIII Baron von Hügel tried to persuade the Vatican to accept critical scholarship. But Pius X in *Lamentabile Sane Exitu* decreed that Scripture in all its parts was immune from error, and proscribed a series of opinions which have come to be established in all non-Roman and non-fundamentalist biblical scholarship. The Papal Biblical Commission, established in 1902, decides disputed points of biblical interpretation. According to the *Catholic Encyclopedia* ("Biblical Commission") it has ruled, for example, that the Pentateuch is substantially the work of Moses, and that the author of the Fourth Gospel is the disciple John.

Thus a considerable strand of history may not be studied by the methods of historical scholarship. Further, Christian history is not understandable apart from specific providential preservation of particular ecclesiastical institutions. The extent of the *a priori* doctrinal factors thus governing historiography is rather large.

Despite the rigid path prescribed by Roman officialdom, a number of Catholic scholars have thought creatively about history. Perhaps the greatest of these has been Baron Friedrich von Hügel (d. 1925), whose influence reached far beyond his own communion. Although he held many of the propositions condemned by Pius IX and X, he believed in keeping critical thought subject to constructive and traditional affirmations and rejected modernist excesses. Partly for these reasons, partly because of his lay position, he managed to avoid the difficulties of his friends Loisy and Tyrrell, while yet developing his thought with independence. Generally more conservative than von Hügel has been a second movement, neo-scholasticism, which is flourishing now. Its representatives give a place both to old wisdom and to new knowledge and viewpoints. A third development has come out of Anglo-Catholic thought in Great Britain. Here a group of vigorous thinkers, most famous of whom is the poet T. S. Eliot, has given attention to the problems of history and civilization. Unchained to Thomism or to papal authority, these thinkers have nevertheless 'worked within a generally Catholic tradition emphasizing some of the ideals of "Christendom." In all of these movements there is some modification of those characteristics which gave Thomism its non-historical bent.

II. INCREASED CONCERN WITH HISTORY

To many an enthusiastic modern the notion of returning to a medieval system of thought implies a disrespect for history. Thus the very word *Neo-Thomism* is a symbol of obscurantism. It is even worse when Jacques Maritain writes: "I am not a neo-Thomist. All in all, I would rather be a paleo-Thomist than a neo-Thomist. I am, or at least I hope I am, a Thomist." [1] What Maritain is stressing, however, is not so much medievalism as the permanent character of truth which he finds expressed in a "perennial" Thomism. Though philosophical investigation is "indefinitely progressive," Thomist rationalism and metaphysical principles are permanently true. This is not to "immobilize history," but simply to recognize that truth "does not flow away with history." The mind, says Maritain, is "above time"—and especially the mind of Aquinas. [2]

Within the freer thought of Anglo-Catholicism the developmental principle has been thoroughly accepted and applied to doctrine, but without giving up the central insistence of traditional Christianity. Christian faith, says T. S. Eliot, has a history and development; but such change does not imply "the possibility of greater sanctity or divine illumination becoming available to human beings through collective progress." [3]

Even within the church of Rome some scholars are inclined to credit Maritain with the excessive zeal of the convert. The eminent historian de Wulf, for example, acknowledges that any particular mind is, to a considerable degree, imbedded in its time. He is quite willing to indicate weaknesses in scholasticism, particularly at the point of neglect of history. But within scholasticism he sees the capacity for evolutionary development. Modern science, for example, "has stripped the walls of the old scholastic edifice of a whole pile of decayed and mouldering plaster." And the study of modern thought will "enable the new scholasticism to benefit by many a theory accepted in modern

---

[1] *Existence and the Existent*, p. 1.

[2] *The Angelic Doctor* (New York: Sheed and Ward, 1938), pp. vii, xiv, xviif. Maritain has said that "the doctrine of the Angelic Doctor is so lofty, and so solidly coherent that it cannot suffer the slightest diminution of its specific determinants without losing its efficacy to penetrate reality." In *Essays in Order*, p. 34.

[3] *Notes Towards the Definition of Culture*, pp. 27–28.

164   MODERN CATHOLIC IDEAS OF HISTORY

philosophy, to correct its own errors and to make good its own shortcomings." [4]

It was Baron von Hügel who most skillfully made a place for an appreciation of history while remaining true to the main principles of Thomism. Admiring St. Thomas as the most comprehensive and deep of theologians, von Hügel could present Thomist ideas vividly to Protestants too inclined to dismiss Aquinas as a dry system-builder. But he found missing in Aquinas (and in Augustine) the historic sense. "Official theology" he criticized for lagging, "angry or superstitious," behind the post-medieval development of "Historical sense and Method." His own writings, von Hügel hoped, were "steeped in" a sense of conditions, growth, contingencies—yet against the background of an apprehension of the unconditioned, abiding, and absolute. In Christianity he saw the possibility of a real appreciation for both. [5]

Von Hügel turned his penetrating mind to the problem of relating the scientific and philosophical concern for the repeatable and the universal to the historical concern for the particular. The mainstream of the philosophical tradition he found concentrated upon the universal. "Yet, against all this mass of authority and tradition, there is every man's continuous experience, that all our ultimate interests and standards, all our valuations of life and of men, ever and intrinsically, suppose and refer to the particular and unique." [6]

The Old Testament documents show how the variety of history is distorted when handled by minds (e.g., of the Priestly historians) insisting upon the clarity and mathematical balance of non-historical attitudes. History, though it cannot approach

---

[4] *Scholasticism Old and New*, pp. 210, 189. It may be recalled that Father Tyrrell, in his plea for modernism, made the same assertion without avail, emphasizing that Aquinas was in his time an innovator and a modernist. However, de Wulf and the modern neo-scholastics retain much more of the content of scholastic thought than did Tyrrell.
[5] *Essays and Addresses*, First Series, pp. xvf.; Second Series, p. 250.
[6] *Essays and Addresses*, Second Series, p. 30.

the universality of philosophy and natural science, has a superior "vividness, depth, and reality." A real religion, therefore, "will at least include the Historical, and will presumably express itself, and its expressions will have to be studied, at all events in the first instance, according to the method, categories, and ideals of History."[7]

Anticipating the emphasis which Protestantism was to rediscover, von Hügel saw the "sheer happenedness" at the basis of Christianity. Thus his "modernization" of St. Thomas was at the same time a criticism of the Catholic modernists who wished a philosophy of religion built on the basis of a philosophical cosmology or general religious experience, apart from historical documents. "For Christianity, surely, is not simply a doctrine—however true—of certain laws and principles of the spiritual life. . . . But precisely the central conviction and doctrine of Christianity is the real prevenience and condescension of the real God —is the penetration of spirit into sense, of the spaceless into space, of the eternal into time, of God into man."[8] Thus Christianity requires history as the soul requires the body.

Other Catholic thinkers have similarly found a historical outlook, shared in part by both modern and biblical thought, which requires a shift in the more static categories of Thomism. Fulton Sheen has suggested that modern ethical and metaphysical skepticism may be overcome by conviction coming out of historical crisis. "History has begun to displace science as the window through which the mind envisages reality, for science is only a record of *what is happening*, whereas history is a record of what matters."[9] Taken with full seriousness, this idea calls for a more radical renovation of Catholic orthodoxy than Sheen, with his Thomist natural theology, is ready to make.

---

[7] *Ibid.*, p. 34.
[8] *Ibid.*, pp. 109, 108.
[9] *Philosophy of Religion* (New York: Appleton-Century-Crofts, 1948), p. 250.

Christopher Dawson, the historian, advocates revising traditional outlooks in view of the modern sense of history. Although Christianity, unlike most religions and philosophies, makes possible a historical sense, such a sense did not come into its own until the Romantic movement and the nineteenth century. And, although it needs criticism, it is basically a significant gain.[10] Thus Dawson, when he writes of "natural theology," as in *Religion and Culture,* ignores the traditional Thomist arguments and appeals instead to the religious experiences of men in various historical cultures. And the Christian scriptures, he points out, are records of history rather than expositions of doctrine.

For Dawson the chief problem of a Christian interpretation of history, since it finds its focus in the history of a particular people (Israel or the church), is to give adequate significance to the rest of history. In the Bible, in St. Thomas, and in Dante, Dawson finds the bases for a recognition of the independent value of the whole of history; and Dawson's own writings develop the theme. Thus he writes with complete appreciation of the history and religion of any people, whether primitive or civilized; yet he has a deep sense of the special divine vocation of the Christian church.

III. ETERNITY AND TIME

Modern Catholicism's increased concern for history has taken place against the background of Thomist metaphysics. Without abandoning the doctrine of the *totum simul* of God and the glorification of contemplation and the mystical vision, Catholicism has aimed to give due emphasis to time and historical activity.

---

[10] See *Progress and Religion,* pp. 26ff.; *The Kingdom of God and History* (Oxford Conference Book), pp. 197ff. Dawson, though an admirer of Aquinas, acknowledges that his thought requires considerable reconstruction. See *Progress and Religion,* pp. 181–84.

Certainly a philosopher like Maritain cannot be accused of failure to take seriously the problems of history and politics. Repeatedly he stresses the social responsibilities of Christians in all the personal and group relations of industrial civilization. He distrusts the "supra-temporal faith" which shuns the historical.[1] Yet, standing in the Aristotelian and Thomist tradition, Maritain finds the "pure essence of the spiritual" in contemplation,[2] which stands at the peak of the hierarchy of activities. Similarly, he shares the Thomist regard for the mystical vision as the pinnacle of Christian experience.

Much of Catholic metaphysical and historical doctrine focuses in the conception of *totum simul*. For a great deal of modern metaphysics the idea of total simultaneity is scarcely a live option. Yet in Catholic thought it is not the abstract or sterile doctrine that it may seem at first glance. Thomist natural theology depends on the conception of first cause, which is not merely first in a series but is the origin of the being of all things and provides a real explanation for them. Likewise Catholic (indeed Christian) religious faith is directed toward a God who is the Alpha and Omega, who is and was and is to be. Thomist metaphysical confidence, unshaken by Kantian skepticism and unsatisfied with a purely existential answer, is determined to make a coherent theory which will do justice to its intellectual and religious apprehensions. Thus any conception of a God who emerges, or comes to consciousness, or develops into the fullness of experience through the time process is abhorrent. Hegel's *Weltgeist*, Alexander's *Deity*, Bergson's creative *Durée*, or Whitehead's *God Consequent*—all leave metaphysics without a final explanation and faith without final assurance. God, to be truly God, must transcend time.

Even the critic who may regard this doctrine as a useless

<hr/>

[1] *Ransoming the Time*, p. 196.
[2] *Essays in Order*, p. 47. *Ransoming the Time*, Ch. X.

remnant of scholasticism is likely to be surprised at the vividness
with which it emerges from the writings of Baron von Hügel.
The Baron was concerned to preserve the significance of time
and history within God's eternity. Hence he insisted that history
was the absolutely necessary correction against the delusions of
false mysticism, which denies time for the sake of eternity. But
he revelled in the exalting thought of the God who is "Pure
Eternity, Sheer Simultaneity," "the purely Simultaneous and
All Present," who unlike us is "the ultimate non-successive Reality," who is "at bottom unchanging, an overflowing richness of
ever simultaneous life." [3] Creatures possess a partial simultaneity,
i.e. they can in a limited way unite past and future in the experience of the present; and this partial simultaneity rests in
God's pure simultaneity.

In the richness of von Hügel's thought this conception enhances rather than denies the significance of time. Eternity is no
timeless monotone, but a real variety-in-unity which incorpo-
rates the "work, pain, and joy" of concrete actuality into a fullness of experience. Personality "can only be achieved in time,
across helps and obstacles, joys, sorrows, actions, productions,
graces, temptations, victories—all demanding time, succession."
History and life derive their meaning, both from a movement to
the future, and from a direct, present relation to the source of all
meaning. "For we each of us already form, at our best, one particular link in but one great chain from earth to heaven; yet each
little link is also, severally, already linked directly to Heaven
itself."

History, in the significant meanings of the word, depends on
successiveness, but also on a degree of interpenetration of past

---

[3] Von Hügel's principal discussions of the *totum simul* in relation to his-
tory are in his *Essays and Addresses*, First Series, Ch. III; Second Series,
Chs. II, III. The quotations above are from First Series, pp. 133, 215;
Second Series, pp. 52, 65–66.

and future; the past is "operatively present" at any time. So the complete interpenetration of past and future will "in no way abolish even the least of the valuable resultants of the Succession in History, or be in any sharp antagonism with what now looks like mere Process, but which, to be truly Historical, is even now something more than such mere succession." The *totum simul* is not the denial of history, but the "mighty harmony in Eternity."[4] The most clear "recognition" of the temporal by the Eternal comes in certain varying "incarnational" acts throughout history, in which "the Non-Successive God Himself condescends to a certain Successiveness."[5] Indeed the belief in *the* Incarnation prevents any radical denial of the importance of history.

More recently Erich Frank, devout and profound if sometimes unorthodox Catholic philosopher, has similarly tried to combine the dynamic aspect of time with the simultaneity of eternity.[6] Whether these suggestive and imaginative ideas can be made into a rational metaphysics and theory of history remains a problem. If for God the whole of history is instantaneously present, are futurity, freedom, and the new real? Does history really matter? Maritain, more systematic in his metaphysics than von Hügel or Frank, insists that we can maintain "the unforeseeableness of concrete becoming" along with the God of St. Thomas.

If He knows all things from all eternity, and the feather which tomorrow will fall from the wing of a certain bird, it is not because the history of the world should be only the unfolding of a *ready-made scenario*. It is, on the contrary, that all the moments of the whole of time are present for the divine Eternity, who sees in its own instant, and hence always, everything creatures do, have done,

---

[4] The foregoing quotations come from Second Series, pp. 52–55, 65–66.
[5] First Series, p. 94.
[6] *Philosophical Understanding and Religious Truth*, Ch. III. Cf. "Time and Eternity," *Review of Metaphysics*, II (1940), 39–52.

will do in the very instant that it *happens*, and hence in an eternal freshness of life and newness.[7]

Metaphysicians and logicians must decide whether such a statement can be consistently maintained. For the understanding of history it is clear that Catholicism is eager, within the limits of Thomism, to do justice to the importance of history.

IV. WHAT HAPPENS IN HISTORY

Catholic tradition has never lost the confidence that God governs history. It has not, on the whole, been inclined to equate His providential plan with the various secular faiths in progress, and it has usually remembered that this mysterious plan is not readily discernible. But recent Catholicism shows two differing tendencies to describe the course of history. The first sees evidence of God's governance in the course of observable events—in the history of the secular and pagan world, in the development of the institutional church, and in the establishing of Christian civilization. The second finds providence understandable only as God's mysterious plan of salvation, which may be quite incomprehensible to the observer of history.

The two tendencies are not utterly distinct; both are represented in the thought of some philosophers. But the difference is clear enough to serve as a guide.

A. THE DISCERNING OF PROVIDENCE

The first of these viewpoints is advanced in confident terms in one Catholic study of history:

History is the realization of a great divine plan, a vast supernatural process, more God's than man's. We do not mean to exclude the economic, sociological, idealistic or political theories of interpretation of history, provided that they are made subservient to the super-

---

[7] *Ransoming the Time*, pp. 82–83.

natural purpose of the human race. . . . The history of man without
Providence is inexplicable.[1]

The writer goes on to give an actual sketch of human history to
show how it illustrates this plan. In doing so he criticizes common views of progress and points instead to a "spiritual progress"
attained through religion and the church.

Such an assured reading of the plan of history stands in
contrast to the more reserved attitude of a thinker like Baron von
Hügel. With his strong appreciation for the variety of history
and the insights in different religious outlooks, von Hügel could
make no hasty generalizations about the plan of history. Yet he
did see history as the unfolding of a providential purpose, with a
rationale and a teleology. History shows a progress of religion
which "with increasing purity and power" brings certain basic
convictions. Any such progress is tortuous and slow, "at its best
spiral rather than straight," interrupted by reactions of violence
or complacence, but none the less real.[2] There was nothing glib
in von Hügel's understanding of history, but it was essentially
confident.

Neo-Thomism is bound to resist the dogmas of progress since
it generally assumes a retrogression of both thought and culture
since the high tide of medievalism. Intellectually speaking, Descartes, Kant, and the positivists are the agents of disintegration.
Culturally speaking, the Renaissance, Reformation, and Enlightenment mark the main steps. Among others Jacques Maritain,
particularly in his earlier writings, has delivered polemics against
these modern movements.

But despite his critiques of modern anthropocentric culture,
Maritain has kept a surprisingly large place for progress. "We
should not forget that in virtue of a natural law of growth and as

---

[1] Joseph Schrembs, "The Catholic Philosophy of History," in a symposium
by the same title, edited by Peter Guilday. P. 4.
[2] *Essays and Addresses*, First Series, pp. 90–96; Second Series, pp. 38–39.

a consequence of the leaven of the Gospel deposited in humanity, a certain progress takes its course in the heart of that [modern] civilization."[3] This progress includes scientific and industrial achievements, and intellectual, artistic, and spiritual "means and technique." There are even advances, if not in moral life itself, in the setting and conditions of it, as certain accepted practices of the past come to be disapproved. The eternal natural law is apprehended with progressive clarity throughout history.[4]

Maritain adopts the theory of cultural lag—a doctrine of social evil which is peculiarly the product of secular humanism. At the "root of our unhappiness" is the fact that "technical progress has outstripped the mind." Maritain's remedy, however, is not that of the American pragmatists who, on the basis of a similar analysis, call for an extension of scientific method to include social problems. Maritain hopes for a "heroic effort of spiritualization" by which men will utilize technical advances for the sake of genuine progress.[5]

If Maritain has moved a considerable distance from Aquinas, he returns to tradition in his understanding of God's providential sovereignty. "God has no opposite, . . . all is borne on irresistibly by the tide of His providence." Indeed, the devil is active; history has a fundamental ambivalence:

For Christianity, the truth about the world and the earthly city is that they are the kingdom at once of man, of God, and of the devil . . . the history of the temporal city, divided between two opposing final ends, leads . . . at one and the same time to the kingdom of perdition and the Kingdom of God.[6]

---

[3] In *Essays in Order*, p. 15. Cf. *The Rights of Man and Natural Law*, p. 30, where Maritain describes a creative energy in history which counters the destructive tendencies.
[4] *Essays in Order*, p. 16; *Ransoming the Time*, p. 40.
[5] *Ransoming the Time*, p. 130.
[6] *True Humanism*, pp. 84, 101–102.

Using a biblical insight which is peculiarly relevant to modern movements, Maritain suggests that various anti-Christian movements may, in God's providence, serve His purposes and contribute to progress. On the basis of this viewpoint, as we have noticed (Ch. V), Maritain views "atheism," including communism, with far greater perceptiveness than most Roman Catholic critics. Thus our present historical purpose must be, not to return to medievalism, but to move forward to Christian civilization, for which St. Thomas has given us the principles.[7]

Like Maritain, Christopher Dawson is a convert to Rome who has steeped himself in the spirit and literature of Catholicism. But as a professional historian he develops his ideas with somewhat more independence than do the church's philosophers and theologians. Early in his career (before he had read Spengler) Dawson worked out a flexible cyclical interpretation of history, but fitted it into a more general developmental pattern of the whole of history.[8] Development, for Dawson, is not equivalent to progress—certainly not in any religiously significant sense. Intellectual and scientific development may coincide with real cultural loss. Further, in Dawson's genuinely historical viewpoint there are no "dark ages." Each age of history is working on its own problems; none can be regarded as inferior because it does not satisfy the queries of another time. Nevertheless, this development, if not "from the lower to the higher," has been "from

---

[7] Essays in Order, pp. 17–18, 23. Maritain's idea of a Christian civilization includes a good many modernisms which he does not find in Aquinas. It is avowedly more pluralistic and diversified in organization and outlooks. It gives up the medieval demand for a unity of faith. And Maritain, who criticizes the "abstract" democracy deriving from Rousseau and supports a "Christian democracy," is a genuine democrat in ways which the Middle Ages had not conceived. See his many books on politics, freedom, natural law, etc.

[8] Dawson elaborated the theory in a paper in 1922, which in 1933 was published in Enquiries into Religion and Culture. The theory is also sketched briefly in Progress and Religion, Ch. III.

the confused to the distinct." Man has fulfilled the "natural vocation of the human mind," which is "the progressive *rationalization* of matter by the work of scientific intelligence." [9]

Against the background of this long view of history, modern progressive interpretations appear as a rather sudden eruption of a new theory, understandable in its own setting but not to be taken overly seriously. In *Progress and Religion* Dawson shows how these modern theories really form a new religion—a new heresy, requiring as much faith and as many postulates as any religion. Dawson finds one tangible and convincing body of evidence which supports the religion of progress: recent centuries have seen a remarkable development, not only of industrial civilization, but also of democratic institutions, of humanitarian movements and universal education. But this outburst of activity, so far from affording the basis for an interpretation of universal history, represents "an exceptional and indeed unique achievement of a single society at a particular stage of its development. It is not necessarily more permanent than the other achievements of past ages and cultures." And, impressive though it is, many penetrating observers have doubted that it represents a true progress in which men are "happier or wiser or better" than in other times.[10] The collapse of the dreams of nineteenth-century liberalism and the discovery that evil too is progressive have hit our world with shattering effect.

Dawson's own interpretation of secular history stresses the significance of spiritual power as the organizing center and creative force of civilization. Its loss in advanced civilizations brings weakness and artificiality. "The whole history of culture shows that man has a natural tendency to seek a religious foundation for his social way of life and that when culture loses its spiritual basis it becomes unstable." [11] Not only the "interpretation" but

---

[9] *Progress and Religion*, p. 94. *Essays in Order*, p. 235.
[10] *Progress and Religion*, pp. 7–9.
[11] *Religion and Culture*, p. 217.

even the writing of history seems to require understanding of this spiritual factor:

> History is not to be explained as a closed order in which each stage is the inevitable and the logical result of that which has gone before. There is in it always a mysterious and inexplicable element, due not only to the influence of chance or the initiative of the individual genius, but also to the creative power of spiritual forces.[12]

Christianity played this creative role in the development of Europe, as other religions have in the various civilizations. Modern civilization, in rejecting the faith which formed it, is endangering its whole life.

Dawson is aware of one problem raised by this relationship between religion and culture. A religion, to have creative cultural significance, must avoid either a purely negative attitude toward culture or an identification of religion with the particular culture so as to idolatrize the culture.[13] At this point Dawson, who is quite appreciative of the historical significance of all the great religions, finds Christianity particularly significant in its avoidance of either of these tendencies. Its God is transcendent to culture, but does not deny the work of culture, like the deities or metaphysical systems of some of the Eastern religions.

All this analysis of civilizations and religions has not yet touched what to Dawson is the final touchstone of the significance of history. For history has its mysterious and unpredictable aspects, which are an affront to historical rationalism. "The real meaning of history is something entirely different from that which

---

[12] *The Making of Europe* (New York: Sheed and Ward, 1945), p. 25. T. S. Eliot, who acknowledges his indebtedness to Dawson, similarly sees religion as the unifying and creative force in cultural development. He also emphasizes the incalculable aspect of cultural creativity, which can never be simply the product of deliberate effort. (See *Notes Towards the Definition of Culture*, pp. 17–18, 24–25.) Eliot makes this insight part of a more deliberate conservatism than Dawson shows.
[13] *Religion and Culture*, p. 206.

the human actors in the historical drama themselves believe or intend." [14] Here Dawson moves in the direction of the tendency in modern Catholicism which stresses the mysterious, unobservable character of providence. The tragic character of history, the hiddenness of its meaning, evokes one of the most mature statements of his understanding of history:

> Thus in comparison with the optimism of liberalism the Christian view of life and the Christian interpretation of history are profoundly tragic. The true progress of history is a mystery which is fulfilled in failure and suffering and which will only be revealed at the end of time. The victory that overcomes the world is not success but faith and it is only the eye of faith that understands the true value of history.
>
> Viewing history from this standpoint the Christian will not be confident in success or despondent in failure. . . . None knows where Europe is going and there is no law of history by which we can predict the future. Nor is the future in our own hands, for the world is ruled by powers that it does not know, and the men who appear to be the makers of history are in reality its creatures.[15]

In the midst of the frantic spirit which accompanies much modern thought about history, the best of Catholicism stands with a feeling of maturity. It represents a tradition which has never succumbed to some of the illusions of recent centuries, and does not have to reject them excitedly at this late date. Although a historian like Dawson moves in a different world from that of Pius IX with his *Syllabus of Errors,* he can nevertheless insist that the real error was with those who, in their confidence in "Liberalism and Progress and Modern Civilization," denounced or ridiculed the Pontiff.

Further the church of Rome has the advantage, as it appears to its adherents, that it can point to a solution to the problem of

---

[14] *Religion and the Modern State*, p. 81.
[15] In *The Kingdom of God and History* (Oxford Conference Book), p. 216.

history—short of Protestantism's final reliance on the mysterious sovereigny of God. Beside, and in contrast to, the solutions offered by Communist materialism, by the American combination of liberal democracy and standardized mass civilization, by the various European traditions, the Catholic like Dawson can offer a specific cultural and religious tradition. In the return to this definite tradition, and the visible, historical institution which embodies it, he finds an answer to the problems which beset the history of man today—and in all ages.[16]

B. THE MYSTERY OF PROVIDENCE

The second viewpoint on providence in recent Catholicism takes up the side of the Augustinian heritage which Protestantism has emphasized and stresses the inscrutability of God's hidden providence. The thinkers already considered have not ignored this viewpoint, but have retained the Catholic confidence that reason can discern something of the rationale of history—in the development of a divine institution, in progressive apprehension of natural law, or in the creative power which religion exerts within a civilization. Another group of Catholic thinkers finds evidence of providence only as faith apprehends history as a story of salvation.

A real recognition of the unfathomable ways of God appears in the writings of the German Catholic Theodor Haecker, a translator of Kierkegaard, whose profundity is acknowledged by European Protestants, though he is little known in America. Haecker finds several levels or orders of history, the final of which is the history of salvation. As in all Catholicism this supreme order does not deny the place of lesser natural orders, but for Haecker it finally makes them insignificant. When man is confronted with the ultimate meaning of history—salvation—all the lesser meanings of cultural achievement become indifferent.

---

[16] *Essays in Order*, pp. xii–xvi, xix, xx.

No doubt Neanderthal man did not look like Belvedere Apollo, but he too was a spiritual person whose Salvation mattered. Some of those Neanderthal men, who before the Incarnation obeyed, as far as in them lay, the direct commands of God, will on the Last Day of history and of Judgment rise up transfigured against certain highly cultivated and civilized enemies of God.

For Haecker the meaning of history is expressed in terms which have nothing to do with general progress, institutional developments, the rise and fall of civilizations, or the growth of religion. "It is not the history of families, nor of races and nations, nor of cultures that holds within itself the final meaning of history, but only the history of the Salvation of persons in the Kingdom of God." [17]

Another German Catholic philosopher, Peter Wust (d. 1940), interprets history against an unusual background which combines a Kierkegaardian analysis of man's spiritual despair with more normative Thomist conceptions. Wust sees history running quite counter to Hegel's idea of the development of freedom. The momentum of fate continuously increases and encroaches upon freedom, until at an unforeseen moment a creative personality—perhaps a St. Francis—arises with power to upset the course of events.

Whether God will raise up a St. Francis for our world, or whether our sick Western Culture is doomed, we cannot know. The duty of the Christian is renewed inner faith and evangelism; it is for God to determine what generation will gather the harvest. The meaning of history is hidden:

. . . history, in its deepest sense, does not consist merely of secular happenings but . . . is always at the same time a sacred process, a spiritual happening. For it is only on the surface that history is a *motio physica* of wars, battles, national disorders, political catas-

---

[17] "The Unity of History," *The Dublin Review*, CCXIX (1946), 47, 48.

trophes, and so on. Below, in the depths that are accessible to the mind alone, it is a truly majestic *motio metaphysica voluntatis*, a passionately stirring will-drama of the spirit.

There is, nevertheless, one known point in this view of history and the future: ". . . even if Western culture were destroyed, the Christian work of salvation and its natural-supernatural institution, the Church, would survive the ruin intact." [18]

At this point of definite foreknowledge of an otherwise mysterious history, Wust raises a difficult problem. From the viewpoint of the philosopher or historian, he affirms on doctrinal grounds what must be left for a future empirical judgment to determine. And from the viewpoint of the non-Roman theologian, he compromises doctrinal certitude by asserting in the name of faith something which might be disproved by the course of events.

These difficulties, implicit in most Roman Catholic doctrines of history, are avoided by the late Erich Frank. Clearly more Augustinian than Thomist, his writings were received more favorably by Protestants than by Catholics. Frank rejected decisively the various modern substitutes for providence, like the doctrine of progress. The whole problem of history is symbolized for Frank in the figures of Caesar and Christ. Caesar was the political genius whose intellect and ambition subjugated the world. "If we measure the greatness of an individual by the durability and consequence of his accomplishment, Caesar undoubtedly is the greatest character in history." As if secretly in tune with fate, he was master of his historical situation, and his death could not destroy his work.

All attempts to find a moral rationale of history founder on the facts of the Caesars. Whatever moral forces rise against them are shattered. Yet Caesar was totally unable to bring the ancient world the faith it needed; this Christ did. So Frank can say: "In

---

[18] "Crisis in the West," in *Essays in Order*, pp. 101, 142.

Christ, not in Caesar did the truly creative power in the history of that age manifest itself."

But the historians of his age did not notice Christ, and historians since have not known how to deal with him, because the significance of Christ does not fit the categories in which history is written. The experience wrought by Christ

is beyond the reach of historical method. It is an experience of the soul, of the spirit, accessible only to him who holds the belief that in all those events which seemed of little importance a new truth had come into the world, a truth through which he who has faith in it may become a new man.

The relation of Christian faith to history is thus paradoxical. This faith, says Frank, "has been *the* driving force of history ever since"—whether men followed or violently opposed it. Yet it establishes no earthly kingdom. "In this world, it is always Caesar who is bound to be victorious, while Christ will for ever be crucified." [19]

Thus what happens in history, in Frank's understanding, is knowable only to faith. One is not to speak of God's providence in terms of causality, or to illustrate it from the development of political and social institutions. It is a purely religious idea with a solely spiritual meaning. But eyes of faith can recognize God's activity in history, even in the movements of rebellion against God.

This viewpoint clearly rejects any attempt to impose a pattern upon history, to determine in advance or even to explain in retrospect the way God works in history. It does not encroach upon the historian's domain in determining the events of history—whether past or future. The question it raises is whether a Christian conception of providence can, without losing its

---

[19] *Philosophical Understanding and Religious Truth*, pp. 124, 126, 127–28, 130.

essential character, ignore the realm of politics and social change and cling only to a religious certitude.

Catholicism, with its sense of organic community and historical institutionalism, has long regarded Protestantism as too "individualistic." It is therefore surprising to see Haecker, Frank, and (to a lesser extent) Wust establish religious views of history by turning from the movements of men and nations to the emphasis on individual experience. The more orthodox Monsignor Ronald Knox, facing the threat of atomic energy, takes a similar direction. He finds neither faith nor evidence affording grounds for predicting whether history will grow better or worse; and he rejects apocalyptic faith as too irresponsible and too close to the fantasies of millenarian sects. So he finds that "hope in the theological sense is concerned only with the salvation of the individual believer, and the means which will help him to attain it." [20] Looking at society and history, he proposes, as "a kind of Platonic myth," the conception of a divinely willed "progress towards the millennium." But he rejects any notion that the mythical progress has much correspondence to historical progress.

Again the Czech-American scholar Bodhan Chudoba sounds the individualistic concern. He sees no evidence that history brings an increase of good or evil, of happiness or unhappiness. "The drama of every human personality," he writes, "is enclosed in the frontiers of the individual human conscience." Like all Protestant or Catholic thinkers he rejects autonomous individualism—the secular creed declaring man's independence of God and neighbor. But historical communities have little importance in his theory of history. The "core of the Christian conception of history," then, is a "drama in which the love of each individual person may be manifested independently." [21]

---

[20] *God and the Atom,* p. 121.

[21] *The Meaning of Civilization,* pp. 60–61, 66. Cf. p. 312. Chudoba is a scholar with a tremendous breadth of interest for the many aspects of culture. He has fervent concern for historical values. But when he comes finally to state the *meaning* of history, his answer says little about *history*.

Certainly the awareness of mystery and the sense of the need to probe deeply for a meaning of history is closer to biblical perspectives than are any confident attempts to link providence with general progress or glibly stated patterns. One can only ask—without implying any pat answer—whether Christian faith must give up the prophetic-Augustinian belief that God's sovereignty does express itself, however hiddenly, in the rise and fall of nations as well as in the lives of the faithful.

V. ECCLESIASTICISM AND ESCHATOLOGY

Roman doctrine has never formally modified the literal apocalyptic expectation of the New Testament. Those Protestant theologians who have recently revived eschatology most vividly will frankly acknowledge that their literal historical expectations differ considerably from those of Jesus of Nazareth or Paul, his apostle. This admission orthodox Catholic theology does not make. Standard textbooks (e.g., the well-known Baltimore Catechism and more intellectualized books) give highly detailed descriptions of future apocalyptic events, including the fire that torments the damned, with no hint that their language might not be literal.

Nevertheless, as we have seen, ecclesiasticism may blanket the significance of eschatology more thoroughly than the abandonment of literalism. One writer sums up the problem of history in the expansive statement: "The Catholic Church alone provides the complete answer to man's infinite strivings."[1] No doubt the "complete answer" includes the entire eschatological doctrine; but the sense of ecclesiastical finality overcomes the sense of expectation and mystery.

In another respect ecclesiasticism has engulfed eschatology. Nearly all non-Roman biblical scholarship has agreed that Jesus

---

[1] Joseph Schrembs, "The Catholic Philosophy of History," in the book by the same title, ed. by Peter Guilday. P. 7.

probably expected an early end of history; the result has been an enriching discovery of the meaning behind the literally-misleading New Testament symbolism. But most Roman Catholic writings conform with Pius X's condemnation of such a teaching about Jesus. The rejected doctrine is doubly dangerous: it undermines the contention that Jesus deliberately founded the church of Rome, and it destroys conceptions of divine revelation which must assume that Jesus was infallible.

Baron von Hügel was one of the independent minds who saw meaning in the discoveries of the New Testament scholars. Never pretending to understand completely Jesus' apocalyptic teachings, he saw in them a clue to significant truth:

I love to accept this great doctrine, this great teaching of our Lord's; for I see it is a part, and a very great part, of His own mind. It is a teaching *peculiar* to our Lord. The sudden arrival of the Kingdom, the choice between good and evil, the immense warnings, the abiding consequences of sin, all these are bound up in this great teaching of our Lord's. . . .

To the deepest Spirituality God, the next world, death and the judgment, all these are very near, so that to our Lord's mind these things are all *now*. . . .[2]

Philosophers like Karl Adam and Jacques Maritain represent more orthodox doctrine, qualified both by their liberal spirits and their historical awareness. The church, says Adam, "is a society awaiting the parousia, and her nature is fundamentally eschato-

---

[2] Reported by von Hügel's niece, Gwendolen Greene, "Thoughts from Baron von Hügel," *Dublin Review*, CLXXXVIII (1931), 254–60.

As John Baillie points out (*The Belief in Progress*, pp. 195–96), Tyrrell, for all his modernism, did not accept the doctrine of progress. Instead, he welcomed Schweitzer's New Testament scholarship with its emphasis on Jesus' apocalyptic expectations. Tyrrell found apocalypse, interpreted symbolically, to offer a religiously profound understanding of history. It is curious to note that the orthodox Monsignor Knox takes for his "Platonic myth" a more modernist conception than did Tyrrell, who took a biblical myth.

logical."[3] Maritain describes the church as the "commencement" of the Kingdom, the "chrysalis," the Kingdom itself "existent and living, but veiled and in a state of pilgrimage."[4] Both writers, while laying great stress on the fact that the present Kingdom of God is a visible, papal institution, do not overlook the *"not yet"* of the Christian belief about history. Nevertheless the crash of apocalypse is not here. The difference between the present institutionalized Kingdom and the future Kingdom is the difference between incomplete and complete, unfinished and consummated—not the difference between a history with its violence and pretensions and idolatries extending even into religious institutions, and the Kingdom in which God's righteous sovereignty is revealed as the meaning of history.

T. S. Eliot's Anglo-Catholicism shows how a more apocalyptic mood is released in Catholic thought once the Roman doctrine of the church ceases to control historical thought. Eliot is thoroughly the traditionalist, desiring the Catholic goal of a Christendom with an established church and a religious temper pervading society. But history has a more open future than for the adherents of Rome; only time can tell what will happen, even to the church. It is quite possible that Christian society and Christian institutions will succumb to the corrosion of secular influences.[5] And, although all Catholics know that no imaginable Christendom is a perfect society, Eliot is more Protestant than most:

But we have to remember that the Kingdom of Christ on earth will never be realised, and also that it is always being realised; we must remember that whatever reform or revolution we carry out, the result will always be a sordid travesty of what human society should be—though the world is never left wholly without glory.[6]

---

[3] *The Spirit of Catholicism* (New York: Macmillan, 1933), p. 78. *Cf.* pp. 71, 73, 223.
[4] *True Humanism*, pp. 94–95.
[5] *Notes Towards the Definition of Culture*, p. 126.
[6] *The Idea of a Christian Society*, p. 60.

Once again the thought of a historian clarifies in concrete terms the Roman Catholic doctrine of history. Christopher Dawson has come increasingly to appreciate the significance of New Testament apocalypse, but he applies it to history by ecclesiastical means. The "key to the Christian understanding of history" is the Incarnation, and the Incarnation "finds its extension and completion in the historic life of the Church." The "foundation of this divine society" gives history an "absolute value" and a "transcendent end." [7]

Something of the apocalyptic spirt of discontinuity is present in Dawson's thought: "The Kingdom of God is not the work of man and does not emerge by a natural law of progress from the course of human history. It makes a violent irruption into history and confounds the work of man." But this Kingdom of God is still identifiable with the church, "the supernatural society through which and in which alone humanity could realize its true end." [8]

If ancient Jewish apocalypse was faith in the savior who was to come, Catholic apocalypse is primarily faith in Him who has come and in the supernatural institution which continues His incarnation. Most Protestants would agree on the significance of the church as the community which transcends (certainly in spirit and at least partially in fact) the divisiveness of history— the barriers between living and dead, between nations and races and social classes. But Protestantism knows that the church introduces new divisiveness, and is convinced that an institution composed of a particular group of people is an inadequate source of the meaning of history. So the Protestant looks for the meaning of history past the church to the Lord of the church. He is confident that the gates of hell will fall before the Lord, but thinks that they often do prevail against—or even come to

---

[7] *Religion and the Modern State*, p. 97.
[8] In *The Kingdom of God and History* (Oxford Conference Book), pp. 205, 210.

encompass—the historical institutions which claim to be the church.

In Christopher Dawson's mature Catholicism, there is considerable freedom from the pretensions in Romanism which disturb outsiders. But in his tragic interpretation of history, the rock certainly is the church. It is not, to be sure, the *success* of the church, for "the cross is her victory." But "the Christian interpretation of history depends on the continuation and extension of the incarnation in the life of the church," conceived fully, concretely, organically. "She has been the guest and the exile, the mistress and the martyr, of nations and civilization and has survived them all. And in every age and among every people it is her mission to carry on the work of divine restoration and regeneration, which is the true end of history."[9]

---

[9] *Ibid.*, pp. 214, 216–17.

CHAPTER VII

THE REDISCOVERY OF BIBLICAL

ESCHATOLOGY

CONFRONTED by the problems of history in our age, contemporary thought has rediscovered in striking fashion the significance of prophecy and Gospel. The renewed interest in biblical concepts of history has marked the thought of men with the greatest variance in religious ideas—men so diverse as Paul Althaus, John Baillie, Karl Barth, Nicolas Berdyaev, Edwyn Bevan, C. H. Dodd, Walter Horton, Reinhold Niebuhr, William Temple, Paul Tillich, and Arnold Toynbee, to mention only a few. So pervasive has been this renewed concern that to dismiss it as an aspect of a particular "neo-orthodox" movement is foolish. When in 1937 a group of several writers of various national and denominational backgrounds contributed essays to the Oxford Conference Book, *The Kingdom of God and History*, all criticized the assumptions of progressivism and turned in a more biblical direction.

Two great stimuli have done much to evoke this new interest: the course of modern history and the work of New Testament scholarship.

First, history itself has forced men to reconsider their assumptions about it. A swelling undercurrent of protest against the reigning optimism of the nineteenth century had been represented by Schopenhauer and Nietzsche. When Oswald Spengler combined brilliance and perversity in his dramatic prediction of doom, he found a responsive twentieth-century audience.

The theological protest was expressed most brilliantly in the nineteenth century by the little-known Kierkegaard, who in a minor language was blasting Hegel's philosophy of history. The twentieth century saw an increasing number of voices in theology making more and more radical criticisms of the prevailing assumptions. Among them was a Swiss Christian socialist, a young pastor in the town of Safenvil, who found it impossible to pronounce easy assurances from his pulpit when, as he later said, "it required only a little imagination for me to hear the sound of the guns booming away in the north." [1] Turning to the New Testament he found Paul's eschatological faith; the result was Karl Barth's famous *Römerbrief*. Although only one thousand copies of the first edition were printed (in 1918, the same year as Spengler's *Der Untergang des Abendlandes*), the message caught fire and Barth became the prophet of a theological revolution.

The new interpretations of history made doubly effective the second stimulus—the discoveries concerning biblical eschatology made by Johannes Weiss and others. In 1906 Albert Schweitzer published his study of research into the life of Jesus; by 1910 the English translation, *The Quest of the Historical Jesus*, appeared. Henceforth it was impossible to go on appealing to "the historical Jesus" as a figure whose main ideas were those of the nineteenth and twentieth centuries. Schweitzer's own radically eschatological portrait of Jesus was to undergo considerable criticism and change; but the apocalyptic elements in the Gospels could no longer be ignored or regarded as metaphorical statements of progressivism.

The work of New Testament critics was at first an embarrassment to the church. Schweitzer himself, finding little help in

[1] Karl Barth, *The Epistle to the Romans*, author's preface to English edition, p. v.

his rather bizarre picture of the historical Jesus, took inspiration from a living Christ of faith for one of the great lives of Christian service. But with the undermining of long-established assumptions about history, the biblical outlook became less a stumbling block than a release and a source for creative attempts of theology to grapple with the problems of history.

I. THE INADEQUACY OF "PROGRESS"

Theological attacks on the assumptions of progressivism do not, as is sometimes assumed, deny the fact or the possibility of progress. Most theologians are willing to make a quite empirical analysis of history to determine what progressive developments can and cannot be discovered. They deny that progress is inevitable, that history is a story of the elimination of evil from human affairs, or that progress offers an adequate center of the meaning of history.

Biblical thought from the beginning has had appreciation for the realization of the historically new and unprecedented; but in itself, it would not have led to the expectation of the amazing technological achievements of the human race. These developments have transformed many aspects of historical life. For example, medicine, agriculture, and architecture have done much to modify the dependence of man upon nature. Communication and transportation have widened human intercourse until, *from the viewpoint of technology*, global community is an easy possibility. Inventions have so affected labor and production that in many areas of the earth all classes of society are in part leisure classes and can be educated; hence democratic political processes are made possible in ways inconceivable to the ancient Greeks or to medieval Christendom. Thus "progress" has wrought major changes in political, cultural, and social history of the human race.

But even this indisputable technological progress requires qualification. In principle, once man has invented the wheel, to take an example, the achievement can be passed on to all later generations, who are enabled to go on to new accomplishments. Actually technology has not so simple a developmental history. It is entirely possible, for instance, that the Babylonian system of irrigation, which made possible one of the most ancient civilizations, finally failed for reasons connected with the social organization and morale of society, and that in the break-up of that civilization technological achievements were lost for a long time to come. There is considerable evidence that many techniques have been discovered or invented repeatedly, in various areas and periods of history, and that many accomplishments have been lost for centuries or permanently. Whitehead judges that the technological achievements of the ancients, at their best, probably surpassed those of their successors until the seventeenth century.[1] Similarly it is certainly possible that many contemporary achievements belong to what Toynbee calls "the temporary Western technological scaffolding" which will fall away in time.

But granting the permanence of some technological gains, to what extent do their cultural effects constitute "progress"? Since the advent of atomic energy, the threat to civilization from its own achievements needs no elaboration. There are other threats than those of destruction through the insanity of modern warfare. Spengler's vision of a society dependent upon its small minority of technicians, the "priests of the machine," has had at least some justification in the course of events; cries for decentralization and spreading of responsibility are almost ineffectual against the technological drive toward uniformity and central control. One need not accept Spengler's whole thesis, that ages of technological advance are ages of cultural decline, to agree

---

[1] *Adventures of Ideas*, p. 33. Christopher Dawson writes: "In all essentials Babylonia, in the time of Hammurabi, and even earlier, had reached a pitch of material civilisation which has never since been surpassed in Asia." *Enquiries Into Religion and Culture*, p. 107. Cf. Arnold Toynbee, *A Study of History*, I, 424–40; Morris Cohen, *The Meaning of Human History*, pp. 195–96, 236–37.

that sometimes progress in techniques accompanies retrogression in human relations.[2]

When we turn to non-technological aspects of history, the case for a progressive interpretation becomes still more dubious. Technical inventions, once the product of genius, can soon be mass-produced by quite ordinary people. But it is not true that once an Aeschylus or Shakespeare has produced a drama, anyone who takes the trouble to acquire the know-how can turn the trick. Nor is it evident that because a St. Francis or a Schweitzer has lived, it is easy for succeeding generations of men to fashion lives of the same spiritual quality. The wind bloweth where it listeth, and the incalculable element of "grace"—whether in cultural or spiritual terms—is not always cumulative.

Most significant of all, in the critiques of progressivism, is the recovery of certain insights which philosophers of history, with their *a priori* developmental principles, had overlooked. Psychology since Freud has realized that the problems of human personality are far deeper than assumed by simple developmental philosophies. And sociologists and historians have become increasingly aware of the diversity and relativity of all human achievements, in contrast to the ideological claims of men who think they are approaching the pinnacle of history. These secular insights, when seen within a Christian context, reaffirm two ancient doctrines: the sinfulness and the finitude of man before a holy and infinite God.

Thus the theological critique of progress, so far from being merely a pessimistic reaction to temporary historical difficulties or a retreat into religious obscurantism, appeals to facts and judgments corroborated by much of secular thought. Nevertheless, its most incisive and inclusive formulations come from its

---

[2] Many aspects of the industrial revolution are evidence of this point. A specific instance is the perpetuation of slavery, encouraged by the invention of the cotton gin. Toynbee records a similar phenomenon in the development of Greek agriculture. *A Study of History*, I, 168.

religious perspective. Thus Karl Löwith, one of the most radical
and penetrating of the critics of progress, writes:

. . . man's historical experience is one of steady failure. Christianity,
too, as a historical *world* religion, is a complete failure. The world is
still as it was in the time of Alaric; only our means of oppression and
destruction (as well as of reconstruction) are considerably improved
and are adorned with hypocrisy.[3]

If such a statement seems to ignore the entire cultural and
humanistic aspect of history, the author would reply that the
cultural achievements of men, though very real, do not change
the character of the basic problems of historical existence. Some
theologians, as a matter of fact, have given considerable attention
to cultural-historical achievement.[4] But it is the dynamic power
of evil, reappearing continually on higher levels of achievement
and infecting the most civilized and moral attainments of man,
which has impressed many recent thinkers. It has led to renewed
appreciation of the parable of the tares and the wheat, and the
picture of the anti-Christ as the symbol of the cumulative and
dynamic effect of evil which, like good, comes to its culmination
at the End of history.

The emphasis of continental Protestant theology is brought

---

[3] *Meaning in History*, p. 191. For an even more severe judgment see
Berdyaev, *The Meaning of History*, p. 198.
[4] Numerous writings refute the charge that Christian writers are making
a blanket attack upon "progress." Paul Tillich distinguishes quite carefully various human endeavors with progressive significance from those
where history shows no general progress. See *The Kingdom of God and
History* (Oxford Conference Book), pp. 113–14. Reinhold Niebuhr
shows real appreciation for modern developmental thought, which has
pointed out truths too long unrecognized by Christianity; but he finds
that certain exaggerations and errors have betrayed it into illusory confidence. See *Faith and History*, Chs. V, VI. *Cf.* Emil Brunner, *Christianity and Civilisation*, I, 57–58; *The Divine Imperative*, pp. 281–82. Also
C. H. Dodd, in *The Kingdom of God and History* (Oxford Conference
Book), pp. 36–37. Also Herbert Butterfield, *Christianity and History*,
pp. 96–97.

out in Brunner's use of the pluperfect tense: "The belief in progress had played out its fatally dazzling role, and Western humanity, which had staked all hope on this one card, found itself facing the nothingness of despair." [5] If American thought has not been so radical, there has been dramatically increasing criticism of progressive assumptions in most theological and considerable philosophical literature.

One further inadequacy is often noted by the critiques of progress. Even though the progressive interpretation of history could be maintained, it would be from the Christian perspective an inadequate source of meaning for history. As Henry Sloane Coffin puts it, man "is not just a link in the existence of the human race. . . . He is not mere fertilizer for the soil of the nation from which harvests will be reaped in days ahead." [6] If history is interpreted as progress toward a goal, a collectivist outlook upon mankind gives the only possibility of meaning. To use Kant's terms, personality is conceived as a means rather than an end. Or in Brunner's figure, man is like a single frame cut from a motion-picture strip, while "abstract humanity" is the real subject of the drama.

These various critiques of progress, especially the more radical ones, raise the question of whether they have forgotten the Christian awareness of the dynamic forward thrust of history. Brunner says, "If a man does not believe that through his action things will become better, he cannot act at all." [7] But this emphasis sometimes seems denied in the writings of Brunner and his more radical colleagues. If the meaning of history is to be found in an eschatological future and if man is not to be regarded

---

[5] *Christianity and Civilisation*, I, 68.

[6] *God Confronts Man in History*, p. 127. Berdyaev makes the point with biting emphasis in *The Meaning of History*, p. 193. Cf. Edwyn Bevan and Paul Tillich in *The Kingdom of God and History* (Oxford Conference Book), pp. 58, 113; Emil Brunner, *Christianity and Civilisation*, I, 57.

[7] *The Divine Imperative*, p. 282. Cf. p. 236.

merely as a means to that end, then the "future" must somehow become contemporary for present-day mankind. Either human personality must in some way participate in a future which resolves the problems of history (an immortality which evades history does not solve the difficulty), or the future must in some significant sense invade the present and offer realization to men now living. Both of these views may be found in the Christian tradition and are being reemphasized today.

II. SOME CHARACTERISTICS OF HISTORY

In rejecting progress as the key to history, Christian thought insists that history cannot be understood except as the story of men living in a divinely initiated and consummated drama. The religious significance of history is not simply to be read from the facts; it is known only through grace and faith, through repentance, trust, and commitment which enable man, the actor within history, to perceive something of the meaning of history. Nevertheless, there are in the Christian conception several ideas which make connection with the empirically observable character of history and which can be stated, at least in part, in terms which are relevant to philosophical and common-sense views of history. Five such ideas will be considered here.

1. *History is concerned with human activities, which can neither be equated with nor utterly separated from natural processes.*

History, as Collingwood points out repeatedly in *The Idea of History*, is humanistic; it is the story of human affairs. Natural history—the story of the geological development of the earth or the evolution of primates—is not the same as human history. (The Ionic word, ἰστορίη, originally obscured the difference between natural and human history. But since Herodotus the word history has usually, in its precise sense, been reserved for human history.) One visits the Museum of Natural History and the Metropolitan Museum of Art with differing expectations. History is more than process and development because man knows that he has a history. He inquires into its meaning. He makes decisions which direct his own history. When he is a victim of natural circumstances, he knows that he is a victim. Even Marx's naturalism recognized important differentia in human history. Even Spengler's, built on the analogy with the natural life cycle, appealed to action in the "Hour of Decision." Human freedom, thoughtfulness, memory and anticipation, make history what it is.

Yet history is enmeshed with nature, influenced by geography, climate, economics, and biology. There are more remarks about food-getting and geography in the Bible than in most sacred literatures. Theologians and philosophers, however, sometimes forget the dependence of history upon nature, as evidenced by the shock of the famed Lisbon earthquake upon eighteenth-century ideas of history. Collingwood, in his idealist interpretation of history, says:

. . . whether or no there is such a thing as nature, as distinct from spirit, at least it cannot enter as a factor into the world of spirit. When people think that it can, and speak . . . of the influence of geography or climate upon history, they are mistaking the effect of a certain person's or people's conception of nature on their actions for an effect of nature itself . . . rational action is free from the domination of nature, and builds its own world of human affairs, Res Gestae, at its own bidding and in its own way.[1]

But nature has put an end to the history of some communities and presumably will to history as a whole (unless the human race beats her to it); and this, to put it mildly, is an effect of nature.

We may recall Pascal's remark that if Cleopatra's nose had been a bit longer, the course of world history would have been changed.[2] Dean Inge says: A microbe "had the honor of killing

---

[1] The Idea of History, pp. 200, 318.
[2] Pensées, No. 162. Cf. J. B. Bury's essay, "Cleopatra's Nose," Selected Essays.

Alexander the Great at the age of thirty-two, and so changing the whole course of history." [3] Clearly this sort of reasoning can be overdone, but it is more likely to be overlooked. To Collingwood such notions imply a "bankruptcy of historical method." [4] But theology can do justice to their truth. History is not independent of disease, famine, the cruelty of nature, and the biological life cycle which sets limits to the historical time of every man. The theological concept which expresses this relation of historical man to nature is the doctrine of the creation of man, from the dust of the earth, in the image of God.

2. *History is event-ful. It is made up of concrete unrepeatable acts.*

As a consequence of freedom historical activities are individual, unique, creative. They are also destructive, but destruction is not mere dissolution. Men cannot build and take apart civilizations, as they might endlessly combine and separate salt and water with no evident change in the chemical constituents because of the process they had been through.[5] In Spengler's vivid metaphor, the expanse of the waters of history is periodically broken by the rise of a civilization, which runs its course and vanishes, leaving the face of the waters once more "a sleeping waste." But historical destruction does not restore the primitive situation. Where there has been history there have been

---

[3] "The Idea of Progress," in *Outspoken Essays*, II, 166. Inge misses the Christian idea of history when he lets such facts persuade him to devalue history along Neo-Platonic lines.

[4] *The Idea of History*, p. 80.

[5] It is interesting to note that whereas in the past history has often been interpreted in natural categories, the modern elaboration of specifically historical categories has been so pronounced that nature is now often interpreted by historical categories. *Event* is a key word in many philosophies of nature, and some metaphysicians suggest that each event—including those we call atoms—has individuality and a historical character. There may well be value in such an interpretation. It does not, however, conceal the great difference between the cultural-historical and the metaphysical writings of a Whitehead. History still differs from nature.

unrepeatable human activities, remembered or forgotten. Whether
the witness be the impact of a Socrates upon centuries of human
life, or the huge mystery-ridden stone figures on Easter Island,
something unique has taken place.

So Brunner writes:

The characteristic element in history is not that something happens
—even in the clouds all kinds of things happen, but there is no history there—but that something is *done*. . . . History is made where
decisions are made.[6]

History is not the unfolding of an eternal rationale. There is
in it what Brunner calls the "irrationality of the absolutely factual," what we have seen von Hügel call "sheer happenedness."

What this means to the practicing historian is indicated by
Carl Becker, who quotes Rousseau's challenge: "Is it simple, is
it natural that God should go in search of Moses to speak to
Jean Jacques Rousseau?" Becker's disarming answer is: "Well,
frankly, we do not know."[7]

It is, of course, in the idea of revelation that this general
doctrine gets its specifically Christian emphasis. Thus, says Karl
Barth, the historical event (and specifically the revelatory event)
is not to be conceived "with the enlightenment" as "a special
case under a rule, or the realisation of a general possibility"; it
is "sheer event, with no court of reference above it."[8] This does
not mean that one must accept accounts of historical events on
authority without investigation. All the historian's carefully

---

[6] *Man in Revolt*, p. 440.
[7] *The Heavenly City of the Eighteenth-Century Philosophers*, p. 46.
Becker is not making a declaration of his own belief. He is simply saying
that historians must be empirical.
[8] *Church Dogmatics*, I/1, 378. Cf.: "The man who is hankering after
the so-called 'eternal verities' had best, if he is determined not to be con-
verted, leave his faith uncontaminated with Christian faith. Revelation
is a *hic et nunc*, once and for all and unique, or it is not the revelation
to which Holy Scripture bears witness." *Credo* (English tr.), p. 80.

developed criteria for handling historical evidence may be used. But no theory of rationalism is entitled to determine what should have happened, assuming that therefore that is what did happen. If empiricism is compatible with an existential relation to historical facts, contemporary Christian interpretations of history are empirical; they may, as a matter of fact, be more empirical than many so-called empiricisms which conceal nests of *a priori* assumptions.

3. *History is a story of conflict.*

If history is not simply a group of harmonious processes, but includes countless decisions, the result is conflict. And if human nature is perverted by sin, conflict is intensified. Men may find ways of settling their conflicts. They may cooperate. But against all theories of history which discern "through the ages" any obvious "one increasing purpose," Christian eschatology says that history is a battlefield of cross purposes, of schemes and counterschemes, of disruptive as well as harmonious tendencies.

From the Christian viewpoint, of course, the most fundamental of all conflicts is that between good and evil. To say this is not to force a pattern upon history or reduce its diversity to a single antithesis, because the conflict between good and evil is not conceived as a struggle of particular "good" men and groups against the wicked. It is emphatically a struggle that crosses all party lines and claims the soul of each man. In observing history theology recognizes that in the conflict between good and evil, judged by any standards that can measure the dominance of purely historical power, evil has its triumphs as truly as does good.

4. *What happens in history is seldom what is intended.*

It is seldom that plans are accomplished in history in anything like the way they are envisioned. Surely no man—wicked tyrant or noble idealist—planned the history we have lived through. Sometimes for better, sometimes for worse, the deliberate decisions of men result in events which were never decided upon. Decisions at Yalta, Potsdam, and around the world were made in a twilight where their outcome was invisible. One can, of course, analyze all this quite matter-of-factly by saying that the event is the resultant of a variety of planned decisions and errors, plus certain factors of nature which might or might not have been foreseen. But this is simply sophisticated language for what men have always sensed about history, often in profound ways. The Greeks had their Fates and their mysterious *peripeteia*, the reversal of fortunes following *hybris*. The Hellenistic age had its *Tyche* and *Fortuna*. Shakespeare had his "destiny which shapes our ends"; Marx, his dialectic; Hegel, his "cunning of reason." Atomic scientists write of the events leading to Hiroshima with as vivid a sense of fate as can be found in Greek tragedy. All these conceptions point to something overlooked by those who say, "The future will be exactly what men make of it." [9]

This feature of history is the secular aspect of the Christian idea of providence, which acknowledges a hidden governance of history. When wrongly used the doctrine may intrude upon the determination of historical fact; but, says Collingwood, "the recognition that what happens in history need not happen through anyone's deliberately wishing it to happen is an indispensable precondition of understanding any historical process." [10]

5. *History has no immanent rationale, no simple coherence or unity, no inherent and autonomous meaning.*

If the preceding propositions are taken seriously, it follows that all attempts to make history fit a philosopher's preconceived pattern, or some partisan's "historical destiny" are suspect. Polybius' cycles, Vico's spiral, Joachim's three ages (or their secularization in Comte and others), sectarian apocalyptic expectations,

---

[9] Shirley Jackson Case, *The Christian Philosophy of History*, p. 91. *Cf.* pp. 112–13. *Cf.* the reference to Dewey, p. 22, above.
[10] *The Idea of History*, p. 48. See index, "Providential history." Also pp. 53, 95, 116–17.

Hegel's dialectical movement of the *Weltgeist*, Marx's materialistic dialectic, Spencer's inevitable progress, the revised cyclicism of Spengler, Sorokin, or Toynbee's magnificent drama—none is adequate. The very term "philosophy of history," in the sense of a rational comprehension of history's conflict and variety, is dubious. Whatever the eschatological drama may represent, it is not a schematization of history or a chart and timetable of the future. Barth's radical refusal to predict the future, sometimes even to plan for it, is extreme; but, perhaps in moderated form, it has its theological and factual justification.[11] Similarly common sense and historical experience might qualify Karl Popper's assertion that "everything is possible in human affairs."[12] But theology keeps a profound sense of the unknowability of the future and the impossibility of discerning reliable patterns for history.

Eschatological theology criticizes particularly attempts to show any simple moral meaning or coherence in history. It agrees with E. Harris Harbison, the Princeton historian, when he says: "The prophetic interpretation of history is more convincing in the prophets, who never stopped to write actual history, than in the chroniclers, who did. It is easier to say that God acts in history than to say precisely where and when."[13] Christian apocalypse, as a matter of fact, was born out of the faith of those unwilling to reject prophetic insight, but unable to find it neatly

---

[11] When questioned during the war about plans for post-war reconstruction, Barth replied with friendly amusement at the attempt of Americans to foresee the unknowable future. If his answer then seemed irresponsible, we need only think how useless much of the war-time future planning has become. Nevertheless it is likely enough that some of the world's current woes are due to a past lack of serious concern for the future.

[12] *The Open Society and Its Enemies*, II, 185. Popper's entire book is a sometimes brilliant, sometimes erratic attack upon "historicism," defined as any attempt to understand the laws of historical development and thereby to predict the future.

[13] "The Problem of the Christian Historian," *Theology Today*, V (1948), 388–405.

illustrated in history. Perhaps the best illustration of the point is Kierkegaard's ridicule of Hegel's philosophy of history:

There were philosophers even before Hegel who took it upon themselves to explain existence, history. And it is true of all such attempts that providence can only smile at them.

But Hegel . . . how the gods must have laughed! A miserable don like that who had seen through the necessity of everything and got the whole thing off by heart: ye Gods! [14]

One is entitled to ask whether some recent theology (in company with some philosophical existentialism) does not over-emphasize the chaotic character of history, just as previous generations exaggerated its harmony. Constructive impulses in history deserve attention along with the destructive. But theology has well realized the dangers of a tender minded reading of history.

The preceding five ideas may be summed up in the proposition: *History is not the solution of the human problem, but part of the problem demanding solution.*

Niebuhr sums up the dominant modern idea of history as "the belief that historical development is a redemptive process." [15] It is this belief which he, with many another, rejects. History with all its achievements, says recent Protestantism, brings to a penetrating focus the problems of conflict, sin, and frustration.

Various thinkers have tried to find some schematism or over-arching idea which makes sense of the human story, but few have convinced many beyond themselves. By and large it may be agreed that while there are purposes in history, there is no pur-

---

[14] *The Journals of Soren Kierkegaard* (A Selection Edited and Translated by Alexander Dru. New York: Oxford, 1938), Entry 1323, July 1854. Hegel, it must be acknowledged, realized better than many modern rationalists the irrationalities of history, which might be conceived as a "slaughterbench" for the virtue and happiness of men. See *Philosophy of History*, p. 21.

[15] *Faith and History*, p. 2.

pose of history sufficiently obvious to convince any large proportion of the actors in history. Thus far skeptic and theologian agree.
As Karl Löwith writes in the conclusion to *Meaning in History*:

> The problem of history as a whole is unanswerable within its
> own perspective. Historical processes as such do not bear the least
> evidence of a comprehensive and ultimate meaning. History as such
> has no outcome. There never has been and never will be an imma-
> nent solution of the problem of history.

Such a view is a view of despair, if it is assumed that history
is its own be-all and end-all. This assumption, of course, is not
accepted by Christianity. Christian faith, from the New Testament onwards, affirms that historical life is never utterly bereft
of meaning, but that confused flashes of meaning, which sometimes illumine and sometimes are blotted out by history, find their
only conceivable coherence in a source not contained within
history.

The idea is expressed clearly in the writings of an American
philosopher, usually regarded as a naturalist, but sensitive to
human problems and the significance of faith. The justification
of life he found in "faith in Elsewhere." "That 'elsewhere' is
where there is a light which is never lit and is never put out and
which clarifies all darkness." Distrustful of all doctrinal formu-
las, he rejected any attempt to pin down this justification literally.
But, he said, "It means that Here and whatever happens Here is
for the sake of Elsewhere—for God's glory, not for an earthly
purpose." [16]

The Christian understanding of history, although many of its
propositions can be stated in terms quite understandable, often
agreeable to secularism, actually understands history only in
terms of God. The finite and sinful finds completion and redemption only in Him. "History is not an autonomous process
which secretes its own meaning as it goes along, like a cosmic

---

[16] Frederick J. E. Woodbridge, *An Essay on Nature*, pp. 321–22.

endocrine gland. . . . History is a process with an author, who lies outside it, that is to say outside time. It had a beginning and will have an end, both of them determined by its author; and it is only in relation to what lies outside itself that it has a meaning." [17]

III. GOD AND THE COMPLETION OF HISTORY

A. THE UNITY OF HISTORY

The problem of *universal history* and its answer have changed little since Augustine's day (See Ch. II, Part III above). Historical research has simply intensified the problem, as it has shown the centuries of geographic and ethnic diversity. In the by-ways of history are many blind alleys, down which cultural and ethnic groups have gone, losing their connection with the rest of history, finally having their cultural achievements wiped out by natural or historical disasters so that they contribute nothing to the mainstreams of human history. More and more obviously the writing of history has become a selective process determined by the historian's viewpoint, and viewpoints are so diverse that the variety of histories produced can no more be added together into a universal history than can apples plus cities plus love affairs be totalled (See Ch. I, Part II above). The combination of ignorance and pretension which enabled most early civilizations to conceive history as the story of themselves and their gods is less excusable—though hardly less prevalent— than ever. At just this point, we have noted, the protests of the historical pluralists must be taken seriously.

In Christian theology, history is conceived in universal terms because the universal God is its originator and stands at its End.

---

[17] Martin Wight, "The Church, Russia and the West," in *The Ecumenical Review*, I (1948), 38. Since theological writings on history often seem to come from a different world from that of the practicing historian, it is interesting to note that the above statement, within a penetrating theological discussion, comes from a colleague of Arnold Toynbee in the Royal Institute of International Affairs at London.

This universal God is never, in historical conflicts, the champion of one people against others, but rather the transcendent judge of all men. No single perspective within history can be the focal point of a universal history; every attempt to view history in terms of the destiny of any one people or cause is an idolatry. Such pretension was broken in principle as early as the eighth century B.C.: "Have not I brought up Israel out of the land of Egypt and the Philistines from Caphtor, and the Syrians from Kir?" (Amos 9:7.) The God who is truly transcendent, before whom all nations are as drops in the bucket and all righteousness is as filthy rags, who is yet concerned for all His people, is the Lord of universal history.

Further, the final symbol of God's activity within history is in Christianity the cross of Christ—a symbol which can never be claimed by any one group, despite attempts of wretched religious egotism so to claim it. For the cross stands for judgment upon the guilt of all men and the promise of redemption for all who are contrite. "In Christ there is neither Jew nor Greek." Creation and fall, Christ, and Eschaton are the three fixed points in eschatological interpretations of history. The first and last stand on the fringe of history and are clearly universal. Christ partakes of the particular character of a historical event, but is a judgment on all particularisms.

Thus Christianity finds it possible and necessary to conceive of the unity of history. Barth has written:

Unless . . . there exists a living perception of the one constant significance of all human occurrence, history becomes merely a sequence of epochs and a series of civilizations: it consists of a plurality of different and incommunicable elements, of separate individuals, ages, periods, relationships and institutions; it teems with phenomena which charge about in all directions.[1]

---

[1] Epistle to the Romans, p. 145. Cf. H. D. Wendland in The Kingdom of God and History (Oxford Conference Book), p. 150.

"Faith in God," says Niebuhr, "is faith in some ultimate unity of life, in some final comprehensive purpose which holds all the various, and frequently contradictory, realms of coherence and meaning together."[2] Increasingly Protestantism finds that only eyes of faith can recognize a unity of history which gives meaning to the many parts.

B. THE REDEMPTION OF HISTORY

In Christian faith the God who unifies history also redeems it. All attempts to redeem history from within are doomed because they are tainted with the evils they seek to overcome. Nations, classes, churches join the long succession of would be messianic saviors of history; but all need salvation themselves.

If all Christianity promises redemption as a divine gift, the particular emphases of eschatological thought are two. First, redemption is part of historical experience but is always incomplete, awaiting the End. Second, redemption must not negate history; it must be a redemption of history.

(1) Within history there are judgments which crush the egomaniac pretensions of would be lords of history, but judgment is always incomplete; the full vindication of God's justice awaits the future. Similarly there are in history real evidences of grace healing the wounds caused by sin, actually transforming personal and community life. There are real renewals of life, creative activities which break the chain of past guilt and permit a fresh start. Yet history can never entirely escape the burden of a guilty past and a guilty present. Redemption awaits the future.

Theologians sometimes seem to stress the incompleteness of redemption with wearying effect. But in an age when confident ideologies have repeatedly promised the redemption of history,

---

[2] *Discerning the Signs of the Times*, p. 154. Cf. *Faith and History*, Ch. VII.

this negative message has been an important point of criticism. One young Christian leader writes:

There is literally a universe of difference between this testimony that history will have a verdict delivered on it—and that we know who the Judge is, though the verdict itself is hidden—and the view which sets the end of history within history itself. . . . The only safeguard against totalitarian claims on the part of the state or party —or church—is the recognition that state and party—and church— have a calling to fulfil and a reckoning to give, and that the issue will not be settled within the human and historical order.[3]

It is in exactly such terms that protest has been made, often in heroic action, against the totalitarian claims of our day.

Nor is this emphasis entirely a negative one. It has made hopefulness possible when all historical prospects were dismal. Of the most thorough and dramatic of those who insist that redemption within history is incomplete, it has been said: "Barth has indeed taught many what *hope* means. For those who accepted it [the theology of crisis], it became a message of joy and a call to go forward. The overwhelming dimensions of God's world-embracing plan began to dawn upon them."[4]

(2) Eschatology promises the redemption *of* history. Here is one reason for the polemic against mysticism which is so frequent in recent theology. Even theologians like Tillich and Berdyaev, who are friendly to mysticism, have a dynamic element in their mysticism and are usually careful to distinguish it from the mysticisms which seek to escape from history. Difficult as the eschatological imagery may be, it seeks to preserve, rather than to rub out, the importance of the historical. In the apocalyptic vision "the kingdom of the world has become the kingdom of our Lord and of his Christ, and he shall reign for ever and ever" (Rev. 11:15).

---

[3] Alexander Miller, *The Christian Significance of Karl Marx*, p. 75.
[4] W. A. Visser 't Hooft, *The Kingship of Christ*, p. 35.

William Temple, taking the crucifixion of Christ as the key to the Christian understanding of redemption, writes:

the Christian scheme of redemption affirms, not only a preponderance of good over evil, so that the temporary victory of evil is wiped out by a more decisive victory of good, but the conversion of defeat itself into triumph . . . *the future does not merely disclose in the past something which was always there, but causes the past, while retaining its own nature, actually to be, in its organic union with its consequence, something which in isolation it neither is nor was.*[5]

It is this principle of transformation *in* historical experience which is the clue to the Christian hope for redemption of history.

IV. ETERNITY AND TIME: THE FUTURE AND THE PRESENT

A. CONCRETE EXPERIENCE AND RATIONAL FORMULATIONS

Any understanding of history involves an often subconscious apprehension of time in its relation to eternity, as the folk lore and burial customs of many a primitive (or civilized) people reveal. Yet attempts to rationalize the experience result in the most abstruse of metaphysical theories. Experience is clearly a composite of permanence and flux, so that a modern cosmologist can find "the complete problem of metaphysics" formulated in the hymn lines:

> Abide with me;
> Fast falls the eventide.[1]

But the attempt to solve the problem confirms Augustine's perplexity—he is quite sure what time is, until he tries to explain it and finds he cannot.

---

[5] *Nature, Man and God*, p. 210. Cf. Brunner, *Man in Revolt*, p. 453.
[1] Alfred North Whitehead, *Process and Reality* (New York: Macmillan, 1929), p. 318.

Insofar as recent Protestant thought differs from the Catholic views of time already considered, it is likely to be at two points: eschatology, convinced that "now we see through a glass darkly," is more skeptical of the adequacy of metaphysical theories; and eschatology, conceiving God not as the unmoved mover but as the Lord of history, lays more stress on the dynamic character of time.

In Christian belief the eternal God creates time and history, and brings them to an end. In the beginning, God; at the end, God. Creation and history depend on God; He does not depend on them. But God's eternity is not a static changelessness. He accomplishes purposes in time. Time is no mere moving image of His eternity (Plato), no mere measure of motion (Aristotle). Historical time, in particular, is directed time, time of decision, irreversible and unrepeatable time. History is no pale realm of unreality but is integral to God's purpose. It is, to be sure, dependent upon God, who alone is self-sufficient; but, says Temple, "if there were no History, or if History were other than in fact it is, the Eternal would not be what the Eternal is. . . . The historical is . . . a necessary self-expression of a Being whose essential activity is at once self-communication and self-discovery in that to which He communicates Himself." [2]

The thought of Karl Barth is particularly interesting on this issue because Barth in his tempestuous spiritual pilgrimage has tried various alternatives. In a famous self-characterization in 1921, he wrote: ". . . if I have a system, it is limited to what Kierkegaard called the 'infinite qualitative distinction' between time and eternity." [3] But as he became increasingly distrustful of existential philosophy and sought to rely more and more ex-

---

[2] William Temple, *Nature, Man and God*, pp. 447-48.
[3] *The Epistle to the Romans*, p. 10. The statement comes from the preface to the second edition. To those familiar with the later Barth, it is surprising to notice that he attributes many of the modifications in this major revision of his original work to the influence of Plato, Kant, and Kierkegaard.

clusively on the Bible, his viewpoint changed. The many echoes of Platonism increasingly dropped out of his thought. His homiletic writings stressed the gulf between God and man in terms of sin, not of metaphysics; and his systematic writings criticized his earlier works and took up more biblical conceptions.

In the later writings the human crisis is no longer conceived in such "vertical" terms as the permanent situation of crisis, in which history has no great significance in God's plan of salvation. The eventful character of history and the importance of time are taken more seriously. Not time and eternity, but this age and the coming age are contrasted. The drive toward the future shows itself in the stress on the future—expressed in the serious symbolism of the second coming of Christ. [4]

Barth now stands—strangely for him—in a mediating position. On the one hand are the theologians who lean toward the classical position; Temple, for instance, despite his insistence on the value of history, holds that "the Eternal is not successive." [5] On the other side is the contention of Oscar Cullmann, Barth's colleague at Basel, that the biblical view of time is strictly linear —an endless succession of aeons with no conception of eternity except that of endless duration. [6]

Barth answers these viewpoints by holding that God is eternal but that His eternity is not timeless. The very statement that *God reveals Himself* is equivalent to saying that *God has time for*

---

[4] *Credo*, pp. 72, 143–44 (Eng. tr., pp. 82, 166–67). The main shift in Barth's eschatology was paralleled or anticipated by the German theologians Paul Althaus and Karl Heim.

[5] *Nature, Man and God*, p. 447.

[6] Cullmann maintains that Barth still has not overcome the philosophical taint of conceiving a fundamental difference between time and eternity. See *Christ and Time*, esp. pp. 62–63. Barth's criticisms of Cullmann may be found in his *Kirchliche Dogmatik*, III/2, 532, 578ff. Cullmann's criticisms, if not entirely convincing, at least point out unintentionally that neither Barth nor Cullmann—nor any other theologian—can discuss theological problems without raising and taking a stand on philosophical issues.

us. The stumbling block of revelation is the belief in God in time, God in history. But this is exactly what theology must affirm: God's revelation is the event of Jesus Christ. The Word became flesh; the Word became time. In a typically expressive statement Barth cries out: "God would not be God for me if he were only eternal in himself, if he had no time for me." [7]

If God were time-less, He would have no *life*. Yet in His eternity, present, past, and future interpenetrate instead of succeeding one another. He is pre-temporal, super-temporal, and post-temporal. Or stated differently, eternity involves a simultaneity which does not exclude successiveness, and a successiveness which does not exclude simultaneity.[8]

If Barth's language is confusing, even contradictory, it is no more so than that of many a thinker who, mindful of the Kantian antinomies, has tried to analyze the significance of time. The rationalist can conceive eternity consistently in terms either of pure timelessness or of infinite duration. When the theologian rejects these alternatives, it is not out of a perverse love of paradox but out of a respect for the richness of historical experience which refuses to be bound by the rationalist's *a priori* categories. Historical experience, so obviously subject to time, nevertheless unites past and future experience in a partial but real simultaneity. In memory the past is not merely recollected; it becomes part of the present. Similarly purposes are not merely future intentions, but at any moment do much to create present actuality.

If man is able to say anything at all intelligible about the eternity which grounds and surrounds his existence, but which he cannot know, the statements must be in the form of inade-

---

[7] *Kirchliche Dogmatik*, III/2, 630. *Cf.* I/2, 54–68. *Cf.* Brunner, *Revelation and Reason*, pp. 403–404.
[8] *Ibid.*, III/1, 72; III/2, 524–25, 578. Brunner writes of "'the fullness of the time' in eternity" (*Man in Revolt*, p. 450); *cf. Christianity and Civilisation*, I, Ch. IV. See also Reinhold Niebuhr, *Faith and History*, Ch. III; Paul Tillich, *The Interpretation of History*, Part II, Ch. II and Part IV, Ch. III. Also, the Catholic thinkers considered in Ch. VI above.

quate symbols which have a greater existential than theoretical value. It is the conviction of faith that our fragmentary personal lives and our more inclusive but still fragmentary human history are completed in eternity. Completion must mean the transforming but not denying of the temporal and historical. This is the religious content of the more theoretical statements that eternity is neither succession nor timelessness, that it transforms temporality without annulling it.

B. CHRISTIAN SYMBOLISM: "ABOVE" AND "AT THE END"

The symbolism of Christian eschatology is not abstruse. It sprang from the life of a people. It was the natural language for which many a journalist reached in recent years when trying to express the significance of the release of atomic energy. But the symbolism makes difficulties when, as in recent theology, men wish to take it with full seriousness, at the same time avoiding literalistic illusions. The problem is evident in a thinker like Barth, whose writings reveal a great sophistication but frequently use biblical language in such a way as to give comfort to less imaginative literalists who hang on his words.

One attempt to avoid the errors of literal expectations has been to "platonize" eschatology, to place the Kingdom of God "above" history as a symbol of eternal truth and judgment, instead of in the future at the "end" of history. This tendency— the opposite of Barth's—manages to avoid certain literalistic misconceptions. But with the change in language comes a change in the interpretation of experience.

Thus Berdyaev, the most Platonic of any recent eschatological thinkers, wishes "to make the perspective of life independent of the fatal march of time, of the future which terrifies and torments us." Creativity and hope he finds in an "escape from time," a "victory over time." [9] His Eastern Orthodoxy comes closer to Protestant understandings when he says: "The Kingdom

[9] *The Destiny of Man*, p. 187. *The Meaning of History*, p. 200.

of God comes not only at the end of time but at every moment
. . . the paradox of eschatological consciousness is that the end is
both put off to an indefinite time in the future and is near to
every moment of life." But the main emphasis is on the "vertical"
relationship: "Eternity and eternal life come not in the future
but in a moment, *i.e.* they are a deliverance from time, and mean
ceasing to project life into time." [10]

Berdyaev's conception runs the risk of losing any sense of the
creativity of history and the directed character of historical time.
Actually as we analyze historical experience, we find it at any
given moment temporally incomplete. The political decisions of
any nation as well as the personal decisions of an individual have
much of their meaning in connection with a foreseeable future.
When the life of a person is cut off unexpectedly—particularly
the life of a child or youth—those who know that person experience a real sense of the incompleteness of the lost life. To a considerable degree this incompleteness is felt as something that
the future might have completed; plans might have been realized,
preparations ended with achievements. But in other aspects no
extent of time would realize the potentialities of the lost life;
continued existence would have brought frustration as well as
realization. And no imaginable increase in duration through an
endless time would change this incompleteness.

Here we have the justification for symbols of eternity which
include both the "future" and the "above." "Eternity," says Niebuhr, "stands over time on the one hand and at the end of time
on the other." [11] And, it may be added, the idea of "above"
is as much a symbol as the idea of the "future." Because of the
dominance of the Greek tradition in Western philosophy, many

---

[10] *The Destiny of Man*, pp. 368, 333. Paul Tillich can say with Berdyaev
that "the ultimate stands equally close to and equally distant from each
moment of history." (*The Interpretation of History*, p. 280.) But Tillich,
especially in his doctrine of *Kairos*, stresses also the dynamic character of
history.
[11] *The Nature and Destiny of Man*, II, 299.

a thinker who could not mention the "Last Judgment" without
a smirk can talk of "eternal values above history" in full seriousness. Actually, "above" has about the same reference to the
spatial arrangements of our solar system as the "end" has to our
calendars. Neither symbol is any more intellectually respectable
than the other. The symbol of "above," with its appeal to universality, admittedly has attracted many of the great minds in
the history of human thought. But some of these same minds, as
von Hügel reminded us, have had a corresponding difficulty in
doing justice to the particular. The eschatological symbols do
justice to the dynamic aspects of history submerged by the Platonic symbolism. There is religious profundity in Spinoza's
view of life *sub specie aeternitatis*; but there is not the biblical
sense of the forward thrust of history.

C. CHRIST AND THE FUTURE

The Christian future is always conceived in terms of the
Christ who has come. Memory and anticipation illumine the
present. The double emphasis is expressed in a document of
the World Council of Churches:

The Christian faith leaves no room for . . . despair, being based on the
fact that the Kingdom of God is firmly established in Christ and
will come by God's act despite all human failure.[12]

The point is not simply that Christ has inspired men to transform history. The history which crucified Christ continues largely
in its crucifying ways. But to confront Christ is to find the one
focus which brings the blurred events of history into meaningful
significance; He is the revelation of the God who originates history and ends it. The "cross of Christ," as Tillich describes it, is
"the event of history, in which this divine judgment over the
world became concrete and manifest."[13] As the understanding

[12] Report of Section II, on "The Church and the Disorder of Society."
First Assembly of the World Council of Churches, Amsterdam, 1948.
[13] *The Interpretation of History*, p. 32.

of history requires some perspective or viewpoint, Christ furnishes a point of absolute significance, which is not another ideology, conformable to our wishes, but a judgment on our ideologies.

The significance of Christ is sometimes expressed in doctrines of "realized eschatology," which take several forms. In the thought of C. H. Dodd, Christianity finds "the fulfilment of history in an actual series of events within history—namely the life, death and resurrection of Jesus Christ, and the emergence of the church as the bearer of his Spirit . . . in the coming of Christ we have the conclusive entrance of God into history, which prophecy and apocalypse had associated with the End." Dodd thoroughly subordinates the element of expectancy in Christian thought. "The Kingdom of God is not something yet to come. It came with Jesus Christ, and in its coming was perceived to be eternal in its quality." [14] The emphasis usually given to the return of Christ at the *parousia* is here transferred to the church, which gains a semi-Catholic significance. Protestant historical thought by and large, though it has been placing increased importance on the church, refuses to go to the extent of Dodd.

A difficult but influential conception of realized eschatology is found in the thought of Barth and many influenced by him. It is expressed in the formula that the reconciliation of the world is "*already accomplished* in Jesus Christ but is *still hidden*." [15] Despite Barth's great emphasis on the eschatological fulfillment of history in the future, the sovereignty of Christ in the present is to be taken with absolute seriousness:

---

[14] *The Kingdom of God and History* (Oxford Conference Book), pp. 25–26, 37. Cf. *History and the Gospel, Parables of the Kingdom.* An extreme realized eschatology is expressed by Martin Wight, who regards history since Christ as an "epilogue." *The Ecumenical Review*, I (1948), 38.
[15] *The Knowledge of God and the Service of God*, p. 236.

... although at present the glory of the Kingdom of God is held out to us only as a hope, yet the Kingly Rule of Christ extends not merely over the Church as the congregation of the faithful but, regardless of whether men believe or not, over the whole of the universe in all its heights and depths; and it also confronts and over-rules with sovereign dignity the principalities and powers and evil spirits of this world.[16]

From this point of view neither the proportions of the victory, which is cosmic in scope, nor the reality of the continuing struggle may be overlooked. Faith discerns that the decisive events are past; but the enemy must still be fought and many do not realize that the climax has come.

It may be asked whether it does not confuse the issues of history to emphasize a *cosmic* victory, and to insist that Christ is in actuality King over a world which defies him and in which only the faithful can discern His reign. There can be no doubt that this is the intellectual form of a faith which in Europe grew powerful under persecution. But recent theology in general would find more agreement with the World Council statement quoted above, or with Barth's unelaborated statement that "He who is to come is no other than He who was and who is."[17] However the expressions and emphases may vary, the Christian confidence concerning history is always a confidence in a Kingdom which has come in Christ, but which awaits its consummation in God's future act.

V. THE KINGDOM OF GOD AND HUMAN CULTURE

How important, in the last analysis, is the history of politics and culture? Nations and cultures come and go. None lasts forever. Are they, therefore, in the last analysis unimportant to

---

[16] *A Letter to Great Britain*, in *This Christian Cause*. In addition to Barth, see Gustaf Aulén, *Christus Victor* (tr. by A. G. Hebert. London: S. P. C. K., 1931); Visser 't Hooft, *The Kingship of Christ*, Ch. V; Karl Löwith, *Meaning in History*, pp. 188–89.

[17] *Kirchliche Dogmatik*, III/2, 588.

God's purposes? Or is part of the divinely given meaning of history expressed in them?

At one extreme Karl Löwith writes:

> As an eschatological message of the Kingdom of God the theology of the New Testament is essentially unconcerned with the political history of this world. . . . Such a theological understanding of the history of mankind cannot be translated into world-historical terms. . . . World-historical establishments and upheavals miss the ultimate reality of the Christian hope and expectation . . . the message of the New Testament is not an appeal to historical action but to repentance.[1]

Critics of such a statement should remember that the man who sees the "meaning of history as the meaning of suffering by historical action"[2] may be better prepared to bear historical responsibility than one who has fed on false hopes. However, the main stream of Protestant thought would reject Löwith's viewpoint.

From the opposite wing Emil Brunner, in his Gifford Lectures, declares that Christianity can enter into the life of a culture as part of its "culture-transcendent presuppositions" and thereby influence all aspects of the thought and activity of a people. The transcendent Kingdom of God can never be identified with any historical social order; there cannot be, for example, a "Christian Europe" in any full meaning of the phrase. Yet "in the course of some fifteen centuries something like a Christion civilisation has been created."[3] That is, Christianity, even in superficial and impure forms, has so formed the consciousness of Western culture that unique conceptions of individual personality, of justice and community, even of metaphysical issues, are assumed even where Christianity is not explicitly accepted. Brunner's ethics has always assumed that a religious-cultural

---

[1] *Meaning in History*, pp. 189, 196.
[2] *Ibid.*, p. 3.
[3] *Christianity and Civilisation*, I, 4–5, 1.

dualism is as untenable as a soul-body dualism, and that the Kingdom of God, though in no sense a "goal of culture" does enter into cultural history.

Between Brunner and Löwith lies a wide range of judgments. Perhaps the broadest and most profound theological appreciation of the whole of culture has come from Paul Tillich. Typically reinterpreting traditional concepts in non-traditional language, Tillich gives the following definition:

> The Kingdom of God is a symbolic expression of the ultimate meaning of existence. The socal and political character of this symbol indicates a special relation between the ultimate meaning of existence and the ultimate meaning of human history.[4]

Thus the significance of eschatology cannot be limited to any narrowly defined "religious" area. Aesthetic, philosophic, and mystical experiences may offer glimpses of the Kingdom. His breadth of outlook and freedom in reinterpreting biblical concepts have made Tillich the *bête noire* of continental theologians, for whom it is amusing that he is sometimes called "neo-orthodox" in America. But Tillich is more distinctively Christian than he sometimes seems to European theologians. History "is ultimately to be interpreted in terms of salvation." "Salvation is actualized in history whenever a demonic power in social or individual existence is overcome by the divine power which has become visible in Christ." But historical salvation is only fragmentary. "Primarily and above all salvation is judgment passed upon world history."[5]

Eschatology gets its most direct reference to history through Tillich's concept of *Kairos*—the New Testament word used to stand for meaning-filled time. Although the appearance of Jesus the Christ represents the unique and non-recurring *Kairos*, there are other periods of special *Kairos*. These are the times of

[4] *The Kingdom of God and History* (Oxford Conference Book), p. 116.
[5] *Ibid.*, pp. 120, 124.

creative possibility, recognizable not by general criteria but only by a semi-mystical "daring faith."

To the pragmatic American mind, accustomed to look for the practical possibilities in every situation, this doctrine has some difficulties. Tillich is right if he is suggesting that a far-reaching creative movement, like the Renaissance or the Reformation, cannot be launched simply by raising funds, appointing committees, and getting radio time. Similarly, primitive tribalism does not flower into civilization simply by trying. There is a "grace" of the situation which makes possible great cultural achievements, whether individual or social. But it is too negative to say, as Tillich does now:

Instead of a creative *kairos*, I see a vacuum which can be made creative only if it is accepted and endured and, rejecting all kinds of premature solutions, is transformed into a deepening "sacred void" of waiting. This view naturally implies a decrease of my participation in political activities.[6]

One might better recognize that, however uncreative our decade may be, Congress is continuously debating proposals of incalculable effect on future history. And Christian faith always faces unlimited opportunities to express itself in social life.

Barth is perhaps right in saying that Tillich has been too much determined by "the pseudo-eschatological 'situation' of the years immediately after the [First World] War."[7] But Barth's own doctrine, which allows theology to say nothing about many political events, until the sudden moment when it must give an unequivocal *Yes* or *No*, is subject to the identical criticism.

---

[6] "Beyond Religious Socialism," *The Christian Century*, LXVI (1949), 733. The doctrine of *Kairos* is developed in *The Interpretation of History*, Part II, Ch. II.

[7] *Church Dogmatics*, I/1, 83. Tillich uses the expectant fervor of the German religious socialist movement following the First World War as his principal illustration of a "special *Kairos*." May it not be that as he probably overestimated the potentialities of that period, he may be underestimating the present?

The curious twists of Barth's own thought, since his early dissatisfaction with religious socialism, are understandable only when traced historically.[8] A professor at Bonn, Barth responded to the Hitler menace with a series of bold pamphlets entitled *Theologische Existenz Heute,* starting in June, 1933. Explicitly assuming the lawful authority of the government, Barth said nothing about wrong politics as such. His scathing journalism attacked the group of churchmen, known as "German Christians," who perverted the Gospel and church organization to give political support to the Nazi movement. The job of the church was simply to proclaim God's Gospel, said Barth, and the duty of theological professors was to ignore the government and go on teaching as if nothing had happened.

Barth was a principal inspirer of the Confessional Church's Barmen Declaration of 1934, which on theological grounds affirmed boldly the Lordship of Christ and denied final loyalty to any earthly ruler. In 1935 the government dismissed Barth from Bonn, for insubordination—particularly for refusing to take the oath of allegiance without qualification. That same year in lectures in Holland (dedicated to resisting pastors) Barth announced: "The Lordship of Christ is not only a so-called religious Lordship; as that, it is very much an ethical, yes, a political Lordship."[9]

This doctrine of Christ's Lordship was amplified in the Gifford Lectures of 1937–38. Although the state's only duty to the church is that of providing *freedom,* the church claims "the political order as an order *for the service of God.*"[10] A pamphlet in 1938 declared that the church should not regard state politics

---

[8] Visser 't Hooft summarizes the major shift toward increasing social responsibility in Barth's doctrinal thought. (*The Kingship of Christ,* pp. 38–53.) My account will deal with Barth's practical response to historical situations.

[9] *Credo,* p. 52 (Eng. tr., p. 56).

[10] *The Knowledge of God and the Service of God,* p. 221. Cf. pp. 218–32.

as "a night in which all cats are grey," and announced that the state belongs in the Christological sphere, being established on the doctrine of justification.[11]

As the Nazi military threat mounted, Barth startled the theological world with his letter to Professor Hromadka of Czechoslovakia. In stirring language he expressed his hope that the sons of the Hussites would show flabby Europe, paralyzed by pacifism, that there were still men in the world. To those accustomed to Barth's insistence on the absolute transcendence of the divine, the next words came with a shock:

Every Czech soldier who fights *will do this also for us and—I say it with all reservation—he will do it also for the Church of Christ.*[12]

Despite sharp criticism from friends and foes, Barth refused to backtrack on the statement.

The theme was continued in a group of letters to French Protestants, to Great Britain, and to American Christians.[13] Addressing the British in 1941, Barth objected to fighting the war in the name of Western civilization, social justice, or freedom;

[11] *Church and State* (tr. of *Rechtfertigung und Recht*), pp. 31–34, 44. The "Christocentric doctrine of the state" is described by Visser 't Hooft, *The Kingship of Christ*, pp. 135–39. The doctrine represents a startling reversal of much continental thought, especially Lutheran. The denial of any general revelation or natural law, providing standards of political morality, leads to the appeal to the Gospel as the basis of the state and justice. The doctrine has difficulties when only a minority of citizens are, in any precise sense, Christians. Brunner criticizes it in *Justice and the Social Order*, pp. 271–72.

[12] Written in September, 1938. Reported by E. G. Homrighausen in *The Christian Century*, LVI (1939), 678. Barth reaffirmed the language in a lecture in December on *The Church and the Political Problem of Our Day*.

[13] During these years Barth joined a secret Swiss defense organization and cooperated in the care of refugees, especially Jews. At the age of 54 he became an armed soldier, doing sentry duty on the border, completing a tour of duty as a captain in 1942. See S. M. Cavert's introduction, *The Church and the War*; Barth, "How My Mind Has Changed," *The Christian Century*, LXVI (1949), 299.

rather the reason was "simply the resurrection of Jesus Christ."
Resistance to Hitler finds "a really sure foundation only when we
resist him unequivocally in the name of Jesus Christ." After
these words it may seem a fine distinction to state emphatically
that "the church" does not wage war and that this war is not a
crusade waged in behalf of the Kingdom of God.

Is there any rationale to explain this violent shift? Barth
thinks so. He opposed Nazism not primarily because it was a
bad government (although he did not hesitate to call the roll of
its sins); basically national socialism was idolatry, claiming to be
"a *religious institution of salvation*." At the moment when an
earthly sovereignty demands final allegiance and acknowledges
no God except itself, the First Commandment immediately assumes a political significance. The message of the absolute transcendence of God over all political causes suddenly, with seem-
ing contradiction, becomes a political message. Then political
decisions become unequivocal:

Is this choice a political one? . . . Yes; by all means it is a political
choice: It is a choice where I would rather say 'No' with the crudest
democratically-minded fellow citizen than 'Yes' or 'Yes and No' with
the most pious fellow Christian! What is a choice of faith if it never
becomes a political choice? [14]

Prophetically Barth said at this very time that after Hitler
his attitude might seem to revert to the old one. This is exactly
what has happened. In his famous address to the Assembly of
the World Council of Churches at Amsterdam, 1948, Barth
proclaimed "God's design" as the Kingdom established in Christ.

Should we not see that 'God's design' therefore does not mean the
existence of the church in the world, its task in relation to the
world's disorder, its outward and inward activity as an instrument
for the amelioration of human life, or finally the result of this

---

[14] *The Church and the Political Problem of Our Day*, pp. 41, 58. Cf.
"How My Mind Has Changed in This Decade," *The Christian Century*,
LVI (1939), 1134.

activity in the Christianization of all humanity and, consequently, the setting up of an order of justice and peace embracing our whole planet? [15]

We can agree when Barth castigates the opinion "that man is the Atlas who is destined to bear the dome of heaven on his shoulders." But we wonder when he wishes to reject "every thought that the care of the church, the care of the world is *our* care." What was it but such care when Barth urged the Czech soldier to fight *"for the Church of Christ"*?

Reinhold Niebuhr, while paying tribute to Barth for his rediscovery of the "final pinnacle of the Christian faith and hope," criticizes him for ignoring the foot hills in which most of history is lived. Acknowledging the contributions of his theology to the crisis of the struggle against tyranny, Niebuhr finds it irresponsible now, offering no guidance for Christian statesmanship.[16]

Niebuhr himself has consistently held that Christian love, although not in itself a social and political program, is relevant to every level of human experience. God's Kingdom is not attainable in history; it is genuinely eschatological. But, says Niebuhr: "Ideally the faith and hope by which the church lives sharpen rather than annul its responsibility for seeking to do the will of God amid all the tragic moral ambiguities of history." [17]

In his volume, *Faith and History*, Niebuhr affirms that faith brings genuine renewals of individual and collective life and is thus constantly significant for the historical situation. Further, there are no fixed limits to the possibilities of solving problems of politics, economics, or world organization—any of the specific problems which arise in history. But conflict, sin, and the fragmentary character of all historical meaning—all these remain. Every claim to overcome them is an idolatry. So eschatological

---

[15] *The Christian Century*, LXV (1948), 1330.
[16] "We Are Men and Not God," *The Christian Century*, LXV (1948), 1138–40.
[17] *Faith and History*, p. 238.

faith is required to save history from pretense and to offer the fulfillment which history itself cannot produce.

Clearly one cannot generalize glibly about the relation of the Kingdom of God to history in contemporary thought. On specific issues there are stern, perhaps dangerous, conflicts. Yet there is wide agreement on the basic proposition, as enunciated at the First Assembly of the World Council of Churches, that in Christ "God has established His Kingdom and its gates stand open for all who will enter. Their lives belong to God with a certainty that no disorder of society can destroy, and on them is laid the duty to seek God's Kingdom and His righteousness." [18]

---

[18] Report of Section III: "The Church and the Disorder of Society."

CHAPTER VIII

TOYNBEE'S MODERN SYNTHESIS

NOTABLE among recent attempts to draw together the frayed strands of the thread of history is Arnold Toynbee's imposing philosophy of history. The grandeur of its scope, the breadth of its scholarship, and the timeliness of its concern for the survival of present civilization have all contributed to its dramatic influence.

Worked out over a period of years,[1] Toynbee's thought includes suggestions of many interpretations of history, with acknowledged indebtedness to classicism and the Bible. In the most general terms it emphasizes two diverse but equally evident aspects of history: first, a number of movements in varied forms of rise and decline—of communities, states, civilizations; second, certain lines of continuity which run through the patterns of rise

---

[1] The plan for *A Study of History* (London: Oxford University Press) was jotted down on half a sheet of paper in 1922. The full work was sketched out in 1927–28 (*SH*, IV, viii). The first three volumes, covering the geneses and growths of civilizations, were published in 1934 (revised edition, 1935). The second three volumes, on the breakdowns and disintegrations of civilizations, appeared in 1939. Toynbee's duties in the British Foreign Office during the war interrupted his work, but in 1948 he published *Civilization on Trial* (London: Oxford University Press), a collection of essays, most of them written during the previous year. These and a few still later essays, and his Bampton Lectures in America (delivered at Columbia University, April, 1948), offer clues to the further development of his philosophy of history. He is now working on a final three volumes of *A Study of History*.

and fall, lines which in at least some cases take a progressive direction. As Toynbee develops these themes and their interrelations, suggestions emerge of three different philosophies of history: (1) the theme of challenge-response, in a cyclical setting; (2) the theme of general, though not constant, progress; (3) the ecclesiastical-apocalyptic theme. The three, and the possibility of a consistent relationship among them, require investigation.

I. CYCLES WITHOUT DETERMINISM

Toynbee's first and most obvious interpretation of history is his famous stress on challenge and response. It leads to a cyclical interpretation of history, which generally follows classical patterns, except that there is no necessity involved in it. Civilizations are not biological organisms, ordained to grow and decay. Rather a civilization rises when a society responds successfully to a challenge of environment, physical or social. It continues to develop as long as it faces successive challenges with creative responses. The time comes when, usually because of too great rigidity, it fails to make creative responses, clinging instead to some "ephemeral technique" or "institution" which has served it in the past but does not answer its new difficulties. Its "creative minority," which once inspired society with its leadership, becomes a "dominant minority," trying to browbeat society into obedience. Plagued by problems of war and class, the civilization moves toward death. A "time of troubles" is usually met by a "universal state" which postpones the decay but finally itself succumbs.

But in all this there is no necessity of cultural death; civilizations die "by suicide." Their possibilities of growth are actually limitless; there are no bounds upon the progress which society may achieve. At times Toynbee becomes quite voluntaristic, and we get the impression that the real meaning of history is found in creative response to challenge. The odds are strong that any civilization will come to its time of failure, as evidenced by the fact that almost all of them have.[1] But we need not succumb:

we are not compelled to submit our fate to the blind arbitrament of statistics. The divine spark of creative power is instinct in ourselves; and if we have the grace to kindle it into flame, then the stars in their courses cannot defeat our efforts to attain the goal of human endeavors.[2]

A renewal of religion might save our own civilization from paralysis in the face of challenges. The immediate challenge to our contemporary civilization is to solve the problems of war and class, and "put the secular super-structure back onto religious foundations."[3]

At other times the voluntarism, though still evident, is more qualified. In an apt, but somewhat enigmatic statement, Toynbee expresses the belief that "with God's help, man is master of his own destiny, at least to some extent in some respects."[4]

In this cyclical interpretation, then, each civilization has its opportunity to work out its own salvation. Unlike Spengler, Toynbee allows for civilizations to influence each other in many ways, but each is responsible for its own inner life. Usually each follows the cycle which seems set for all, but there is always the possibility of creatively breaking the typical pattern.

Two questions are raised by this theme in Toynbee's interpretation of history. First, does history disclose such neat pat-

---

[1] SH, IV, 122 (S, p. 276).
[2] SH, IV, 39 (S, p. 254). Cf. V, 22 (S, p. 367). More recently, writing on the theme, "Can Western Civilization Save Itself?", Toynbee says that on a statistical basis, analogous to that of life insurance, our risk is high; but, emphatically rejecting determinism, he says that we are not fated to perish. Commentary, VII (1949), 103–10. Cf. "Does History Repeat Itself?", in CT. (The answer is that it does, but does not have to.)
[3] CT, p. 39. For the hope of a saving religious revival see SII, V, 193–94 (S, pp. 402–403); VI, 320–31 (S, p. 554).
[4] CT, p. 30.

terns? At times Toynbee makes great allowance for the variety of history. By considering all sorts of geographical, social, and spiritual factors, he attains a much broader interpretation than the single-track schemes of a Marx or Spencer. And by emphasizing contacts between civilizations, with their infinite variety of outcome, he avoids the rigid schematism and arbitrary pronouncements of Spengler. Yet the result is an over-all pattern which is so nearly a stylized blue-print that the civilizations can be lined up in parallel columns with their main events pigeon-holed in proper places.

The schematism becomes particularly rigid when Toynbee traces the decline of a civilization through the process of routs and rallies. While making no claim for absolute universality, he finds a "standard run" to consist of three and a half beats: rout-rally-rout-rally-rout-rally-final rout. But can the infinite variety of history, with the multitude of causes that contribute to the downfall of civilizations, be so confined in a scheme?[5] A great many historians here find Toynbee's system entirely too conventionalized, and even the amateur must wonder whether the materials of history fit the mould so exactly.

The second question concerns Toynbee's belief that civilizations die by suicide. Are civilizations never simply crushed by the superior power of a militant foe? In those cases where a civilization has been destroyed, Toynbee usually tries to show

---

[5] The reader of Toynbee, who is naturally interested in trying to discern his own historical destiny through Toynbee's analysis, finds himself baffled at one especially obvious point. In Toynbee's scheme the second and most evident rally is the formation of a universal state which establishes a *Pax Oecumenica*. Toynbee states emphatically that our Western civilization, now in its "time of troubles," has not reached the point of its universal state. (*SH*, IV, 3–4; VI, 314ff.) But in his table of universal states one finds Western civilization credited with two universal states— the Napoleonic Empire and the Danubian Hapsburg Monarchy—each with its *Pax Oecumenica* (VI, 327). The latter suggestion with all its implications leads to a more pluralistic and less schematic view of Western civilization than Toynbee usually gives.

that it had already passed the critical point of breakdown. Somewhere in its previous history he finds a critical error. But on Toynbee's own doctrine of "original sin," we can expect to find evil in a society at any time we choose to inspect it. So it is not surprising that in any case of the destruction of a civilization, inspection will disclose some prior inner failure. Many would agree when Toynbee argues against Gibbon that the failure of Rome came well before the Golden Age of the Antonines. But sometimes the flaw in a civilization seems hardly commensurate with the penalty of destruction.[6]

II. A LARGER PROGRESSIVE DESTINY

The second theme is suggested early in *A Study of History* but developed especially in the second three volumes, where Toynbee deals with the disintegrations of civilizations and is forced to ask whether they serve any purpose. Here he suggests that the cyclic movement of civilizations may be like the movement of the wagon wheel which, by describing its circle around the hub, carries forward the wagon. In such a way the rise and fall of civilizations may carry forward some larger destiny. In nature the "sombre cycle of birth and reproduction and death has made possible the evolution of all the higher animals up to Man himself." The repetitive movement of the weaver's shuttle carries along the development of the pattern. So it may be that the major movement of history "is not recurrent but is progressive."[1]

At this stage Toynbee does not describe in any detail what this major movement may be, except to call it, in some sense,

---

[6] The Dutch historian P. Geyl finds Toynbee's evidence unconvincing on the theme of "suicide" and attributes the interpretation to a "distaste for the idea that spirit should succumb to violence." Geyl's well-known critique of Toynbee makes several incisive criticisms. It should not be overlooked, however, that Geyl has his peculiar set of presuppositions no less than does Toynbee. See Geyl, Toynbee, and Sorokin, *The Pattern of the Past.*

[1] *SH*, IV, 36–37 (*S*, pp. 253–54).

"the process of civilization." When Toynbee thinks in these more progressive terms he subordinates his stress on the twenty-one individual civilizations to a new pattern of three successive generations of civilizations.[2] Through these three generations there has been a development, aided by advances in technology and communication, toward the unity of mankind. The major event of our age, when viewed in retrospect, will be its first step "towards the unification of mankind into one single society."[3] So far is this from a cyclic occurrence doomed to probable destruction that Townbee suggests that future mankind may have difficulty even conceiving the parochialism in which we live.

In this new situation mankind may evolve a system of world order—not the "universal state" of the past in which a strong ruler has imposed order on a usually grateful people to stall off the disintegration of their civilization, but a genuinely cooperative achievement. For example, there is the prospect that even a partial success of the United Nations "might open out quite new prospects for mankind, prospects that we have never sighted before during these last five or six thousand years that have seen us making a number of attempts at civilization."[4] By the challenge of the present social crisis we "might be stimulated to invent something quite new in the field of international politics or of social affairs in general—to rise to some quite new standard of good behavior that would transform the situation to such an extent that these precedents [of past cycles] would cease to be relevant to our case."[5]

Occasionally, though not often, Toynbee becomes quite romantic in his future hopes. Usually a severe critic of common progress theories, he can sometimes echo them with the best of moderns. He hopes that we may reach a "stage of social progress"

[2] SH, I, 172–73 (S, p. 42). CT, pp. 225–52.
[3] CT, p. 216.
[4] CT, p. 128.
[5] Commentary, VII (1949), 108.

where war will be utterly obsolete—where "physical warfare of one man against another will have been translated into a spiritual warfare of all men united in the service of God against the powers of evil."[6]

The two themes we have found so far in Toynbee are not necessarily contradictory. They correspond to the much less precise popular view that history moves along with its ups and downs, but making a net gain. Yet the reader of Toynbee cannot avoid the impression of strikingly different moods in his cyclicism and his progressivism.

III. ECCLESIASTICAL FUTURISM

Related to the second theme, yet quite different in substance, is a third one. Its elaboration is promised for the final three volumes of the *magnum opus*. But enough suggestions of it have been offered that we can begin to plot its curve.

In the closing pages of the published portion of *A Study of History* Toynbee deals with the combined repetitive-progressive theme and suggests that history is the work of a mighty weaver with purposes not immediately obvious. As civilizations are woven together and then unravelled, perhaps some debris of the process, some by-product, may prove to be the important result. Possibly we may find "the birth of something new, and not just the rebirth of something that has lived and died any number of times already."[1] And Toynbee indicates that the clue is to be found in the universal churches formed in dying civilizations. The clue is followed up most thoroughly—and most speculatively—in the famous Burge Lecture of 1940, where Toynbee probes for the ultimate meaning of history, especially in the decline of civilizations.[2]

---

[6] *SH*, IV, 649. Cf. *SH*, I, 464.
[1] *SH*, VI, 324; cf. p. 174 (*S*, pp. 556–57, 532). Cf. *CT*, p. 159.
[2] Toynbee points out sometimes that the lecture was delivered at a portentous hour of history when earthly hopes were quite insecure. (The

Toynbee had long held the theory that a disintegrating civilization falls into three groups: a dominant minority (the creative minority with its creativity gone), an external proletariat, and an internal proletariat. (Proletariat refers not simply to an economic group but to any people who are "in but not of" a civilization.) The internal proletariat, stimulated by suffering, creates a higher religion and a universal church. The religion is often the product of an encounter between civilizations (e.g., Christianity, of encounter between Syriac and Graeco-Roman worlds). The universal church, Toynbee held in his first three volumes, may serve the function of preserving the life and the heritage of the old while it forms the womb for a new civilization. Now Toynbee rejects this "rather patronizing view." He finds evidence that the relation between religions and civilizations varies in different generations of civilizations—that fully developed higher religions develop only between civilizations of the second and third generations.

From this point Toynbee moves to the bold thesis that the rise and fall of civilizations is subsidiary to the growth of religion, as ages of suffering bring new insight.

If religion is a chariot, it looks as if the wheels on which it mounts towards Heaven may be the periodic downfalls of civilizations on Earth. It looks as if the movement of civilizations may be cyclic and recurrent, while the movement of religion may be on a single continuous upward line. The continuous upward movement of

---

date, May 23, 1940, was about ten days prior to completion of the evacuation of Dunkirk.) But the basic ideas are reaffirmed in a 1947 introduction to a pamphlet edition of the lecture. This introduction frankly states that the author is going beyond any empirical evidence, seeking guidance, as man has always done, by faith. *Christianity and Civilization* (Wallingford, Pa.: Pendle Hill, 1947), pp. 6–7. The essay has also been reprinted in *CT*. Further references will be to this latter printing.

religion may be served and promoted by the cyclic movement of
civilizations round the cycle of birth, death, birth.[3]

The thesis is audacious enough that a theologian would
scarcely dare offer it. It is worth noting that Whitehead had
written fifteen years before: Religion "is the one element in
human experience which persistently shows an upward trend.
. . . The fact of the religious vision, and its history of persistent
expansion, is our one ground for optimism. Apart from it, human
life is a flash of occasional enjoyments lighting up a mass of pain
and misery, a bagatelle of transient experience."[4]

Toynbee's theory of religious progress, however, is considerably more novel than Whitehead's. He goes on to suggest that
civilization, having produced the higher religions, has done its
job. Perhaps our Western civilization is simply a thrice-told tale,
a vain repetition of the past, and its disintegration should not
worry us greatly. Nor need we expect it to produce another
higher religion,[5] for that task of civilization has been accom-

---

[3] CT, p. 236. In SH, IV, 585–88, Toynbee had thrown out the question,
for a later answer, of whether the breakdown of civilizations is a true
catastrophe. The essay, "My View of History," suggests that the cycles
of civilization carry forward a divine plan as "the learning that comes
through the suffering caused by the failure of civilizations may be the
sovereign means of progress." (CT, p. 15.) The theme of learning
through suffering, taken from Aeschylus, and often interpreted bibli-
cally, is a basic one in Toynbee. See SH, I, 271–99 (S, pp. 60–67).

[4] Science and the Modern World, p. 47. Herbert Butterfield cogently
argues the direct opposite of Toynbee's thesis: "And neither do I know
of any mundane fulness of life which we could pretend to possess and
which was not open to people in the age of Isaiah or Plato, Dante or
Shakespeare." Christianity and History, p. 66.

[5] In A Study of History Toynbee had already commented on the fact
that Western civilization in its decline seemed to be producing no out-
standing new religion. He suggested that the reason might be that, despite the persistent efforts of Western secularism to get rid of it, Christianity still flowed in the veins of the West. Ubiquitous and protean, its
influence has been evident even in the movements which challenged it.
And among the American Negroes it had found new life within a group
of the Western internal proletariat. SH, V, 188–94 (S, pp. 400–403).

plished. Perhaps the function of Western civilization will be to furnish the world-wide society in which Christianity, fructified by the best in other higher religions, may be left as the heir of all religions.

Most startling of all is the idea that "the Christian Church as an institution may be left as the social heir of all the other churches *and all the civilizations.*"[6] This raises a number of puzzling questions. Are religions or churches in any sense alternatives to civilizations, or are they rather not incommensurable with civilizations? Living in a given civilization, I can choose which church (if any) I wish to unite with. Or, within a given church, I can even choose a civilization. And, belonging to a church and a civilization, I can choose which will have my primary loyalty, or how they will share my loyalty. But how can I make any religion or church take the place of a civilization?

An answer has previously been suggested in *A Study of History,* with its hint that universal churches may be "representatives of another species of society which is at least as distinct from the species 'Civilizations' as the civilizations are distinct from primitive societies."[7] Clearly this must be a visible, institutional church. It is, very baldly, a church which will take over the still necessary functions of Caesar—a church of sacrament and hierarchy, of the tough and enduring forms of Catholicism.

What are we to make of this new species of society? In the absence of any real evidence that history is moving in this direction, we may ask whether such a development would be desirable. Toynbee had once written of the stultifying effect of the dominance of a universal church. He had shown great admiration for the medieval Roman church, but had seen its disastrous error to be Hildebrand's taking of the sword.[8] How will his projected

---

[6] *CT,* p. 240. Italics mine. *Cf.* a more recent statement that the future of mankind lies with the higher religions rather than with the civilizations which have given them birth. *CT,* p. 159.

[7] V, 23 (S, p. 368); *cf.* IV, 350 n. 2.

[8] *SH,* I, 474; IV, 537–38, 545–46 (S, pp. 353–55).

church avoid these two errors, if it is to be an institutional church replacing civilization and still providing somehow for the work of Caesar? One might imagine many a heretic and pagan gasping for a breath of fresh air in this milieu. And one might wonder whether such heretics and pagans might not sometimes be the publicans and sinners who will enter the Kingdom of God before the orthodox.

This ecclesiastical theme in Toynbee stands in striking contrast to other themes. Once Toynbee talked of the possibility of a couple billion more civilizations rising and falling, like the twenty-one thus far, during the life of man on earth.[9] Now he sees the succession of civilizations giving way to a single universal church, with no mention of its decline and fall. Once it seemed that a new breath of religion might revitalize our Western civilization and save it from the doom which had confronted all others. Now it seems that such a service would be no favor, since it would prolong what is destined to be an obsolete form of social organization. The Promethean theme of struggle to meet new challenges has given way to an ecclesiastical hope that feeds on the failures of civilizations to meet their challenges. Nor are these contrasts simply between old and new ideas in Toynbee. In his recent essays we find some of his most voluntaristic statements, in which penetrating logic and ardent hope look for the means of saving this civilization.

We must not apply too rigid a logic to a philosophy which is still in development. Some of Toynbee's earlier apparent inconsistencies have been brought into coherent synthesis, and we must wait for the completion of *A Study of History* to make any final judgment. Further, Toynbee is on the edge of certain fundamental problems of religion which are in no case easily answered. To demand relentless consistency may be to use the foolish logic of Paul's opponents who urged sin that grace might abound

---

[9] *SH*, I, 462–64; IV, 10.

more exceedingly.[10] Yet clearly there are contrasts here which raise difficult problems.

IV. THE UNRESOLVED PROBLEM IN TOYNBEE

For Toynbee salvation is quite clearly the issue of history. As in every Christian interpretation the crucial problem is that of relating the Kingdom of God to history, salvation to the course of events.

At this point Toynbee's analysis presents a marked contrast: the life of the spirit differs decisively in its relation *to the rise* and *to the fall* of civilization. The advance of a civilization involves a spiritual *elan* within the creative minority, which responds magnificently to challenges and refuses to petrify. The decline of a civilization demands an act of grace redeeming the suffering of history. The rise of civilization glorifies the heroic and military virtues (though they alone may not be adequate); the fall glorifies the Christian virtues.

The growing civilization moves forward with the creative spirit that is only intensified by obstacles, whether physical or social. War is one of Toynbee's most common examples. Militarism, if overdone, is fatal; and the criterion of growth of a civilization is never conquest of its external environment (physical or social), but progress in increasing self-determination.[1]

---

[10] To use a remark which was not intended for publication, I may mention a conversation in which I asked Toynbee how he reconciled a double emphasis that runs through his writings: (1) that we may, by heroic striving to meet our problems, avoid a disaster to this civilization; (2) that the decline of this civilization is merely a thrice-told tale whose only value is to lead us through suffering to deeper religious insight. With his typical sincerity and openness, Toynbee would not claim to have a complete answer. But the Christian, he suggested, will always feel a social responsibility and a genuine desire to struggle for the well-being of society and civilization. On the other hand, when history confronts him with tragedy, he will find in it the means to a closer approach to God.
[1] SH, III, 174–217 (S, pp. 198–208).

Nevertheless military strength and heroism are almost always necessary.[2]

But for the declining civilization militarism is suicidal and the sword is utterly useless, except to prolong the uncreative universal state. They that take the sword, however circumspect their intentions, are sure to perish by the sword. The Christian God of redemption is the source of salvation for disintegrating civilizations, whereas the Promethean spirit is the creative force in rising civilizations. Considering the rise of civilizations, Toynbee is largely Pelagian, stressing the power of the active, indomitable will; when he turns to the fall of civilizations, he becomes Augustinian. (Thus the first three volumes have the biblical motto: "Work . . . while it is day." For the second three the motto changes: "Except the Lord keep the city, the watchman waketh but in vain.") The two viewpoints are linked by the fact that *hybris* or the *sin* of pride is always disastrous, but the differing emphases are clear.

Since every rising civilization faces the threat, usually the actuality, of disintegration and death, the issue of salvation is most critical in the time of decline. Here Toynbee discusses dramatically the succession of would-be saviors who appear. There is the savior *of* society—the savior with the sword, the most futile of all the candidates. There are the various saviors *from* society—the archaist, proposing escape into an irrevocable past; the *futurist*, substituting a utopian dream for actuality; the various philosophers and mystics, proposing detachment from the troubles of society. All fail. The only hope is the savior who promises "transfiguration" of society, the God Incarnate in a man. Again there are many candidates, but as their promises are

---

[2] See discussion of "The Stimulus of Blows," *SH*, II, 100–112 (*S*, pp. 108–11).

Toynbee is aware of the problem in his ambivalent attitude toward conflict and discusses it in an annex, "Militarism and the Military Virtues," *SH*, IV, 640–51.

examined all prove their futility—save Jesus of Nazareth
alone.[3]

Exactly here the crucial problem arises. In what sense is this
Kingdom of God an answer to the problem *of history*? Toynbee's
answers are rich in suggestions but—thus far—lacking in precision. On the one hand, the *Civitas Dei* is the very opposite of
withdrawal and escape from the world, of the "detachment"
dreamed of by philosophers. It is positive, not negative; an ad-
venture rather than an asylum; an expansion and transfiguration
rather than a negation of the experiences of history. It is no "act
of truancy" but a bold initiative "to save the City of Destruction
from its doom by converting it to the Peace of God."[4] But on the
other hand, we cannot really expect history to attain the Peace
of God. The one true savior *from* society does not allow himself
to become the savior *of* society, thereby doomed to failure. His
success is in showing "the way into an Other World, out of range
of the City of Destruction."[5]

For the reconciliation of these two opposing ideas, we can
only wait. At one point Toynbee poses exactly the question of
whether the New Jerusalem can be brought down to earth and
refers us to the answer—in a yet unpublished volume.[6] The key
to the answer, the connecting link between the Kingdom of God
and the best hope of earth, is apparently the church. The envisioned future church, we have seen, will have to perform the
functions of Caesar. Its institutional forms will be "a mundane
feature which makes the Church Militant's life different from
that of the Kingdom of Heaven,"[7] but they are necessary here.

So the church clearly is not the answer to the quest for the
meaning of history. But it is related to the answer:

Therefore, while the replacement of the mundane civilizations
by the world-wide and enduring reign of the Church Militant on

[3] SH, VI, 259–78 (S, pp. 544–47).
[4] SH, V, 394–97 (S, 438–39). SH, VI, 167.
[5] SH, VI, 279.   [6] Ibid., p. 279, n. 3.   [7] CT, p. 243.

Earth would certainly produce what to-day would seem a miraculous improvement in those mundane social conditions which the civilizations have been seeking to improve during the last six thousand years, the aim, and test, of progress under a truly Christian dispensation on Earth would not lie in the field of mundane social life; the field would be the spiritual life of individual souls in their passages through this earthly life from birth into this world to death out of it.[8]

Although the future universal church is sometimes romanticized beyond any reasonable bounds,[9] Toynbee is aware of its limitations. In his "Christianity and Civilization," where he glorifies it most strongly, he is aware of "original sin"; he sees no perceptible variation in the stuff of human nature over the whole span of history; and he does not expect the future church to purge human nature. But he sees the possibility of spiritual progress in "the opportunity to souls, by way of the learning that comes through suffering, for getting into closer communion with God, and becoming less unlike Him, during their passage through the world."[10] Elsewhere describing history as a "province of the Kingdom of God," he sees it affording "an accumulative increase in the means of Grace at man's disposal in this world."[11]

But does history show this form of "progress"? It is easy to see how this age may be the heir of the spiritual insights of Plato, the prophets, and the Buddha; or how the Christian may find himself the heir of the insights into the meaning of Christ discerned by Paul, Augustine, Aquinas, Luther, and Wesley. Yet

---

[8] Ibid., p. 248.
[9] Toynbee once let slip the words: "although the Church may actually never yet have expressed Christianity to perfection, there is at least no inherent impediment here to the attainment of a perfect harmony, since the Church has been called into existence for this purpose and no other." SH, V, 80, n. 3 from p. 79.
[10] CT, pp. 241, 248–49. Cf. p. 263.
[11] "The Meaning of History for the Soul," CT, p. 263.

are the means of grace any more available to him than they were to the communities which St. Paul visited?

Toynbee raises these difficulties in trying to relate history and salvation without the illusions which find salvation in history and without the otherworldliness which finds history insignificant for salvation. His conclusions, whatever their difficulties, occur within an attempt to preserve the essential Christian theme: belief in a Kingdom of God which is not the same as history, but which enhances the meaning of history.

V. TOYNBEE'S SIGNIFICANCE FOR CHRISTIAN THOUGHT

Toynbee's philosophy of history is often taken as a justification of the ways of God to man. It offers an interpretation of history in which spiritual factors are determinative, in which sin is the source of destruction, in which men learn and are redeemed through suffering. But with all these affirmations it is not—and for the most part does not pretend to be—a theodicy or a doctrine of providence.

To begin with, Toynbee's idea of salvation implies a redeeming, loving God, but his conception of creativity does not. In the discussion of the geneses of civilizations in the first three volumes of *A Study of History*, there is a strong tendency toward Bergsonian naturalism. We have here not a God who is Lord of history, but a restless, dynamic, blind forward surge of nature in her creative acts. The prodigality of nature may lead to trial after trial, with success coming perhaps after the hundredth or thousandth time.[1] The impression is of the fecundity, not the purposefulness of nature and history.

---

[1] *SH*, II, 275 (*S*, p. 141). At this and many other points the first three volumes show a tendency to equate nature and history. Collingwood, who had available only these three volumes, criticized Toynbee's "ultimately naturalistic" conception of history. (*The Idea of History*, pp. 159–65.) Reinhold Niebuhr takes up Collingwood's criticism and adds to it. (*Faith and History*, pp. 110–12.) At many points Toynbee's later writ-

The Bergsonian and biblical conceptions may seem to unite at the turning point in the history of a civilization. For the start of the breakdown may be described in two sets of terms. (1) In Bergsonian language it is the failure of the creative *elan*. A civilization has become mechanical, has lost its flexibility. Instead of meeting new challenges with appropriate new actions, it goes on trying the obsolete methods that have worked for other challenges. (2) In biblical terms the same facts can be described as the sin of pride (or in Greek terms as *hybris*). We see the sin of idolatry (of an ephemeral self, institution, or technique), and the pattern of κόρος, ὕβρις, ἄτη (satiety, pride, destruction). Here is a conception of judgment in the biblical tradition.

But we have already noted some problems in the idea that civilizations always die by "suicide." And even if the pattern of judgment on sin should hold up, it applies at best to powerful, mature civilizations. It does not deny that history has shown a vast quantity of arbitrary, irrational ruthlessness which has wiped out many a society. Toynbee points out examples of large social groups, if not complete civilizations, which have been destroyed by cruel military power.

Perhaps for these reasons Toynbee's own doctrine of providence rests finally not on the destinies of the twenty-one civilizations. His religious understanding of history rests rather (1) on the view of a vast providential plan by which the civilizations prepare the way for a universal church, and (2) on the opportunity for individuals to find salvation in the midst of historical suffering.

Can we then find in Toynbee, not a detailed doctrine of

---

ings qualify or refute the naturalistic implications of his earlier volumes. Yet something of the naturalistic strain occasionally recurs. *E.g.*, in a writing of 1947 Toynbee was willing to draw a qualified analogy between the U. S. Civil War and the spring ploughing with its natural annual recurrence. (*CT*, pp. 32–34.)

providence, but an adequate general Christian understanding of history? Certainly this attempt to review history on the grand scale stands as an immense achievement. Further, it is a basically honest effort, in which the author is quite frank about his perplexities and always willing to follow out a theme even though it may not agree with ideas he has previously developed. But his *Study of History,* so rich in suggestions for religious, political, and historical understanding, is least convincing in its systematization. And the results raise serious problems for a Christian understanding of history.

In the first place, as we have seen, Toynbee has not decided the relationship between the Kingdom of God and history. Historical dynamism and mystical salvation are still at war in his thinking. Repeatedly he protests against withdrawal from history, only to come perilously close to the views he criticizes. Summoning us to action, he proclaims that the stars in their courses cannot prevent our triumph, if only we meet our challenges intelligently and valiantly. Then, looking at signs of decline in our civilization, he pronounces its demise a "thrice-told tale" almost to be welcomed. While we wait for Toynbee's final answer, we may hope for clarification, but may not expect too much. For the Christian myth cannot be neatly systematized; and perhaps the Christian can never draw the precise lines of relation between the prophetic conviction that God rules history and the eschatological faith that God will redeem history.

Second, Toynbee's dangerous ecclesiasticism threatens to subdue his deeper insights. Although he carefully distinguishes between the Kingdom of God and the church and does not try to locate the meaning of history in the church, Toynbee glorifies the institution and its future far more than empirical evidence or Christian faith give warrant. Augustine was more aware that the tares will grow in any institutional church until the day of judgment. Toynbee should, after these centuries, know better than

Augustine the perils of a dominant ecclesiasticism; he sometimes points them out, yet forgets them in his own expectations for the church.

The final error is a confusion between the religious understanding of history and the empirical assessing of facts and probabilities. The problem is at best a difficult one. To separate the two utterly—to say that the Christian historian should forget his faith when he considers history—is to make faith utterly insignificant and, when faith is true, to misunderstand history. To confuse the two is to make bad history and bad religion.[2] On the one hand, the naive attempt to write history without presuppositions has largely been abandoned, and the Christian regards his presuppositions as valid. On the other hand, one's presuppositions dare not take the place of, or do violence to, the evidence.

In Karl Löwith's strong criticism, "Toynbee is neither an empirical historian nor a good theologian."[3] An empirical historian would not allow his religious convictions to affect so completely his predictions about the future destiny of the historical process—even to the extent of seeing the church replace civilization. And a theologian would be more reluctant to foresee and describe God's providential plan.

On this issue Augustine may point the way to a solution. The soaring faith of the African genius worked out an interpretation of history with far less use of the actual data of history than Toynbee, and none of the refined techniques of historiography. Yet he probably did not bend history to serve his theories so much as this modern master of historical scholarship. For Augustine saw the uselessness of trying to fix history within any discernible scheme. He knew that God is *Deus Absconditus*, that his sovereignty is hidden and not to be comprehended in finite patterns

---

[2] See E. Harris Harbison, "The Problem of the Christian Historian," *Theology Today*, V (1948), 388–405. *Cf. Religious Perspectives of College Teaching in History* (New Haven: Hazen Foundation, c. 1950).
[3] *Meaning in History*, p. 14.

but discerned only in the dimension of history to which man may respond in faith. Thus his reading of history could be realistic, his trust in God sure. He could see God's sovereignty worked out in the fall of an empire without surmising that the fall must contribute to a foreseeable improvement in the course of history.

Toynbee knows well the weakness of a natural theology which tries to draw a religious conception of God from the scientific data of physical nature. He knows also, but sometimes forgets, that the historian's data as such do not add up to religious conceptions.

Conclusion

CHAPTER IX

FAITH AND THE SOVEREIGNTY OF GOD

NATURAL temptation and plentiful precedent often lead authors, after examining and criticizing the views of others, to offer the world their own confident answers to questions that have puzzled the ages. Usually the world is a bit more amused, but no wiser, for their presumption. It would be particularly amusing if, after chapters of insistence that human rationality cannot see through the problems of history, this final chapter should pretend to offer the solutions.

But there may be some purpose in looking for a few major convictions which emerge from the examination of many facets of Christian tradition. Inevitably the personal judgments which have repeatedly colored pages of this book will in the process come a bit more clearly into the open.

In the last analysis the problem of history for faith is the problem of the sovereignty of God. If God rules the world, then provisional chaos and meaninglessness finally contribute to His purpose, and history is not in vain. If God does not rule, then whatever achievements may be wrought, the final words pronounced upon history are doom and despair.

Certainly the sovereignty of God is not obvious in history. No body of evidence sufficient to convince the dispassionate observer can be collected. Even to eyes of faith God's sovereignty is seldom clear—else the Old Testament would not have been driven finally to forsake the idea of a conclusive providence. Eschatology arose when men, facing the frustration which history brings, could deny neither intimations of God's sovereignty nor the incomprehensibility of that sovereignty.

It is possible, however, for eschatology to destroy any sense of meaningfulness in history. An other-worldly Kingdom of God may constitute an escape from a history which is given up in despair. Concentration on a "last" judgment and ultimate redemption may crush out all notions of a judgment and redemption in history.

Christian faith has traditionally included belief in the sovereignty of God both as demonstrated in history (a doctrine of providence) and as left incomplete by a history which demands some further redemption (eschatology). The sovereignty of God includes His Lordship over history and a Kingdom of God never fully realized in history. How are the two related? The answer determines one's outlook upon history.

I. DIFFICULTIES IN A DOCTRINE OF PROVIDENCE

A doctrine of providence which keeps the events of history in view is never easy to formulate. In the *first* place, much of what happens in history is apparently the result of blind necessity or blind chance—two forces which may be logical opposites but whose practical meaning is almost the same. Historical purpose is subject to the impersonal processes of nature and to the capricious, inexplicable purposes of particular human beings. The length of Cleopatra's nose, the fog that hung over the battle of Dunkirk, the unique abilities of a Julius Caesar, the peculiar temperament of a John L. Lewis—these are factors in history. Whether personal or impersonal, determined or contingent, they show how particular detail may affect the general course of history.

The impossibility of working out any adequate conception of providence in terms of historical causality is indicated in Edwyn Bevan's attempt. "If a bullet did not kill Napoleon in one of his early battles, it cannot be regarded by a Christian as a mere accident that the position which Napoleon took up on the field was never in the line of a bullet's trajectory: it must have been God's will that Napoleon should survive and influence the course of history in the way he did."[1] Having said this, Bevan must next ponder the question as to whether God governed history, in this case, by supernaturally making the course of bullets swerve in order to avoid Napoleon, or by governing Napoleon's volitions so that he would never be in the position where God knew that a bullet would be coming.

This sort of reasoning leads to the most perplexing conclusions regarding the natural sciences, psychology, and any philosophical conception of the world. Even more serious, it sooner or later reduces the profound meaning of providence to a matter of intellectual gymnastics. Its sole value is to show the difficulties in a great many notions of providence. For once we realize that vagaries of weather or disease germs, trajectories of projectiles, random motions of battle leaders, quirks of personalities, the length of a woman's nose, or the want of a horseshoe nail may affect momentous affairs, we must reason further: if God is not the causal agent in these matters of detail, it is hard to see how He can be the decisive causal agent in great affairs.

Of course, some find evidence of providence in such events as the flight of a seagull within range of a lifeboat filled with men about to starve. Clearly the causation of this sort of rare event lies beyond the possibility of any sort of proof or disproof, or even of very precise statistical evidence, though the scientific mind will have its questions. Again, however, the scientific problem is not so difficult as the religious one: if God does work in such a manner to save men, why does He not do it to many other deserving men who cry out for help? When men claim that

[1] In *The Kingdom of God and History* (Oxford Conference Book), pp. 47–48.

a special providence has saved their lives (implying that providence chose not to save the lives of many others), the intellectual credulity is hardly so troublesome as the spiritual presumption implied. On the other hand, to find no divine meaning in such an event may be evidence less of humility than of ingratitude and religious emptiness.

Hence the Christian doctrine of providence in its deeper forms cannot be primarily a theory of historical causation. It is rather a confidence that God's grace is sufficient to any occasion, that He cares for His people in the midst of the contingencies which buffet their lives, that He is Lord of history—not the main efficient cause. The final aspect of providence, whatever else we may find in the belief, will be known less in the rise and fall of nations than in a divine grace which may be found whatever the course of events. Napoleon might have died at the start of his career, or he might have won at Waterloo; the most fundamental aspects of providence cannot depend on such contingent events.

The *second* difficulty in a doctrine of providence is the problem of evil. It concerns principally the evil wrought by human decisions, perhaps in defiance of God; but it cannot be separated from natural evil, from the famines and epidemics and ice ages and floods which have affected the course of history. The non-concern of nature for human individuals, sometimes for vast numbers of human beings, immediately refutes many notions of providence. And the violence of "man's inhumanity to man" refutes many more. The present generation has been given bold reminders of the ruthlessness of history, a ruthlessness too often forgotten by men who philosophize in comfort about history. If we would look at history as a whole, at the human race as a whole, we must grant that human experience has found about as much evidence for belief in demons and evil spirits as for belief in beneficent gods. Too often the doctrine of providence is merely the ideology of the comfortable and fully deserves the sneers of the Voltaires who see through its comforting illusions.[2]

The most ambitious modern attempt at a providential reading of history has been that of Hegel, who concluded his *Philosophy of History* with the conviction "that what has happened and is happening every day, is not only not 'without God,' but is essentially His Work." Hegel's whole work on history is avowedly a theodicy. He is emphatic in his assertion of providence: "God governs the world; the actual working of his government— the carrying out of his plan—is the History of the World."[3] But this governance of the world has little to do with the welfare of individuals or their conceptions of justice and right. The sufferings of vast masses of the human race are justified by their contribution to the world-historical process in which the idea of freedom is being realized—although those who so suffered had no idea of the purpose of their sacrifice. All this is the very denial of the Christian conception of providence.

Christian thinkers who take seriously the intensity and extent of historical evil are well aware of the threat to the whole idea of God's sovereignty over history. To assert that God reigns over the conflicts and accidents and evil deeds which compose so much of history is either utter nonsense or a genuine triumph of faith. The very meaning of apocalyptic thinking—we have seen—is that God's providence cannot be discerned with any clarity in the tangled events of the past and present, but that faith refuses to deny His sovereignty.

The idea of any "providential ordering of world-historical destinies" has been rejected by one penetrating contemporary

---

[2] It is not only cynics who make bitter attacks on the doctrine. Kierkegaard assailed "gossip and rumor about the righteousness of providence which are invented by human wisdom and circulated by effeminate creatures and eunuchs." *Repetition* (Princeton: Princeton University Press, 1946), pp. 112–13.
[3] *Philosophy of History*, p. 36.

Christian writer, Karl Löwith, in his *Meaning in History*. To ask that providence be evident in the course of history, says Löwith, is like asking with Satan that the Son of God demonstrate his power by throwing himself from the pinnacle of the temple. The Cross is the answer to all assurances about history; suffering is the destiny of those who serve God. The Old Testament idea of God's reign over history must be transformed in Christianity to a personal and individual conception of salvation via the path of suffering.[4]

Löwith offers a profound religious assurance of a victory of faith and of a salvation from the evils of history. But while he asserts the meaning of *life in history*, he denies, in effect, the *meaning of history*. He gives up the hope of finding any significance in the process of history as such. In surrendering the conception of providence, Löwith withdraws to a citadel of faith which he finds invulnerable; but one must ask whether he has not surrendered bastions close to the center of biblical faith.

II. THE VINDICATION OF THE IDEA OF PROVIDENCE

There are positive aspects of the faith in God's sovereignty which, although one could scarcely demonstrate them by an analysis of history, may throw some illumination on the actual character of history. These may be considered in three forms.

A. TECHNICAL HISTORIOGRAPHY AND PROVIDENCE

We have already seen (Ch. VII, p. 199, above) how the general idea of providence—in a thoroughly secularized form, to be

---

[4] *Meaning in History*, pp. 142–44, 195–96. Löwith, like Kierkegaard, in his radical skepticism of certain Christian conventionalities comes close at times to the position of the utter non-believer. His viewpoint on providence may be compared with that of the humanistic skeptic, Karl Popper, who in the name of morality attacks the idea of providence, and uses Kierkegaard in his support. See Popper, *The Open Society and Its Enemies*, II, 256–65.

sure—has been adopted in the practice of most modern historical study. The course of history, it is commonly recognized, is seldom the result of conscious individual or group plans. To a point history can be explained as the resultant of many human political decisions and the influences of nature; from this point, however, history seems to acquire a character of its own which overrules men's planned decisions and gives point to the various suggestions of fate and destiny in most religions.

We need not go all the way with Hegel in his description of the "cunning of reason," or of the "World-historical individual" —the great leader whose desires and actions are unwittingly in tune with the "will of the World-Spirit." At the least we must grant that political leadership—e.g., of a Franklin D. Roosevelt— is successful in large part as, without the long foresight men often yearn for, it hits upon measures which accord with the dimly known, scarcely understood needs of the times. "Thus," says Morris Cohen, "no one planned the British Empire or what is known as the British Constitution, just as no one planned our so-called capitalistic system. Things develop in ways which are not quite anticipated." [1]

Clearly there is no necessary jump from this fact about history to a Christian doctrine of providence. As the Cambridge historian Herbert Butterfield says: "Whether we are Christians or not, whether we believe in a Divine Providence or not, we are liable to serious technical errors if we do not regard ourselves as born into a providential order. We are not by any means sovereign in any action that we take in regard to that order, and not by any means in a position to recreate it to the heart's desire." [2] Such divergent writers as Collingwood, Cohen, and Butterfield are equally aware of the "technical errors" of nonprovidential interpretations of history. Butterfield alone is led to a specifically Christian providential interpretation, and he does

[1] *The Meaning of Human History*, p. 127.
[2] *Christianity and History*, pp. 95–96.

not pretend that the Christian conclusions are read solely from the evidence. Certainly the non-voluntaristic aspects of history do not always work for the creation of good or for the overthrow of evil. One may simply charge them off to the baffling, irrational character of history. But if religious faith discerns in them signs of a meaning, however veiled and dimly perceived, it is asserting the providential character of history.

B. THE CUMULATIVE EFFECTS OF HISTORY

The second aspect of a doctrine of providence, then, will start by asking whether the non-voluntaristic aspects of history can in any way be clarified by the Christian conception of the sovereignty of God. Here we must examine those cumulative effects which, to so great an extent, make history what it is.

We have already seen that, however inadequate progress may be as a religion, history is in some measure progressive. This cumulative progress is most obvious in technology; but technological advance makes possible advance in education and social organization. Many a social development, ranging from family patterns of activity to international politics, is for the first time in all history now possible.

Such development is, of course, not necessarily improvement. Perhaps historical progress resembles the development of music from simple melodies and rhythmic patterns to the magnificent co-ordination of a symphony orchestra. The progress is undeniable; but the value of a melody is not merely that it may some day be co-ordinated in a symphony; and orchestras can on occasion produce a more ear-splitting din than a simple lyre or flute. Again there is undeniable progress represented by the difference between a pow-wow of tribal chiefs and a meeting of the Security Council of the United Nations; but the animosities of the latter may be far more fateful and even more irreconcilable than those of the former.

The musician finds real value and meaning in the development from simple to complex forms. But he will scarcely say that the development constitutes the meaning of music, for that meaning may be expressed at any time in the development.

Perhaps, then, the main effect of progress in history is to heighten the possibilities both for achievement and for disaster. Even disaster, if it comes, will not entirely destroy the cumulative effects of history. It may mean a long-term, perhaps a permanent, set-back of those technological developments which go hand-in-hand with a high standard of living. It is quite possible, though far from certain, that this is the only generation in the whole of history that will dream of two cars in every garage and television in every home. Yet though "the stone age may return on the gleaming wings of science," to use a phrase of Churchill's, the new stone age will not be the old one. It will be post-civilization, not pre-civilization. For better or for worse the effects of some millennia of human historical development will not be rubbed out.

These cumulative effects which start from the externals of technology may be matched by cumulative effects in the inner history of the human race. Like the externally originated effects, these internal ones show an advancing complexity which heightens the possibilities of good and evil alike.

The attitude of Americans toward their historical responsibility today is moulded in large part out of a past history which lives in the conscious and subconscious life of the nation today. It includes creative and vitiating possibilities. American attitudes are born partly of the memory of past national heroes, of old visions of new births of freedom, of compassion growing out of ancient faiths and friendships. And American attitudes are born also of rankling national and racial animosities, of distrusts born of past acts and past prejudices.

History, at this stage of the game, gives no opportunity for a completely fresh start. The attempt to unite Western Europe against a powerful threat is menaced at a dozen points by old hostilities, irrational but powerful. The desperate wish has occasionally been heard in recent years that human hatreds, so long simmering and threatening destruction, might actually erupt and come to a climax. Then, it has been suggested, after the terrors of destruction, some men might make a fresh start, unimpeded by the weight of past error that now hampers the world. But a start among the ruins of a civilization destroyed by fear and hatred is not a fresh start. As World War II left the world with a weight of bitterness and a burden of hostility, so World War III, though it might do a much more thorough job of cleaning things out, would leave its vast burden.

Thus history is a story of social life in which the great deeds of the fathers offer new opportunities for the sons and the sins of the fathers are visited upon the sons—in both cases for many generations.

The question for the Christian then is this: Is God's will accomplished in this cumulative process? Is there evidence of providence?

It might be considered that the increasing opportunities, perhaps even increasing maturity, of history are themselves a realization of God's purpose, whether they be used for good or bad. Part of a parent's purpose is realized in leading the child into the capacity for making weightier decisions—decisions expressive of the child's unique personality. Yet if the child makes its deliberate decisions for evil, much of the parent's purpose has not been realized. So in history cumulative developments of the race may have their part in God's providence, but are hardly the substance of that providence. We must look further for marks of the distinctively Christian teachings of providential judgment and grace.

To at least one distinguished historian of our day, history suggests just such conclusions. Herbert Butterfield finds first the elements of a creative grace. The achievements of history, he finds, are not matters of a moment, but of developments in which millions of people participate, without realizing the accomplishment they are working. These people "are agents of deeper processes than those of which they are aware, instruments of a providence that combines their labours and works them into a larger pattern." One may even find "a providence, in fact, which moves over history with the function of creating good out of evil." Thus many a past catastrophic event is remembered for the larger good which came out of it.

Providential judgment is active too, as history works to break the power of lopsided ambition. Indeed, those who refuse to acknowledge providence because they would like to play its role themselves are the most likely to feel its fury. Butterfield finds in the doctrine of providence considerable practical advice for statesmanship and diplomacy.

These evidences, discernible to any inquiring mind, take on their deepest significance when seen with eyes of faith.

To a religious mind all those providential dispositions which I have attempted to describe must appear as Divine, or the orderings of God Himself; and in the workings of history there must be felt the movement of a living God. . . . All these things considered I do not see why Christians should be shy of trusting in Providence, therefore, floating on it so to speak, leaning on it and making alliance with it, regarding it as a living and active agency both in ourselves and in its movement over the length and breadth of history.[3]

This providential faith of a historian, whose reputation was first established entirely outside of theological circles, comes very close to recent doctrinal statements. Reinhold Niebuhr, for example, in contrast to thinkers like Löwith, affirms a doctrine of providence with a meaning for the life of nations.

God's sovereignty manifests itself first, says Niebuhr, by setting limits to the power of evil. Tyrannies do hold sway for a time; but their triumphs produce the inevitability of a destructive

---

[3] Herbert Butterfield, *Christianity and History*, Ch. V, "Providence and the Historical Process." The quotations are from pp. 97, 98, 111–12.

judgment upon themselves. To be sure, divine judgment does not operate as a simple moral process in history. Historical conflicts are determined by power; and power may be due largely to geography, natural resources, technical and military skills, and other factors having little relation to the moral worth of a nation. But there is an element of judgment in history.

The gracious aspect of divine providence is evident in the possibilities of renewal for a society that sees its sin and repents. The Christian ideas of judgment and grace, so real in the individual life, cannot be transferred easily to fit the lives of nations. The nation does not give up its life for another; it is not born again. But nations experience the same anxiety, pride, lust for power, and idolatry as individuals. In some respects the deaths of nations are even more obviously self-inflicted than those of individuals, and hence more easily interpreted in terms of providential judgment; for the nation is not, like the individual, subject to the biological necessity of death, and it is less the victim of chance vagaries of nature. Niebuhr is unwilling to go as far as Toynbee in holding that civilizations always die by suicide. They may be overwhelmed by superior strength. But, even though rarely, a nation like an individual may achieve a spiritual victory in death.

Niebuhr comes his closest to Toynbee in his analysis of social change as it relates to the survival of a civilization. Both writers find civilizations tending to idolatrize their own achievements and institutions, and therefore to cling to them long after justice and new developments call for change. If the holders of power in a civilization—in our own case, the economically powerful classes, or the white races—can have the grace to see their own pretensions and give justice to those who challenge them, they may actually enhance their own historical possibilities.

There is not as clearly defined an experience of repentance in the life of communities and social institutions as in that of individuals. Yet there is a possibility that old forms and structures of life may be renewed, rather than destroyed by the vicissitudes of history. These experiences establish the validity of the Christian doctrine of life through death for the collective, as well as for the individual, organism.[4]

C. PROVIDENCE AND DIVINE LOVE

The two aspects of providence discussed thus far remain inadequate without the third. For finally the only unambiguous meaning of providence is the personal confession of faith that in any historical situation man can look to God as Lord and Savior. Yet, however much this doctrine belongs to the personal life of the spirit, it says something of history. For human life is confronted with a sharp either-or: "Either there is no pattern of history at all (in which case a cosmic caprice will finally destroy every sense of the meaning of life); or there is a pattern but it is beyond our comprehension and under a Sovereignty which we can only dimly discern."[5]

In a long succession of philosophies of history, men have tried to avoid this decision, claiming to have found other patterns or meanings of history. But events and logic have destroyed the various superficial answers and left the two alternatives in bold relief. The secular alternative has had the virtue of refusing to cover up evil or to deal in vague generalities. But it has left out

---

[4] Faith and History, p. 226. The doctrine of providence which I have summarized is found in Chapters VIII and XIII.

Cf. John Baillie, What is Christian Civilization?, p. 59: "All earthly civilizations are indeed corruptible and must one day perish, the pax britannica no less than the pax romana, and Christendom no less than Babylon and Troy. But if most have perished prematurely, it was largely as victims of their own proud illusions."

Karl Löwith criticizes Niebuhr's viewpoint in a review of Faith and History, in Theology Today, VI (1949), 422–25. In the same issue of this quarterly E. Harris Harbison, the Princeton historian, reviews Löwith's Meaning in History, making an appreciative criticism of it from a viewpoint closer to that of Niebuhr.

[5] Reinhold Niebuhr, "Providence and Human Decisions," Christianity and Crisis, VIII (1949), 185.

the most significant aspects of life. It has excluded, says Paul
Tillich, "those deep things for which religion stands: the feeling
for the inexhaustible mystery of life, the grip of an ultimate
meaning of existence, and the invincible power of an uncondi-
tional devotion." The fateful result was that these things which
"cannot be excluded" came back in the demonic, distorted forms
of modern totalitarian paganisms.[6]

Faith chooses the opposite alternative. It does not, we have
seen, claim to assemble enough evidence that an induction be-
gins to outline the pattern of a meaningful history. It claims only
to respond to a divine love which makes itself known in history
and evokes the trust that events are safe in God's hands. History
does not add up to a doctrine of providence. It sometimes drives
men to one, by blasting all answers except the one—trust in the
mysterious sovereignty of a loving God.

The sovereignty of God is finally the power of the love of
God. It is not the denial of evil which is starkly opposed to
God's love. Indeed, the boldest forms of the Christian doctrine of
providence have refused quite bluntly to deny the reality and
power of evil, to pass over it as a lesser good, or to extenuate it
in any way. They have asserted that divine love is sovereign even
over evil, that "love never faileth," that God alone can complete
the meaning of history as no power of evil can do. Evil can only
destroy. Love can create, can encompass evil, transmute and
redeem it. Though evil can corrupt love and can destroy the
earthly existence of men who would love, it cannot destroy love
and build its own kingdom; it cannot fulfill history. Thus faith
perceives the sovereign love of God, now often known only too
dimly, yet even now possessing the tokens of triumph.

Something like this is what Christianity has usually meant
by the sovereignty of God. Most of the classical theologians have
recognized that divine omnipotence does not mean the power of

[6] The Shaking of the Foundations (New York: Scribners, 1948), p. 181.
Cf. Ch. XII, "The Meaning of Providence."

God to do anything, conceivable or inconceivable. The doctrine of omnipotence is not a set of precise measurements of good and evil, of rational hierarchies subordinating one realm to another, of labored explanations of the origins and future doom of evil. It is the dynamic proclamation of a sovereign claim of God upon the loyalty of his creatures, of an inalienable love, of a power of redemption.

It is not hard to see, when omnipotence is thus defined, why Christian thought has so often coupled the conceptions of the power and the weakness of God. We have seen throughout this study why the conception of God's omnipotent sovereignty is a necessity for Christian thought; if anything is outside God's control, the Christian understanding of history breaks down, for the final context of history is a meaningless one. This is the point which Augustine, Aquinas, and Calvin saw so clearly.

But with all this is the conception of the weakness of God. If its full significance is missed by Aquinas and Calvin, it is seen by Augustine, who in contrast to the "proud" Neo-Platonists glories in the humility of God in the incarnation. It is seen by Luther, in his fascination over the Gospel narratives of the infancy of Jesus. The idea has led in sensitive thinkers like Studdert-Kennedy to belief in a finite God, whose love struggles against other powers. There is something authentic in these emphases, although in the hands of literal-minded metaphysicians they usually turn into barren and confusing theories.

The central tradition of Christianity has been more paradoxical. It is sure that evil is defiance of God, yet that even evil lives only because the source of all things is God. It recognizes in God the majestic power which crushes out evil, yet finds God most truly revealed in the figure of a man suffering on a cross as a victim of evil. It recognizes with St. Paul the cosmic sovereignty of God, but discerns the strength of that sovereignty as made perfect in weakness.

Thus a Christian conception of providence makes three curiously related statements: (1) God's sovereignty is the ultimate power in the universe, and though it is defied by evil, nothing is beyond its scope. (2) God's sovereignty is hidden to mankind, discernible only by faith and then not as a clearly perceptible pattern. (3) God's sovereignty is strangely made manifest in the weakness of love which suffers violence from the forces of evil.

To many an observer the combination of three such statements will seem an impossible rationalization to preserve a dead doctrine. Admittedly it is of little help in formulating a complete and rational metaphysics or philosophy of history—these ventures whose haunting fascination has lured centuries of philosophy to frustration. But in the Christian understanding of life and history the statements are simply a way of stating the vivid experience of faith.

It is not by accident that most recent discussions of providence have found their final form in an echo of Paul's statement in Romans 8:

Who shall separate us from the love of Christ? shall tribulation, or distress, or persecution, or famine, or nakedness, or peril, or sword? . . . No, in all these things we are more than conquerors through him who loved us. For I am sure that neither things present, nor things to come, nor powers, nor height, nor depth, nor anything else in all creation, will be able to separate us from the love of God in Christ Jesus our Lord.

Even such a statement can, of course, be used too glibly. Slums and wars and poverty and psychological disturbances do, as a matter of fact, separate men from the love of God. But it is the conviction of faith that God's grace has resources even for such situations. The supreme example is the crucifixion of Christ—man's utmost act of evil transmuted by divine providence into God's act of redemption.

In the end the doctrine of providence is not primarily a theory about history; but it is relevant at every point to the understanding of history. As Niebuhr puts it,

There are facets of meaning in it [history] which transcend the flux of time. These give glimpses of the eternal love which bears the whole project of history. . . . The Christian faith is the apprehension of the divine love and power which bears the whole human pilgrimage, shines through its enigmas and antinomies and is finally and definitely revealed in a drama in which suffering love gains triumph over sin and death. This revelation does not resolve all perplexities; but it does triumph over despair, and leads to the renewal of life from self-love to love.[7]

III. THE THREE-STRANDED THREAD

We have not in this book discovered the spool on which Henry Adams wished to wind the thread of history. Nor do we expect it to be discovered. But we have found three strands which run through all the knots and tangles of the thread. To faith they are clues to the hidden meaning of history.

The *central* strand of the thread is the eschatological—however harshly the word grates on modern ears. Despite all the dangers of apocalyptic literalism and of other-worldliness, the central meaning of eschatology is essential. Without it we are compelled to say either that history has no meaning (whatever partial meanings we may put into it) or that the meaning is encompassed in some historical movement, process, or method. With it we can say that history derives its meaning from a Kingdom of God. History thus is never bereft of meaning, and it never encompasses its own meaning. For the Kingdom, in Toynbee's phrase, is like "the sweep of a comet's tail through a cluster of planets"; it is here, but its center and origin are not ours to claim.[1]

In its practical meaning the eschatological faith is the answer to fanaticism and to despair. Against fanaticism it insists that no historical movement—national, racial, ecclesiastical, or class—can possess final historical significance or exert a totalitarian claim.

[7] *Faith and History*, pp. 233–34.
[1] *A Study of History*, VI, 131.

Against despair it insists that no historical defeat is ever a final one, that history is never robbed of significance, that faith always has resources for another battle against evil.

Sinful mankind is constantly tempted to appropriate for particular purposes the faith in the supernatural. Many a fanaticism, instead of being quelled by religious loyalties, has been heightened by the assurance that a cause represents the divine program for history. Such pretensions, however, are themselves a refusal to take seriously the eschatological character of faith— the "not-yet" which faith in the Kingdom of God stamps upon all promises of salvation from this-worldly programs, however good. And with all the dangers of distorted religion, in our own time it is clear that most of the threats of totalitarian fanaticism have come from those who have rejected transcendent faith and substituted for the Kingdom of God their own this-worldly programs.

At the other extreme eschatological beliefs may give the excuse for an other-worldliness that takes the seriousness out of history. Such has often been the case in theologies built on Neo-Platonic foundations, where the Kingdom of God became simply a heaven above and in no serious sense a goal of history. But when faithful to its biblical heritage, Christianity has recognized that the Kingdom of God has in a real sense come among us and that its power is here driving men of faith to creative activity in history.

The escape of other-worldliness is hardly our most pressing danger today. There is, in fact, an other-worldliness which may strengthen historical effort, for it gives assurance that no historical defeat is final, that in the most futile situation men may battle gloriously for God.

The *second* strand which we have discerned in the thread of history is the dynamic strand, concerned with creative historical activity. We have noted that in contrast to mystical and cyclical devaluations of history, Christian belief insists that history under a sovereign God moves forward. The tendency of recent centuries to secularize this dynamic conception and to transform it into a philosophy of progressivism has been effectively answered in recent Christian thought. Such thought, we have noticed, does not deny the fact or the possibility of historical progress. But it draws a distinction between human activities which normally develop cumulatively and those which do not. It points to the development of evil along with the development of good. And it regards progress as an inadequate answer to the problem of the meaning of history.

However severe the critique of progressivism, it is not a Christian critique if its result is despair or inactivity. The Social Gospel has undergone revision, but its message is not one to be forgotten. Walter Rauschenbusch was right: there is something false in any idea of the Kingdom of God which paralyzes historical activity now. This insight is incorporated by John Bennett into a Christianity which represents the rediscovery of eschatology:

Instead of assuming that the Kingdom of God is identical with any particular social cause, we can say that we serve the Kingdom of God by serving the cause that seems most fully to embody God's purpose for us. The Kingdom transcends all causes and yet there are causes that point toward it and there are causes that point away from it.[2]

A Christian understanding of history might say that there is meaning in historical progress, but progress is not the meaning of history. The sovereignty of God, which gives history its meaning, ordains that in any historical situation divine grace may evoke responsive love and service. The Kingdom of God may win victories in any stage of history.

[2] *Christianity and Communism*, p. 83.

For our own age progress appears as a possibility, but not as a probability. Even more than most ages, this is a contradictory one. Unprecedented humanitarianism and sordid cruelty, fanatical nationalism and world brotherhood are confusedly mingled. In this situation, loyalty to the Kingdom of God is likely to be more powerful than expectation of progress, as an incentive to a dynamic response to history.

The eschatological understanding of history can exist only in distorted form without the dynamic understanding which seeks this-worldly results. But the dynamic interpretation cannot finally exist at all without the eschatological. On purely naturalistic grounds progressive hopes are finally illusory. "In a span of time which as a cosmic interval will count but as an hour," said William James, our solar system "will have ceased to be." To most people, including most philosophers, this expected fate does not matter much since it is far away. But such a view says merely that an illusion will do provided it is a big enough illusion. If there is a meaning of history, it must be a meaning which bears history, not one which unfolds and perishes with history.

The *third* strand in the thread of history is the ecclesiastical. At this point the church may easily become involved in all the absurdities and blasphemies of the many national or racial groups who lay claim to a destiny involving the whole of history. It is either disastrous or pathetic for any historical collectivity to act as though the immense variety of history came to a culmination in itself; but this claim has been made again and again by secular and religious groups. Any social institution is one of a great many groupings and factors within history; as such it is a part of history, not the goal of history.

Yet goals are themselves present realities. W. E. Hocking has described religion as an "anticipated attainment," a "present possession" of a future goal. Whitehead calls religion "something which is real, and yet waiting to be realized; something which is a remote possibility, and yet the greatest of present facts." Karl

THE THREE-STRANDED THREAD   267

Barth describes the life of the church as a "sharing in the revelation" of Christ, a "sharing in *hope*." [3]

Here in three quite disparate figures is the similar recognition that there must be some present realization of life's ultimate purposes. In the Christian understanding of history the eschatological Kingdom of God is regarded as in some way a present reality. And since the Christian life is never a solitary existence but by its very nature involves the community of faith, this community or *ecclesia* must be regarded as an earnest, a first fruits, or a sign of the Kingdom of God.

To those who are aware of the human frailties of the churches —their limitations and divisions along geographical, political, racial, and doctrinal lines, and their compounding of the individual and social evils in all human life—the claims sometimes made for the church are too absurd to need refutation. Quite clearly Walter Rauschenbusch showed how satisfaction with the church as the embodiment of the Kingdom of God has often taken the dynamic element out of history. Similarly recent theology has shown how the ecclesiastical element has dulled the sharp eschatological insistence that all human institutions stand under the judgment of the heavenly Kingdom.

Yet at the same time Protestantism has been reawakening to the significance of the church. Convinced alike of the wrong in ecclesiastical pretensions and in haughty individualism, theologians have reformulated doctrines of the church and history. They have recognized that faith can create a community which, though composed of sinful men, responds to the power of God and knows His judgment. This community does unite men in love across boundaries of race and nation which often separate. In its truest reality it is a dynamic community, not identifiable

---

[3] See respectively: Hocking, *The Meaning of God in Human Experience* (New York: Longmans, Green, 1929), p. 491. Whitehead, *Science and the Modern World*, p. 275. Barth, in *Revelation*, ed. by John Baillie and Hugh Martin (New York: Macmillan, 1937), p. 80.

by membership rolls, but with boundaries known only to God. Its power is God's mercy, not its own virtue. To take a phrase of St. Paul's out of context, it is made up of "fellow workers for the kingdom of God" (Col. 4:11). Its members are *workers for the Kingdom* because they have already felt the *power of the Kingdom.*

The importance of the church was expressed informally in a letter of the late Archbishop of Canterbury, William Temple:

> I believe that all the doctrinal errors of Rome come from the direct identification of the Church as an organized Institution, taking its part in the process of history, with the Kingdom of God. This is just as bad, theologically, as the view which regards the Church as a mere instrument in preparation for the Kingdom of God. The only wholesome view is one which regards it as being constituted as the Church by the powers of the Kingdom of God within it and yet as being always composed of people still citizens of this world, so that those powers manifest themselves partially and fitfully, and the historical Church is a mixed body.[4]

Like the dynamic strain in the thread of history, the ecclesiastical thread is lost apart from the eschatological. But without the ecclesiastical, the eschatological loses some of its immediacy and power. If the God revealed in Christ is Lord of history, then the community of faith in Him has a share in the meaning of history.

IV. HISTORY AND CONFESSION OF FAITH

In the long sweep of Christian theology there have been relatively few attempts at a theology which has said that human history (or the natural order) simply adds up, without shortage or remainder, to God. It has been more typical of Christian thought to say that nature or history, when viewed in themselves in the agonizing search for a rationale or a meaning, drive

[4] F. A. Iremonger, *William Temple: Archbishop of Canterbury: His Life and Letters* (Oxford: The Clarendon Press, 1948), p. 420.

the seeker to the edge of absurdity or despair. But the same seeker, when grasped by religious faith, can see nature and history as the realm of God's sovereignty.

Herbert Butterfield has stated the case as a historian sees it:

> I do not think that any man can ever arrive at his interpretation of the human drama by merely casting his eye over the course of the centuries in the way that a student of history might do. I am unable to see how a man can find the hand of God in secular history, unless he has first found that he has an assurance of it in his personal experience. If it is objected that God is revealed in history through Christ, I cannot think that this can be true for the mere external observer, who puts on the thinking-cap of the ordinary historical student. It only becomes effective for those who have carried the narrative to intimate regions inside themselves, where certain of the issues are brought home to human beings.[1]

The relation to history of the dramatic concepts in which Christian faith expresses itself may be defined by contrast with two common misunderstandings of them. On the one hand, they are not dictated by the evidence. The evidence of history, we have seen, is too immense and varied to dictate any scheme of interpretation. Equally studious observers come up with the most contradictory over-all interpretations. But on the other hand, the thought-forms are not simply imposed upon a reluctant material. They are not rigid a priori categories, not revealed moulds descended from heaven for the historical thinker to accept unquestioningly.

Instead it might be said that the formulations of Christian mythology are suggested by the materials of history to the mind which approaches them with Christian faith—a faith which itself is generated in the life of a historical community. This faith, of course, is not the acceptance of the authority of a book or an institution. It does not deny any empirical evidence or

[1] Christianity and History, p. 107. Cf. History and Human Relations, pp. 147–48.

acquiesce in any logical contradictions, although it may, with many a philosopher, find reason finally driven to antinomies in seeking to comprehend the world.

An analogy, if it is not pressed too far, may clarify the nature of thought here. In a common test for subtle forms of color-blindness a series of discs, each combining several colors, is shown to observers. When one stares at the discs for a short time, a group of discernible figures emerge from the chaotic background. Different observers see different figures, depending on their ability in color-perception; and the particular figure which an individual sees is the result of the interaction between an external object and personal responsiveness. Perhaps in some such way the materials of history do not *dictate* but do *suggest* to *faith* the strands of coherence by which they may be understood.

The situation has other analogies in modern philosophy. Einstein has frequently said that the source of his scientific passion is the confidence in an undiscovered unity in the world. Dewey has often proclaimed his unconquerable faith in certain methods of inquiry. Most philosophers have some kind of belief in the validity of categories of causality. In each of these cases the particular faith is not dictated by the character of the observable world, but the world offers suggestions which evoke the faith.

Christian faith has its intellectual resemblances to these various faiths. It may often be friendly to them and accept their accomplishments. But it has its distinctive character. Christian faith is the response of the humble and contrite heart when, abandoning pretense and self-deception, it turns in loyalty and trust to the source of its being and the Lord of its life. Here a new context is offered to thought, and the unintelligibilities of history, though not systematized, are invested with meaning. Mystery is not dispelled, but a light is granted by which men may walk. It is a light shining in darkness, which though it does not dispel the darkness, gives the illumination which human life seeks. There is no use explaining further; it is all said in glorious profundity in the Prologue to the Gospel of John.

Hocking has suggested that faith always starts with mystery. It does not solve the mystery, but in the unknown affirms, "It is known." It mounts to real assurance saying, "I know not; but He knows. . . . I cannot, but He can." [2] So, we may recognize, faith is a confession of ignorance and a confession of trust. It is not mainly knowledge. Yet even the phrases, "He knows, He can," are bits of insight and understanding.

Thus it is that Christian faith arrives at a kind of "understanding" of history. We must not claim too much, or too little, for this understanding. We must not claim too much, because it does not solve the myriad problems which only painstaking study of history and disciplined but imaginative interpretation can solve. It in no way removes the need for investigating social causation, for determining economic and geographic influence upon history, for plotting painstakingly the course which a government should take today. It does not "explain" history. It is not, in short, a "philosophy of history," but any philosophy of history which ignores it does so at the peril of incompleteness or downright error. When confronted with other doctrines of history whether those of other worldly religions or this-worldly secularism, of revolutionary hope or resigned complacence—the Christian interpretation cannot demonstrate its truth. It can perhaps point out illusions and dubious premises in other claimants to truth. But finally it is itself a confession of faith.

But exactly because it is a confession of faith, we must not claim too little for it. For faith is the well-spring of life. A Christian interpretation of history, a Christian faith in the sovereignty of God offers and demands a way of life. Within it men may order their lives; for its faith they may—as they have done and continue to do—live and die. Few men would do this for their theory of epistemology or historical causation.

[2] *The Meaning of God in Human Experience*, pp. 237, 238.

Thus understood, Christian faith admits a high degree of agnosticism in history. It is, as a matter of fact, more agnostic than any "philosophy of history" and than most of the implied philosophies of historians. But it ends in an assurance—a trust and a commitment. Admitting a great provisional meaningless-ness in history, it affirms a final meaning.

In the Christian understanding of history we start with mystery verging on chaos: a mystery which we, despite our intelligence, cannot comprehend; a chaos which we, despite our freedom, cannot govern. By faith we affirm: It is comprehended; it is governed. He is Sovereign Lord. And He shall reign forever and ever.

A GUIDE TO SOME LITERATURE
IN THE FIELD

The study of philosophies of history is only in part a study of literature directly on the subject. In larger part it is the study of the assumptions, sometimes deliberate and more often unconscious, of thinkers on many subjects. Most of the great writings in philosophy, theology, history, political theory, epic and dramatic poetry are relevant. This selective *Guide*, however, will include for the most part only writings directly on the subject of this volume.

Although numerous articles have been mentioned throughout the text, this *Guide* includes only books, except in a few unusually important cases. If a book is listed in this *Guide*, the publication data are not included in references to it throughout the preceding text. In the case of books not listed here, publication data have been given with the *first* reference to the work. Quotations in the text are from the editions here indicated.

Titles are here listed under the chapter to which they have *primary* relevance. No title is listed more than once.

CH. I. SOME GENERAL WORKS

A number of books on philosophy of history are related to the whole subject rather than to any particular chapter of this volume. Most of them discuss problems taken up in the introductory and concluding chapters (I and IX) of this book.

Bury, J. B. *Selected Essays*. Cambridge: Cambridge U., 1930.
Butterfield, Herbert. *Christianity and History*. N.Y.: Scribners, 1950.
   History and Human Relations. N.Y.: Macmillan, 1952.
Cohen, Morris R. *The Meaning of Human History*. La Salle, Ill.:
   Open Court, 1947.

Collingwood, Robin G. *The Idea of History*. London: Oxford, 1946.

Flint, Robert. *History of the Philosophy of History: Historical Philosophy in France and French Belgium and Switzerland.* N.Y.: Scribners, 1894.

Hook, Sidney. *The Hero in History*. N.Y.: John Day, 1943.

Löwith, Karl. *Meaning in History*. Chicago: U. of Chicago, 1949.

Mandelbaum, Maurice. *The Problem of Historical Knowledge.* N.Y.: Liveright, 1938.

Nordau, Max S. *The Interpretation of History*. Tr. by M. A. Hamilton. N.Y.: Willey, 1910.

Popper, Karl R. *The Open Society and Its Enemies*. 2 vols. London: Routledge, 1945.

Robertson, Archibald. *Regnum Dei*. N.Y.: Macmillan, 1901.

Shotwell, James T. *The History of History*, Vol. I. N.Y.: Columbia U., 1939.

Simkhovitch, Vladimir G. "Approaches to History." *Political Science Quarterly*, XLIV, no. 4; XLV, no. 4; XLVII, no. 3; XLVIII, no. 1.

Sorokin, Pitirim A. *Social and Cultural Dynamics*. 2 vols. N.Y.: American Book Co., 1937.

Spengler, Oswald. *The Decline of the West*. Tr. by Charles Francis Atkinson. N.Y.: Knopf, 1934.

Troeltsch, Ernst. *Der Historismus und seine Probleme*. Tübingen: Mohr, 1922.

Whitehead, Alfred North. *Adventures of Ideas*. N.Y.: Macmillan, 1933.

Wood, H. G. *Christianity and the Nature of History*. Cambridge: Cambridge U., 1934.

Woodbridge, Frederick J. E. *The Purpose of History*. N.Y.: Columbia U., 1916.

CH. II.   SOME LEADING CHRISTIAN IDEAS—WITH HELP FROM ST. AUGUSTINE

The first source for Christian thinking is, of course, the Bible. Books about the Bible are uncountable, and most recent ones touch on our subject. The pioneer works in this field were those of Albert Schweitzer and Johannes Weiss. Schweitzer's famous book is *The*

Quest of the Historical Jesus, tr. by W. Montgomery (London: Black, 1926). Weiss' mature thought is best represented in his two-volume *History of Primitive Christianity,* tr. by F. C. Grant, et al (N.Y.: Wilson-Erickson, 1937).

Some other important books include:

Bultmann, Rudolf. *Jesus and the Word.* Tr. by L. P. Smith and E. Huntress. N.Y.: Scribners, 1934.
    Theology of the New Testament. Tr. by K. Grobel. Vol. I. N.Y.: Scribners, 1951. (The translation of Vol. II will be published by Scribners also.)

Cullmann, Oscar. *Christ and Time.* Tr. by F. V. Filson. Philadelphia: Westminster, 1950.

Dibelius, Martin. *The Message of Jesus Christ.* Tr. by F. C. Grant. N.Y.: Scribners, 1939.

Dodd, Charles Harold. *The Parables of the Kingdom.* N.Y.: Scribners, 1937.
    History and the Gospel, N.Y.: Scribners, 1938.

Goguel, Maurice. *The Life of Jesus.* Tr. by Olive Wyon. N.Y.: Macmillan, 1934.

Grant, Frederick C. *The Gospel of the Kingdom* N.Y.: Macmillan, 1942.

Klausner, Joseph. *Jesus of Nazareth.* Tr. by H. Danby. N.Y.: Macmillan, 1929.

Manson, Thomas Walter. *The Sayings of Jesus.* Bk. II of *The Mission and Message of Jesus* by Major, Manson, and Wright. N.Y.: Dutton, 1938.

Manson, William. *Jesus the Messiah.* Philadelphia: Westminster, 1946.

North, Christopher R. *The Old Testament Interpretation of History.* London: Epworth, 1946.

Otto, Rudolf. *The Kingdom of God and the Son of Man.* Tr. by F. V. Filson and B. Lee Woolf. N.Y.: Harpers, 1939.

Scott, Ernest Findlay. *The Kingdom of God in the New Testament.* N.Y.: Macmillan, 1931.

Wilder, Amos N. *Eschatology and Ethics in the Teaching of Jesus.* Revised ed. N.Y.: Harpers, 1950.

St. Augustine's complete works are in the *Patrologia Latina*
(Paris: Migne, 1941ff.), Vols. XXII-XLVII. The most important
single work is *De Civitate Dei*. A valuable Latin edition with English
introduction and notes is edited by James Welldon (London:
S.P.C.K., 1924, 2 vols.). There are many English translations of
various writings. The most complete selection is in the set of *Nicene
and Post-Nicene Fathers* (Buffalo and N.Y.: Christian Literature
Co., 1886–88), Vols. I–VIII. This is the translation usually quoted
in this book. Some valuable selections are arranged topically by
Erich Przywara in *An Augustine Synthesis* (N.Y.: Sheed and Ward,
1945).

Of the many books interpreting Augustine, the following are
perhaps most relevant:

Cochrane, Charles N. *Christianity and Classical Culture.* Revised
   ed. N.Y.: Oxford, 1944.
Dawson, Christopher. "St. Augustine and His Age," in *A Monu-
   ment to Saint Augustine* by M. C. D'Arcy, et al. London: Sheed
   and Ward, 1930.
Figgis, John Neville. *The Political Aspects of S. Augustine's 'City of
   God.'* London: Longmans, Green, 1921.
Gilson, Etienne. *Introduction a l'Etude de Saint Augustin.* Paris:
   Vrin, 1931.
Reuter, Herman. *Augustinische Studien.* Gotha: Porthes, 1887.
Scholz, Heinrich. *Glaube und Unglaube in der Weltgeschichte:
   Ein Kommentar zu Augustins De Civitate Dei.* Leipzig: Hein-
   richs'sche Buchhandlung, 1911.

CH. III.   THREE THEMES: THEIR INSIGHTS
AND THEIR DANGERS

Pt. I.   The Church as the Kingdom of God

The most important medieval work specifically on history is Otto
Friesing's chronicle, *The Two Cities*, tr. by Charles C. Mierow
(N.Y.: Columbia U., 1928). But the fundamental works are those
of Thomas Aquinas. The original works are available in various

forms, notably the great Leonine edition. The two most famous writings have been translated by the English Benedictine Fathers and published in London by Burns, Oates, and Washburne: *Summa contra Gentiles*, 5 vols.; *Summa Theologica*, 22 vols. (Also Cincinnati and N.Y.: Benziger.) These are abbreviated, respectively, *ScG* and *ST* in this book. A lesser book, important for our subject, is *The Governance of Rulers*, tr. by G. B. Phelan (N.Y.: Sheed and Ward, 1938). An interesting comparison is offered by Dante's *De Monarchia*, tr. by Aurelia Henry (Boston: Houghton, Mifflin, 1904).

Most interpreters of St. Thomas say little about his conception of history. Three short books give some help:

Leclair, M. St. Ida. *Utopias and the Philosophy of Saint Thomas*. Washington: Catholic U., 1941.
Penta, Clement Della. *Hope and Society: A Thomistic Study of Social Optimism and Pessimism*. Washington: Catholic U., 1942.
Stokes, Ella Harrison. *The Conception of a Kingdom of Ends in Augustine, Aquinas, and Leibnitz*. Chicago: U. of Chicago, 1912.

General help in understanding Aquinas, with indirect help on this subject, may be found in the standard Catholic books on the medieval saint, by such able writers as M. C. D'Arcy, Maurice deWulf, Etienne Gilson, Martin Grabmann, Jacques Maritain, and Hans Meyer.

Some chapters of the two following books contain directly relevant material:

Gilson, Etienne. *The Spirit of Mediaeval Philosophy*. Tr. by A. H. C. Downes. N.Y.: Scribners, 1940.
Patterson, Robert L. *The Conception of God in the Philosophy of Aquinas*. London: Allen and Unwin, 1933.

Pt. II. Radical Eschatology

Luther's works are available in the great Weimar edition (abbreviated *WA* in this book) and the older Erlangen edition (abbr. *EA*). Many works have been translated; some are here listed.

Luther's Primary Works. Ed. by Wace and Buchheim. London: Hodder and Stoughton, 1896. (A convenient but scanty one-volume collection.)

Works of Martin Luther. 6 vols. Philadelphia: Holman and United Lutheran Church in America, 1915–32. (Abbr. *PE.*) (This set includes most of the works which are of greatest importance for our subject.)

Works. Minneapolis: Lenker, 1903–10. (Abbr. *ME.*) (This set of many volumes emphasizes homiletic writings.)

Commentary on St. Paul's Epistle to the Galatians. Philadelphia: Quaker City Publishing House, 1848.

On the Bondage of the Will. Tr. by H. Cole. London: Simpkin and Marshall, 1823.

Luther's Correspondence and Other Contemporary Letters. Tr. and ed. by P. Smith and C. Jacobs. 2 vols. Philadelphia: Lutheran Publication Society, 1913, 1918.

In the inexhaustible literature about Luther, the theme of history has been greatly neglected. Several books shed peripheral light on the subject:

Althaus, Paul. *Kirche und Staat nach Lutherischer Lehre.* Leipzig: Deichertsche, 1935.
    Luther und die politische Welt. Weimar: Böhlau, 1937.
    (See also the very important work of Althaus listed in *Guide,* Ch. VII.)
Holl, Karl. *Gesammelte Aufsätze zur Kirchengeschichte.* Band I. *Luther.* Third edition. Tübingen: Mohr, 1923.
Jordan, Hermann. *Luthers Staatsauffassung.* Munich: Müller und Fröhlich, 1917.
Köhler, Walther. *Luther und die Kirchengeschichte nach seinen Schriften zunächst bis 1521.* Erlangen: Junge, 1900.
Schäfer, Ernst. *Luther als Kirchenhistoriker.* Gütersloh: Bertelsmann, 1897.

Pt. III.   The Hope for Transforming Society

A detailed survey of this whole tendency is John T. McNeill's *Christian Hope for World Society* (Chicago: Willett, Clark, 1937). Sectarian sources can never be complete, but many have been painstakingly assembled. The issues of the *Mennonite Quarterly Review* (Goshen, Indiana) carry translations of many tracts. Extensive collections of continental and English sectarian writings are found respectively in:

Quellen zur Geschichte der Wiedertäufer. Band I, ed. by Gustav Bossert. Band II, ed. by Karl Schornbaum. Vols. XIII and XVI of *Quellen und Forschungen zur Reformationsgeschichte herausgegeben vom Verein für Reformationsgeschichte*. Leipzig: Hensius, 1930, 1934.
The Works of Gerrard Winstanley. Ed. by George H. Sabine. Ithaca: Cornell U., 1941.

The pre-Reformation origins of the dynamic conception of history are brought out in Ernst Benz, *Ecclesia Spiritualis, Kirchenidee und Geschichtstheologie der Franziscanischen Reformation*. Stuttgart: Kohlhammer, 1934.

The numerous books about sectarian origins say little about conceptions of history. An exception is Franklin H. Littell's recent volume, *The Anabaptist View of the Church: An Introduction to Sectarian Protestantism* (Berne, Ind.: American Society of Church History, 1952).

The most complete collection of Calvin's works is in the great *Corpus Reformatorum*. But abundant material may be found in translation.

Institutes of the Christian Religion. Tr. by John Allen. 2 vols. Philadelphia: Presbyterian Board of Christian Education, 1936.
Instruction in Faith. Tr. by P. T. Fuhrmann. Philadelphia: Westminster, 1949.
Tracts Relating to the Reformation. Tr. by H. Beveridge. 3 vols. Edinburgh: Calvin Translation Society, 1844–51.

Commentaries on books of the Bible. Edinburgh: Calvin Translation Society, 1845ff. (The commentaries have been recently reprinted by Eerdmans of Grand Rapids.)

Once again the extensive interpretive literature says little of our subject. But two small volumes by Karlfried Fröhlich deal directly with the theme.

Gottesreich, Welt und Kirche bei Calvin. Munich: Reinhardt, 1930.
Die Reichgottesidee Calvins. Munich: Kaiser, 1922.

CH. IV.   THE IMPACT OF THE IDEA OF PROGRESS

Some classical expressions of the faith in progress in its various forms are listed.

Comte, Auguste. *The Positive Philosophy.* Freely translated and condensed by Harriet Martineau. N.Y.: Calvin Blanchard, 1855.
Condorcet, Marquis de. *Outlines of an Historical View of the Progress of the Human Mind.* Philadelphia: Land and Ustick, 1796.
Dewey, John. *Reconstruction in Philosophy.* N.Y.: Holt, 1920.
    A Common Faith. New Haven: Yale U., 1934.
Hegel, Georg Wilhelm Friedrich. *The Philosophy of History.* Tr. by J. Sibree. N.Y.: Willey, 1944.
Kant, Immanuel. *Perpetual Peace.* (Several translations.)
    Religion within the Limits of Reason Alone. Tr. by T. M. Greene and H. H. Hudson. Chicago: Open Court, 1934.
    Idea of a Universal History from a Cosmopolitical Point of View. (Several translations.)
Smith, Adam. *The Wealth of Nations.* N.Y.: Modern Library, 1937.
Spencer, Herbert. *First Principles.* N.Y.: Appleton, 1880.
    Illustrations of Universal Progress. N.Y.: Appleton, 1864.
    Social Statics. N.Y.: Appleton, 1888. (First published, 1850.)
    Abridged and revised edition. London and Edinburgh: Williams and Norgate, 1892.

Not until the twentieth century did men get enough perspective to study and evaluate the idea of progress. The classic study is Bury's. The most witty and penetrating is Becker's more specialized work.

Becker, Carl L. *The Heavenly City of the Eighteenth-Century Philosophers*. New Haven: Yale U., 1952.

"Progress," *Encyclopaedia of the Social Sciences*, Vol. XII. N.Y.: Macmillan, 1934.

Bury, J. B. *The Idea of Progress: An Inquiry into its Origin and Growth*. N.Y.: Macmillan, 1932. (First published, 1920.)

Fay, Sidney B. "The Idea of Progress." *American Historical Review*, LII (1947), 231–46.

Frankel, Charles. *The Faith of Reason. The Idea of Progress in the French Enlightenment*. N.Y.: King's Crown, 1948.

Hildebrand, George H. (ed.). *The Idea of Progress. A Collection of Readings*. Berkeley: U. of California, 1949.

Marvin, F. S. (ed.). *Progress and History*. London: Oxford, 1916.

Tuveson, Ernest Lee. *Millennium and Utopia; a Study in the Background of the Idea of Progress*. Berkeley: U. of California, 1949.

Christian responses to the idea of progress are evident in this *Guide*, Chapters VI and VII. But a few of the explicit ones, both critical and uncritical, are here listed.

Abbott, Lyman. *The Theology of an Evolutionist*. Boston: Houghton, Mifflin, 1898.

Baillie, John. *The Belief in Progress*. N.Y.: Scribners, 1951.

Case, Shirley Jackson. *The Christian Philosophy of History*. Chicago: U. of Chicago, 1943.

Dawson, Christopher. *Progress and Religion*. N.Y.: Sheed and Ward, 1938. (First published, 1929.)

Drummond, Henry. *The Ascent of Man*. N.Y.: Pott, 1894.

Fosdick, Harry Emerson. *Christianity and Progress*. N.Y.: Revell, 1922.

Inge, William R. *The Idea of Progress*. Oxford: Clarendon, 1920. Reprinted in *Outspoken Essays, Second Series*. London: Longmans, Green, 1932.

Mathews, Shailer. *The Spiritual Interpretation of History*. Cambridge: Harvard U., 1916.

McGiffert, Arthur Cushman. *The Rise of Modern Religious Ideas*. N.Y.: Macmillan, 1919.

Morrison, Charles Clayton. *The Outlawry of War.* Foreword by John Dewey. Chicago: Willett, Clark and Colby, 1927.
Wieman, Henry N. *The Directive in History.* Glencoe, Ill.: Free Press, 1949.

The Social Gospel is best represented by Rauschenbusch. His books most relevant to this theme are listed, followed by three studies of the Social Gospel.

Rauschenbusch, Walter. *Christianity and the Social Crisis.* N.Y.: Macmillan, 1907.
    Christianizing the Social Order. N.Y.: Macmillan, 1912.
    A Theology for the Social Gospel. N.Y.: Macmillan, 1917.
Hopkins, Charles Howard, *The Rise of the Social Gospel in American Protestantism, 1865–1915.* New Haven: Yale U., 1940.
Johnson, F. Ernest. *The Social Gospel Re-examined.* N.Y.: Harpers, 1940.
Visser 't Hooft, Willem Adolph. *The Background of the Social Gospel in America.* Haarlem: H. D. Tjeenk Willink and Zoon, 1928.

Walter Marshall Horton is considered in this book as a prominent heir of the Social Gospel. His spiritual pilgrimage can be traced through his many writings. Those most specifically relevant are listed. See also p. 128, n. 13 above.

Can Christianity Save Civilization? N.Y.: Harpers, 1940.
Our Christian Faith. Boston: Pilgrim, 1945.
Our Eternal Contemporary. N.Y.: Harpers, 1942.
Theology in Transition. Includes an essay and most of two earlier volumes: *A Psychological Approach to Theology,* and *Realistic Theology.* N.Y.: Harpers, 1943.

CH. V.   MARXIST AND CHRISTIAN ESCHATOLOGIES

The most relevant of the extensive primary sources are listed.

Marx, Karl. *Capital,* Vol. I. Tr. by S. Moore and E. Aveling. Ed. by F. Engels. N.Y.: Modern Library. (Copyright, 1906, Kerr.)

(With Friedrich Engels.) *The Communist Manifesto.* Many editions.
A Contribution to the Critique of Political Economy. Tr. by N. I. Stone. Chicago: Kerr, 1904.
(With Friedrich Engels.) *The German Ideology.* Parts I and III. Ed. by R. Pascal. N.Y.: International Publishers, 1947.
Engels, Friedrich. *Herr Eugen Dühring's Revolution in Science.* Commonly known as *Anti-Dühring.* Tr. by Emile Burns. N.Y.: International Publishers, 1939.
The Origin of the Family, Private Property, and the State. N.Y.: International Publishers, 1942.
Socialism Utopian and Scientific. Tr. by E. Aveling. N.Y.: International Publishers, 1935. (A famous pamphlet excerpted from *Anti-Dühring.*)
Lenin, V. I. *State and Revolution.* N.Y.: International Publishers, 1932.
The Teachings of Karl Marx. N.Y.: International Publishers, 1930.

The literature about Marxism is voluminous and represents every conceivable viewpoint. The most relevant and thorough single volume is M. M. Bober, *Karl Marx's Interpretation of History,* second revised ed. (Cambridge: Harvard U., 1948).

The most interesting Christian Marxists are probably Macmurray and Ward. Their most relevant books are listed.

Macmurray, John. *A Challenge to the Churches. Religion and Democracy.* London: Kegan Paul, 1941.
The Clue to History. N.Y.: Harpers, 1939.
Constructive Democracy. London: Faber, 1943.
Creative Society. A Study of the Relation of Christianity to Communism. N.Y.: Association Press, 1936.
Idealism against Religion. London: Lindsey Press, 1944.
Marxism. London: Chapman and Hall, 1935.
The Philosophy of Communism. London: Faber, 1933.
(With others.) *Aspects of Dialectical Materialism.* London: Watts, 1934.

(See also the several *Peace Aims Pamphlets* written by Macmurray, among others. London: National Peace Council.)

Ward, Harry F. *Democracy and Social Change*. N.Y.: Modern Age, 1940.
> *In Place of Profit*. N.Y.: Scribners, 1933.

Among the severe critics of Marxism who appropriate some of Marx's insights are many of the authors listed in this *Guide*, Ch. VII. A few books are specifically on this theme.

Bennett, John C. *Christianity and Communism*. N.Y.: Association Press, 1948.

Berdyaev, Nicolas. *The Bourgeois Mind*. N.Y.: Sheed and Ward, 1933.
> *Christianity and Class War*. London: Sheed and Ward, 1933.
> *The Origin of Russian Communism*. N.Y.: Scribners, 1937.

Lewis, John, et al. *Christianity and the Social Revolution*. N.Y.: Scribners, 1936. (A symposium including advocates and critics of Marx. Contributors include Macmurray and Reinhold Niebuhr.)

Miller, Alexander. *The Christian Significance of Karl Marx*. N.Y.: Macmillan, 1947.

CH. VI. MODERN CATHOLIC INTERPRETATIONS OF HISTORY

In Anglo-Catholicism the "Christendom Group" has given great attention to the social implications of Christianity and thus indirectly to the problem of history. The numerous writings of V. A. Demant, Maurice Reckitt, and Cyril E. Hudson sometimes touch on our subject. The more conservative T. S. Eliot has two short but provocative books which frequently deal with the problem of history.

Eliot, T. S. *The Idea of a Christian Society*. N.Y.: Harcourt, Brace, 1940.
> *Notes Towards the Definition of Culture*. N.Y.: Harcourt, Brace, 1949.

In Roman Catholicism the modernist movement is represented
in the writings of George Tyrrell and the Abbé Loisy. The papal
response is seen in Pius IX, *Syllabus of Errors*, 1864; Pius X, Encyclical *Pascendi*, 1907, and Decree *Lamentabili*, 1907. (Many editions.)

The most important contemporary Roman Catholic writers on
our subject are Christopher Dawson and Jacques Maritain. Dawson,
a historian, has written a great deal on the philosophy of history.
Maritain, a philosopher, deals more indirectly with the subject in
his political and philosophical books. The most relevant works of
these and a number of other Roman Catholic writers of this and
recent generations are listed.

Chudoba, Bohdan. *The Meaning of Civilization.* N.Y.: Kenedy,
   1951.
Dawson, Christopher. *Enquiries into Religion and Culture.* N.Y.:
   Sheed and Ward, 1934.
   The Judgment of the Nations. N.Y.: Sheed and Ward, 1942.
   Religion and Culture. London: Sheed and Ward, 1948.
   Religion and the Modern State. London: Sheed and Ward,
   1935.
   Religion and the Rise of Western Culture. London: Sheed
   and Ward, 1950.
   (See also *Guide*, Ch. IV.)
Dawson, Christopher; Maritain, Jacques; Wust, Peter. *Essays in
   Order.* N.Y.: Sheed and Ward, 1940.
deWulf, Maurice. *Scholasticism Old and New.* Tr. by P. Coffey.
   London: Longmans, Green, 1910.
Frank, Erich. *Philosophical Understanding and Religious Truth.*
   N.Y.: Oxford, 1945.
Guilday, Peter (ed.). *The Catholic Philosophy of History.* A sym-
   posium. N.Y.: Kenedy, 1936.
Haecker, Theodore. "The Unity of History," *Dublin Review*, 219:
   44-48.
Knox, Ronald A. *God and the Atom.* N.Y.: Sheed and Ward, 1945.
Maritain, Jacques. *Christianity and Democracy.* Tr. by Doris C.
   Anson. N.Y.: Scribners, 1944.

Existence and the Existent. Tr. by L. Galantiere and G. B. Phelan. N.Y.: Pantheon, 1948.
Ransoming the Time. Tr. by H. L. Binsse. N.Y.: Scribners, 1946.
The Rights of Man and Natural Law. Tr. by Doris C. Anson. N.Y.: Scribners, 1943.
Scholasticism and Politics. N.Y.: Macmillan, 1938.
The Things that Are Not Caesar's. Tr. by J. F. Scanlan. N.Y.: Scribners, 1943.
True Humanism. Tr. by Margot Adamson. N.Y.: Scribners, 1938.
The Twilight of Civilization. Tr. by Landry. N.Y.: Sheed and Ward, 1943.
von Hügel, Friedrich. *Essays and Addresses on the Philosophy of Religion.* N.Y.: Dutton. First Series, 1921. Second Series, 1926.
Zybura, John S. *Present-Day Thinkers and the New Scholasticism. An International Symposium.* Second revised edition. St. Louis: Herder, 1927.

CH. VII. THE REDISCOVERY OF BIBLICAL ESCHATOLOGY

To include all the relevant books would require a list of most of the theological writings of the present generation. This selective list includes, for the most part, only works specifically on the subject of history. An exception has been made in the cases of Barth, Berdyaev, Brunner, and Niebuhr. Because these four men have had such wide international influence on conceptions of history, the list includes a few of their more general writings which are relevant.

To this list should be added many of the authors of biblical books in the *Guide,* Ch. II.

Althaus, Paul. *Die Letzten Dinge.* Vierte Auflage. Gütersloh: Bertelsmann, 1933.
Baillie, John. *What Is Christian Civilization?* N.Y.: Scribners, 1948. (See also *Guide,* Ch. IV.)

Barth, Karl. *The Church and the Political Problem of Our Day.* N.Y.: Scribners, 1939.

    Church and State. (Tr. of *Rechtfertigung und Recht.*) London: Student Christian Movement, 1939.

    The Church and the War (including "A Letter to American Christians"). N.Y.: Macmillan, 1944.

    Credo. Geneva, 1935. Tr. by J. Strathearn. N.Y.: Scribners, 1936.

    The Epistle to the Romans. Tr. from sixth edition by E. C. Hoskyns. London: Oxford (Milford), 1933.

    Die Kirchliche Dogmatik. Munich: Kaiser, 1932ff. (Several volumes have been published and more are awaited. This is Barth's *magnum opus* and corrects many misconceptions about him. Only the flist half volume has been translated: *Church Dogmatics. The Doctrine of the Word of God.* Tr, by G. T. Thomson. Edinburgh: Clark, 1936.)

    The Knowledge of God and the Service of God According to the Teaching of the Reformation. Tr. by J. L. M. Haire and I. Henderson. London: Hodder and Stoughton, 1938

    This Christian Cause (Letters to the French Protestants and to Great Britain, 1939–41). N.Y.: Macmillan, 1941.

    Die Unordnung der Welt und Gottes Heilsplan. Zurich: Zollikon, 1946.

    (With Eduard Thurneysen, co-editor.) *Theologische Existenz Heute,* Nos. 1–44. Munich: Kaiser, 1933–36.

Berdyaev, Nicolas. *Destiny of Man.* N.Y.: Scribners, 1937.

    The End of Our Times. London: Sheed and Ward, 1933.

    The Fate of Man. London: Student Christian Movement, 1935.

    Freedom and the Spirit. N.Y.: Scribners, 1935.

    The Meaning of History. N.Y.: Scribners, 1936.

    Solitude and Society. N.Y.: Scribners, 1938.

    Spirit and Reality. N.Y.: Scribners, 1939.

    (See also *Guide,* Ch. V.)

Brunner, Emil. *Christianity and Civilization.* N.Y.: Scribners. Vol. I, 1948. Vol. II, 1949.

288　　　　　　　　　　GUIDE TO LITERATURE

The Divine Imperative. Tr. by Olive Wyon. Philadelphia: Westminster, 1947.

Justice and the Social Order. Tr. by Mary Hottinger. N.Y.: Harpers, 1945.

Man in Revolt. Tr. by Olive Wyon. Philadelphia: Westminster, 1947.

The Mediator. Tr. by Olive Wyon. Philadelphia: Westminster, 1947.

Revelation and Reason. Tr. by Olive Wyon. Philadelphia: Westminster, 1946.

Butterfield, Herbert. (See *Guide,* Ch. I.)

Coffin, Henry Sloane. *God Confronts Man in History.* N.Y.: Scribners, 1947.

Davies, D. R. *Divine Judgment in Human History.* London: Sheldon (Christian News-Letter Books), 1943.

Heim, Karl. *Jesus der Herr.* Berlin: Furche-Verlag, 1935.

Jesus der Weltvollender. Berlin: Furche-Verlag, 1937.

Heimann, Eduard. *Freedom and Order.* N.Y.: Scribners, 1947.

Horton, Walter Marshall. (See *Guide,* Ch. IV.)

Künneth, Walter. *Theologie der Auferstehung.* Munich: Kaiser, 1933.

Löwith, Karl. (See *Guide,* Ch. I.)

Niebuhr, Reinhold. *Beyond Tragedy.* N.Y.: Scribners, 1937.

The Children of Light and the Children of Darkness. N.Y.: Scribners, 1945.

Christianity and Power Politics. N.Y.: Scribners, 1940.

Discerning the Signs of the Times. N.Y.: Scribners. 1946.

Faith and History. N.Y.: Scribners, 1949.

An Interpretation of Christian Ethics. N.Y.: Harpers, 1935.

Moral Man and Immoral Society. N. Y.: Scribners, 1932.

The Nature and Destiny of Man. 2 vols. N.Y.: Scribners, 1941, 1943.

Reflections on the End of an Era. N.Y.: Scribners, 1936.

Oxford Conference on Church, Community and State. *The Kingdom of God and History.* A symposium containing essays by H. G. Wood, C. H. Dodd, E. Bevan, E. W. Lyman, P. Tillich,

H. D. Wendland, and Christopher Dawson. Chicago: Willett,
Clark, 1938.

Piper, Otto. *God in History.* N.Y.: Macmillan, 1939.

Rust, E. C. *The Christian Understanding of History.* London: Lut-
terworth, 1947.

Taubes, Jakob. *Abendländischer Eschatologie.* Bern: Francke, 1947.

Tillich, Paul J. *The Interpretation of History.* N.Y.: Scribners, 1936.
        The Protestant Era. Chicago: U. of Chicago, 1948.

Visser 't Hooft, Willem A. *The Kingship of Christ.* N.Y.: Harpers,
1947.

CH. VIII. TOYNBEE'S MODERN SYNTHESIS

Toynbee's most important works are listed. Cf p. 224, n. 1
above.

Toynbee, Arnold. *Civilization on Trial.* N.Y.: Oxford, 1948. (Abbreviated *CT* in this book.)
        A Study of History. London: Oxford. Vols. I–III, second
edition, 1935. Vols. IV–VI, 1939. (Abbr. *SH.*)
        A Study of History. Abridgement of Vols. I–VI by D. C.
Sommervell. N.Y. and London: Oxford, 1947. (Abbr. *S.*)

Geyl, P.; Toynbee, Arnold; Sorokin, P. *The Pattern of the Past.*
Boston: Beacon, 1949. (The book includes two strenuous
critiques of Toynbee, who has limited opportunity to answer one
of them.)

Toynbee has a number of earlier works, but none is strictly relevant. In recent years he has written numerous essays. Most of them
are included in *CT*, but some have come out since. They give clues
to the ideas in the forthcoming final volumes of *SH*, but are not
definitive.

Most popular and semi-popular periodicals and many scholarly
journals have carried articles about Toynbee. A few of these are
rather important for our problem.

Harbison, E. Harris. "The Problem of the Christian Historian: A Critique of Arnold J. Toynbee." *Theology Today*, V (1948), 388–405.

Nichols, James Hastings. "Religion in Toynbee's History." *Journal of Religion*, XXVIII (1948), 99–119.

Sumberg, Theodore A. "Toynbee and the Decline of Western Civilization." *Social Research*, XIV (1947), 267–84.

Tawney, R. H. "Dr. Toynbee's Study of History." *International Affairs*, XVIII (1939), 798–806.

INDEX

Abbott, Lyman, 118, 281
Accident, 46, 249
Adam, 39, 95
Adam, Karl, 183
Adams, Henry, 5, 52, 263
Aeschylus, 191, 232 n.
Aesop, 74
Agnosticism, and faith, 272
Alaric the Goth, 32, 192
Alexander the Great, 196
Alexander, Samuel, 167
Alexeiev, N. H., 149 n., 154 n
Althaus, Paul, 76 n., 187, 209 n.,
    278, 286
America, attitude toward history,
    108, 111, 170
Amos, 154, 204
Analogy, doctrine of, 67, 158
Anderson, Maxwell, 23-24
Anti-Christ, 89, 197
Apocalypse. See Eschatology
Aristotle, Aristotelian, 33, 65 n., 67,
    103, 208
Atheism, 153-54, 173
Augustine, Augustinian,
    and biblical eschatology, 29-33
    bibliography, 276
    and the church, 56-59, 69, 241
    and classicism, 32-34, 36-38, 48,
        50, 55, 59, 101
    and cycles, 36-38
    dynamic theme in, 59-62, 86, 164
    his eschatology and its alterna-
        tives, 23-38
    and Kingdom of God, 53-56, 129
    other-worldliness of, 55-56, 61-
        62, 90 n.
    and philosophes, 106
    and Protestantism, 74, 77-78, 80,
        83, 177, 179
    and sovereignty of God, 45-52,
        77-78, 177, 182, 261

and Thomas Aquinas, 65-67, 69,
    71
three-stranded thread of, 52-53,
    . 62
and time, 55, 67, 207
and Toynbee, 236, 238, 241-42
and universal history, 38-45, 203
Augustus Caesar, 39
Aulén, Gustav, 215 n.
Aztec mythology, 36

Bach, J. S., 21 n.
Bacon, Francis, 96, 111, 112
Bacon, Roger, 66, 87
Baillie, Donald M., 38 n.
Baillie, John, 183 n., 187, 259 n.,
    281, 286
Barbarossa, Emperor Frederick, 86
Barmen Declaration, 219
Barth, Karl, 7, 18 n., 68
    bibliography, 286-87
    on the church, 266 67
    on historical revelation, 197
    on political history, 200, 218-22
    his rediscovery of eschatology,
        187-88, 206, 214-15
    on time, 208-11
    on unity of history, 204
Beard, Charles A., 102, 111-12
Becker, Carl, 24, 103-105, 106 n.,
    109, 127, 197, 280-81
Bennett, John C., 156, 265, 284
Benz, Ernst, 87, 279
Berdyaev, Nicolas, 187
    bibliography, 284, 286-87
    on eternity, 211-12
    on Marxism, 146, 149-52, 155
    on mysticism, 206
    on progress, 192 n.
Bergson, Henri, 167
Bergsonian thought, 239-40
Bernard, Saint, 86

291